CONCISE
INTRODUCTION
to the BIBLE

✹ **AMG** *Publishers*

CONCISE
INTRODUCTION
to the BIBLE

DR. HOWARD VOS

The AMG Concise Introduction to the Bible
Copyright © 1993, 2004 by Howard F. Vos
Published by AMG Publishers
6815 Shallowford Rd.
Chattanooga, Tennessee 37421

ISBN 0-89957-447-5   ISBN 978-0-89957-447-9

First printing—February 2004

Cover designed by Market Street Design, Chattanooga, Tennessee
Interior design and typesetting by Reider Publishing Services, West Hollywood, California
Scanning and formatting of the text by Scribe, Inc., Philadelphia, Pennsylvania
Edited and Proofread by Gloria Penwell, Dan Penwell, and Warren Baker

Printed in the United States of America
10 09 08 07   –EB– 8 7 6 5 4 3

Contents

INTRODUCTION

1 Some Beginning Questions   3

PART I
THE EARLY HISTORY OF GOD'S PEOPLE

2 In the Beginning   25
Genesis 1–11

3 Fathers in Israel: Abraham, Isaac,   45
Jacob, and Joseph
Genesis 11–50

4 Up from Slavery: Moses and the Exodus   51
Exodus 1–15

5 Power in the Desert: The Wilderness Wanderings   57
Exodus 15–Deuteronomy 34

6   "The Lord God Is with You": The Conquest   77
     of the Promised Land
     Joshua 1–24

7   "Everyone Did What Was Right in   83
     His Own Eyes": The Judges
     Judges, Ruth, 1 Samuel 8

8   The Clamor for a King: Saul, David, and Solomon   99
     1 & 2 Samuel, 1 Kings 1–11, 1 Chronicles,
     2 Chronicles 1–9

9   Chaos under the Kings: The Divided Kingdom   117
     1 Kings 12–22, 2 Kings, 2 Chronicles 10–36

10   God Remembers His People: Captivity   137
     and Restoration
     2 Chronicles 36, Ezra, Esther, Nehemiah

PART II

THE PROPHETS OF THE OLD TESTAMENT

11   "Thus Says the LORD": An Overview of   147
     Prophets & Prophecy

12   Prophets of the Assyrian Period   151
     Obadiah, Joel, Jonah, Amos, Hosea, Micah, Isaiah,
     Nahum, Zephaniah

13   Prophets of the Babylonian Period   165
     Habakkuk, Ezekiel, Jeremiah, Daniel

14   Prophets of the Persian Period   181
     Haggai, Zechariah, Malachi

PART III
THE SINGERS AND SAGES OF THE OLD TESTAMENT

15 The Art of Godly Living: Truth in Poetry 189
Job, Psalms, Proverbs, Ecclesiastes,
Song of Solomon, Lamentations

For Further Old Testament Study 206

PART IV
BETWEEN THE TESTAMENTS

16 When There Was No Word from the Lord: The Four
Hundred Silent Years 211

For Further Intertestamental Study 236

PART V
THE LIFE OF JESUS

17 In "the Fullness of the Time": The Resumption
of Revelation 239

18 "Render . . . to Caesar": The World of Jesus and
the Early Church 249

19 The Promised Messiah Comes: The Gospels 255
Matthew, Mark, Luke, John

PART VI
THE GROWTH OF THE YOUNG CHURCH

20 "Power from on High": Acts of the Risen Lord 291
Acts

21 "Grace to You and Peace": Paul's Letters to 299
Young Churches
Galatians, 1 & 2 Thessalonians, 1 & 2 Corinthians,
Romans, Colossians, Philemon, Ephesians,
Philippians, 1 & 2 Timothy, Titus

22   A Better Way: The Letter to the Hebrews   333
     Hebrews

23   To All the Churches: The General Epistles   339
     James, 1 & 2 Peter, 1 ,2, 3 John, Jude

PART VII
THE END OF ALL THINGS

24   "A New Heaven and a New Earth":   355
     The Revelation of Jesus Christ
     Revelation

     For Further New Testament Study   369

Appendix I: A Simple Technique for Learning   371
     Old Testament History

     About the Author   375

Introduction

Some Beginning Questions

MOST of us are vitally interested in answers to the big questions of life. Where did we come from? Why are we here? What makes us tick or what is the nature of human beings? How did we get in the predicament we are in? What is our future? We avidly read all kinds of literature on human beginnings, human psychological makeup, the present state of human affairs, and human destiny. We consider any literature that deals with these questions relevant and timely.

Preeminent among all literature about the big questions of life is the Old Testament. Not only does it report human opinions, but it gives divine insights into all the issues of life. Thus, it gives perspectives and answers available nowhere else. Viewed from this standpoint, the Old Testament is not some book out of the musty past that has only antiquarian interests for a few with a nostalgic bent; but it has a vital, contemporary relevance.

WHAT IS THE OLD TESTAMENT?

The Old Testament is the first part of the Bible and is a collection of thirty-nine documents written by prophets, priests, kings, and other leaders in Israel. All evidence points to the fact that the authors were Hebrews. Originally written in Hebrew and Aramaic, these books have been widely translated into many languages of the world. Although portions of the Old Testament appeared in English earlier, the entire Old Testament was not available to English readers until John Wyclif's translation of 1388; and it was not printed until Miles Coverdale's edition of 1535.

Even after the Old Testament collection was completed, there were not always thirty-nine books in it. For example, Josephus, the Jewish historian of the first Century A.D., spoke of twenty-two books in his day.[1] This does not mean, however, that contents of the collection were different then. The twelve Minor Prophets appeared as one book, as did 1 and 2 Samuel, 1 and 2 Kings, 1 and 2 Chronicles, and other books now divided. The Greek translation of the Old Testament (Septuagint), produced in Alexandria during the third and second centuries B.C., and Jerome's fourth century A.D. Latin translation have been especially important in influencing current division and placement of books in the Old Testament.

Chapter and verse divisions familiar to modern readers did not always appear in the text either. The custom of dividing parts of the Hebrew Old Testament into verses occurred at least as early as A.D. 200 and probably earlier. But verse divisions varied considerably until the tenth century, when the great Jewish scholar Ben Asher edited the Hebrew text with current verse divisions. Chapter divisions in the Hebrew text were adopted from the Latin Bible in the thirteenth century. Probably it was Stephen Langton (d. 1228), archbishop of Canterbury, who worked out these chapter divisions. The first English Bible with present chapter and verse divisions was the Geneva Bible of 1560.

Of course, there were no Old and New Testaments before the coming of Christ. There was only one collection of sacred writings. But after the apostles and their associates produced another body of sacred literature, the church began to refer to Old and New Testaments. Actually *Testament* is the translation of the Greek word *diathēkē*, which might better be rendered *covenant*. It denotes an arrangement made by God for human spiritual guidance and benefit. This arrangement is unalterable; human beings may accept it or reject it but cannot change it. Covenant is a common Old Testament word, and several covenants are described in the Old Testament, the most prominent being the Mosaic. While Israel chafed and failed under the Mosaic covenant, God promised them a "new covenant" (Jeremiah 31:31).

The term *new covenant* appears several times in the New Testament. Jesus first used it when He instituted the ordinance we call the Lord's Supper; by it He sought to call attention to the new basis of communion with God that He intended to establish by His death (Luke 22:20; 1 Corinthians 11:25). The apostle Paul spoke of this new covenant (2 Corinthians 3:6, 14), as did the writer to the Hebrews (Hebrews 8:8; 9:11–15). The detailed description of God's new method of dealing with humanity (on the basis of the finished work of Christ on the cross) is the subject of the twenty-seven books of the New Testament. God's dealing with people in a fashion anticipatory of the coming of Christ is certainly the major theme of the thirty-nine books of the Old Testament, though admittedly, the Old Testament concerns much more than that. Perhaps it should be noted that Latin Church writers rendered the Greek *diathēkē* by *testamentum*, and from them the use passed into English; so old and new covenants became Old and New Testaments.

From what has already been said, it should be clear that the Old Testament is not just a collection of religious essays that inspire antiquarian interest. It is a book that answers many of the big questions of life—where the earth and human beings came from, how sin entered the human race, and especially how the sin problem has been dealt with. It is a record of God's revelation of Himself to humanity, and thus is a revelation of the very nature of God. It discloses the divine plan for humanity's future (see especially the prophecies of Daniel and Isaiah). It details many facets of God's plan of salvation. And it provides examples of God's dealing with unbelievers and believers alike that are relevant for us today. In speaking of numerous Old Testament events and personalities, the apostle Paul said, "Now these things happened to them as a warning, but they were written down for our instruction, upon whom the end of the ages has come" (1 Corinthians 10:11, RSV).

HOW CAN A READER MAKE SENSE OUT OF THE OLD TESTAMENT?

On the whole, the Old Testament follows a logical and easily understood arrangement. In fact, the first sixteen books appear in chronological order. Genesis records the creation of the universe and humanity, the fall of the human race into sin, the beginnings of civilization, and God's decision to call out from a debauched society Abraham, who was to be the father of a people especially destined to stand for the truth. Through Abraham a Messiah would come. The rest of Genesis concerns the activities of the patriarchs in Palestine and, finally, in Egypt where they migrated to escape a famine. The book of Exodus tells how the Hebrews became enslaved in Egypt, dramatically escaped in the Exodus under the leadership of Moses, and began their wilderness wanderings. En route they received the law and the plan for the tabernacle at Mount Sinai. Leviticus, Numbers, and Deuteronomy detail the priesthood and the legal system, continued wanderings of the people, and the conquest of land east of the Jordan River. At the end of Deuteronomy, Moses departed the scene, and Joshua assumed leadership of the Hebrews. The book of Joshua narrates the Hebrew conquest of Palestine. The book of Judges describes events during a subsequent, long period of time when "every man did that which was right in his own eyes" and there was no king in Israel. The story of Ruth takes place during that era (Ruth 1:1) and notes the genealogy of David, the ancestor of the Messiah.

At the end of the period of the Judges, the Hebrews demanded a king like the nations surrounding them. In response, Samuel the prophet, under God's direction, anointed Saul as king. When Saul failed God and was rejected, Samuel anointed David. The books of Samuel tell of these two anointings, the conflict between Saul and David, and David's building of the Hebrew kingdom. The books of 1 and 2 Kings describe the glories of Solomon's reign, the split of the kingdom into the separate kingdoms of Israel and Judah, the fall of Israel to the Assyrians, and the fall of Judah to the Babylonians. Then 1 and 2 Chronicles recapitulate much of this history, beginning with the reign of David and concluding with not only the destruction of the northern and southern kingdoms but also a brief note about the return from captivity under Cyrus the Great of Persia.[2] Ezra, Nehemiah, and Esther detail aspects of Hebrew restoration to Palestine under Persian auspices. Then follows a group of poetical books (Job, Psalms, Proverbs, Ecclesiastes, Song of Solomon) written to a large degree by David and Solomon, but some authorship is uncertain.

The Old Testament closes with a collection of prophetic works divided into writings of the so-called Major and Minor Prophets. These writing prophets all date to the eras of the divided monarchy and the restoration but are not arranged chronologically. Nine wrote during the days of the Assyrian Empire (c. 900–612 B.C.): Obadiah, Joel, Jonah, Amos, Hosea, Micah, Isaiah, Nahum, and Zephaniah. Four wrote during the Chaldean or Babylonian Empire period (612–539 B.C.): Habakkuk, Ezekiel, Jeremiah, and Daniel. And three wrote during the sixth and fifth centuries when Persians ruled the Middle East: Haggai, Zechariah, and Malachi. Generally speaking, the prophets preached moral and ethical conduct in the present and warned the Hebrews and their neighbors of impending judgment for their waywardness. But sometimes they did predict the future in general or very specific terms.

What Does Inspiration Mean?

The concept of inspiration is especially related to 2 Timothy 3:16 which should be translated, "All scripture is God-breathed." When Paul refers to "scripture" here, he has in mind primarily the Old Testament, because several New Testament books had not yet been written and many of those that were transcribed had not yet been widely circulated. If all Scripture is God-breathed, it is exactly what God wanted to say. If it is exactly what He wanted to say, nothing is lacking that He wished to include and nothing is added that He might wish left out. Moreover, the very words He wanted used are there, with all their intimations and innuendoes and implications. Above all, if Scripture is God-breathed, it is completely accurate; for God is the God of all truth and cannot commit error.

In saying that the very words are what God wanted used, we do not mean that He merely dictated to a penman. The fact that there is such a variety of style and vocabulary in the books of the Old Testament and that the personality of the writer shines through so often should be evidence enough that God did not destroy the individuality of the writers. Thus, the Old Testament is a divine-human book; divine truth is passed through the personality and experience of the authors of Scripture. Therefore, we may think of inspiration as a work of God in which He guided the writers of Scripture to pen the exact words He wished recorded. This guidance did not violate the personality of these writers; yet it guaranteed accuracy of doctrine, judgment, and historical and scientific fact.

This view of inspiration is the only one that takes into account all the claims of the numerous biblical references on the subject. We must reject all other theories of inspiration as inadequate. For instance, it is not enough to say that writers of Scripture possessed some special genius or insight, such as that demonstrated by a

Milton or a Bunyan or a Shakespeare. Too much that appears in Scripture is infinitely beyond the comprehension or imagination of the most brilliant or even the most spiritual of men. Nor is it sufficient to say that inspiration is partial—applying only to truths unknowable by human reason and not to the historical sections of the Old Testament. How can we trust the Bible at all if such portions are shot through with error? How can we know that the doctrinal sections are not also unreliable? Neither can we be satisfied that inspiration is merely conceptual-extending to the ideas, but not to the words. Ill-chosen words may mute the force of a concept, change the nature of its impact, or alter the whole direction of its argument. We cannot settle for less than some sort of control over the very words of Scripture and the guarantee of their accuracy.

The Witness of the Authors

It is one thing to assert inspiration of the Old Testament; it is quite another to demonstrate it. Although there is no comprehensive claim of inspiration in the Old Testament, everywhere it is assumed and even asserted. Moses is said to have written down what God had revealed to him: "And Moses wrote all the words of the LORD" (Exodus 24:4; cf. Deuteronomy 27:8, NKJV). Isaiah (Isaiah 30:8) and Jeremiah (Jeremiah 30:2) were commanded to do the same. Several writers were very sure that their pronouncements were God's Word. Moses declared, "You shall not add to the word which I am commanding you, nor take away from it, that you may keep the commandments of the LORD your God which I command you" (Deuteronomy 4:2, NASB).

Jeremiah claimed, "Then the LORD put forth his hand, and touched my mouth. And the LORD said unto me, Behold, I have put my words in your mouth" (Jeremiah 1:9). David asserted, "The Spirit of the LORD spoke by me, and his word was in my tongue" (2 Samuel 23:2). Such expressions as "the Lord spoke" and "the word of the Lord came" are sprinkled liberally throughout the Old

Testament. In fact, the claim is made that such expressions actually occur 3,808 times in the Old Testament. These examples of Old Testament claims of its own inspiration must be added to references that indicate God occasionally wrote by His own hand what He wanted to say (see, for example, Exodus 24:12; 31:18; 32:16; 1 Chronicles 28:19).

The Witness of Prophecy

One of the most remarkable witnesses to Old Testament inspiration is the fulfillment of prophecy. In most cases, hundreds of years before the events, the prophets predicted specific fulfillment. Details concerning the birth, life, death, and resurrection of Christ, the captivity and restoration of Israel, and judgment on numerous cities and empires surrounding Israel are all included in the extensive list of prophetic pronouncements that have been fulfilled. The cumulative effect of these predictions is tremendous. They had to come by divine inspiration; no seer with purely human resources could peer so perceptively, specifically, and accurately into the future.

The Witness of Jesus

The testimony of Jesus Christ is another powerful witness to the inspiration of the Old Testament. One of His most direct statements appears in Matthew 5:17, 18: "Think not that I am come to destroy the law, or the prophets: I am not come to destroy, but to fulfill. For verily I say unto you, Till heaven and earth pass, one jot or one tittle shall in no wise pass from the law, till all be fulfilled." In the larger context of chapter 5, it is clear that He was claiming the Old Testament to be of divine origin and binding on the Jews to whom He was speaking. Apparently He was using "the law" here to stand for the whole Old Testament. In verse 17 He mentioned "law and prophets" but in verse 18 presumably found it unnecessary to repeat "prophets." Elsewhere He used "law" to refer to passages outside the first five books of the Old Testament (called the Law or Torah). See, for instance, John 10:34 where He quoted Psalm 82:6. The Matthew 5:17, 18 reference is especially significant because it appears in the Sermon on the Mount, which even the more severe textural critics acknowledge as a true statement of Jesus Christ. This passage is not an isolated indication, however, because Christ always supported the full truthfulness of Scripture in His parables, miracles, and comments on them, and in His numerous conversations. Hundreds of New Testament passages attest the fact. On occasion He spoke directly of divine inspiration of individual portions of the Old Testament, as for instance in Mark 12:36, where He referred to Psalm 110:1. Three times during His great temptation experience, He made appeal to the authority of the Old Testament to rout the tempter (Matthew 4:4, 7, 10). And He very pointedly remarked that "scripture cannot be broken" (John 10:35); that is, it cannot be annulled or abrogated. Even Jesus' enemies among the Pharisees and Sadducees never accused Him of disrespect toward or questioning of their sacred Scriptures.

The New Testament Witness

Jesus' testimony to divine inspiration of the Old Testament is corroborated and supplemented throughout the rest of the New Testament. Paul, as a good Pharisee, would be expected to support the accuracy and validity of the Old Testament at all times. The writer to the Hebrews likewise subscribed to God's involvement in the process of revelation and inspiration: "In the past God spoke to our forefathers through the prophets at many times and in various ways, but in these last days he has spoken to us by his Son" (Hebrews 1:1, 2, NIV). One of the most significant New Testament passages on Old Testament inspiration is 2 Peter 1:20, 21,

"Above all, you must understand that no prophecy of Scripture came about by the prophet's own interpretation. For prophecy never had its origin in the will of man, but men spoke from God as they were carried along by the Holy Spirit" (NIV). The clear teaching of this passage is that the revelation of God did not come when great religious leaders of the past sought to make some religious pronouncement, but when certain holy men, chosen instruments, spoke as they were moved by the Holy Spirit.

The Witness in Judaism

What the Old Testament claimed for itself in terms of inspiration and what Jesus and the New Testament writers supported in this regard was further attested to in Judaism. The very high regard of Jews for the Old Testament is evident from many passages in the Talmud (a sort of encyclopedia of Jewish tradition), but it is especially spelled out in the forthright statement of the first century historian Flavius Josephus:

> How firmly we have given credit to these books of our own nation is evident by what we do; for during so many ages as have already passed no one hath been so bold as either to add anything to them, to take anything from them, or to make any change; but it is become natural to all Jews, immediately and from their very birth, to esteem these books to contain divine doctrines, and to persist in them, and if occasion be, willingly to die for them.[3]

Before leaving this subject, it is necessary to distinguish inspiration from two other terms. "Inspiration" has to do with accurate reception and recording of God's truth. "Revelation" involves communication of God's message, and "illumination" concerns the Holy Spirit's ministry of giving understanding of truth already revealed (John 14:26).

ARE THE TEXT AND HISTORY OF
THE OLD TESTAMENT RELIABLE?

Some have argued that it does not matter if the Old Testament was inspired in the original writings. They observe that those writings no longer exist and that copyists have made thousands of mistakes as they have reproduced the books of the Old Testament during the almost three thousand years (in some cases) before the advent of printing. As may be suspected, the editing and evaluation of Hebrew texts is a tedious and technical task. It is quite impossible even to provide an introduction to the subject here. We must make generalizations and draw on the conclusions of others.

Until after World War II the only Hebrew text of the Old Testament known was the one standardized between A.D. 500 and 900 by Jewish scholars called Masoretes. The oldest copies of that text in our possession were no older than about A.D. 900. By comparing this text with Greek and Latin and other Old Testament translations dating to a much earlier time, it could be shown that copying of the Hebrew text had been faithfully performed at least since around A.D. 200–300. All of our copies of the Hebrew text coming from A.D. 900 and later are in remarkably close agreement. In this regard, the late William Henry Green of Princeton commented, "The Hebrew manuscripts cannot compare with those of the New Testament either in antiquity or number, but they have been written with greater care and exhibit fewer various readings."[4] Robert Dick Wilson, of the same generation at Princeton, supplemented Green's assertion: "An examination of the Hebrew manuscripts now in existence shows that in the whole Old Testament there are scarcely any variants supported by more than one manuscript out of 200 to 400, in which each book is found. . . . The Masoretes have left to us the variants which they gathered and we find that they amount altogether to about 1,200, less than one for each page of the printed Hebrew Bible."[5] Moreover, "The various readings are for the most part of a trivial character, not materially affecting the sense."[6]

While it is significant that there are few variations among Old Testament manuscripts dating since A.D. 900, one must wonder what happened during the previous two thousand three hundred years (in some cases) of transmission of the text. Something of an answer to such a query is provided by the Dead Sea Scrolls, the first of which were found in 1947. These manuscripts contain much more than biblical texts, but the biblical manuscripts include parts of every Old Testament book except Esther. Especially lengthy portions consist of a complete Isaiah, almost complete Leviticus and Psalms, and an Isaiah manuscript that includes most of chapters 35 through 66 and parts of earlier chapters. The scrolls date between about 250 B.C. and A.D. 70, thus pushing back the history of the Old Testament text about a millennium.

Remarkably, there are very few differences of any significance between the Dead Sea Scrolls and the previously existent Masoretic text. The incomplete scroll of Isaiah is almost letter for letter the same as the Masoretic Isaiah. For instance, in Isaiah 53 there are differences of only seventeen letters, most of which are merely variations in spelling; three letters introduce a word in the scroll copy of verse 11 which does not appear in the Masoretic text; however, this does not change the meaning of the passage. On the basis of the complete Isaiah from the scroll caves, thirteen minor changes were made in the Revised Standard Version of the Bible; but several of these were later thought unnecessary. Admittedly there are passages (notably in 1 Samuel) where some corruption of text seems to have occurred, but in general, it may be said that the text of the Dead Sea Scrolls is essentially that which we have possessed all along. No doctrine has been affected by copyists' changes, inadvertent or otherwise. R. Laird Harris concludes, "Indeed it would be rash skepticism that would now deny we have our Old Testament in a form very close to that used by Ezra when he taught the law to those who had returned from Babylonian captivity."[7] Harris goes on to show that archaeology tends to confirm the accuracy of the text of even earlier centuries than when the scrolls were produced, for instance, in the faithful transmission of names of persons and peoples. He also notes that there is evidence of faithful copying in the transmission of parallel texts in the Old Testament. For example, large parts of Chronicles are found in Samuel and Kings and elsewhere and several Psalms occur twice in that book; such passages can be checked against each other to demonstrate accuracy in transmission.[8]

HISTORICAL ACCURACY OF THE TEXT

But conceivably, even incorrect information may be faithfully copied for a long period of time. Questions are often asked about the historical accuracy of the contents of the Old Testament. Many of these questions arose during the nineteenth century when little specific knowledge about the ancient Near East existed. As rationalistic critics increasingly investigated the Bible, they concluded that it was full of historical errors because history books had nothing to say about most of the peoples and events of the Bible.

But throughout the twentieth century, Near Eastern and classical archaeologists rapidly expanded their efforts. Libraries, palaces, forts, houses, and factories have come to light in increasing numbers. Cities such as Ur, Nineveh, Hazor, and Jericho, which had dropped out of sight, have been at least partially uncovered by excavators. The existence of such ancient peoples as the Hitties or Horites, once doubted, has been confirmed. Likewise, scores of biblical persons and their individual acts have been substantiated by the excavator's pick and trowel. King Ahab did rule over Israel with his wife Jezebel; one may stroll past the ruins of his palace at Samaria. Sargon II of Assyria (Isaiah 20:1) was no figment of the prophet's imagination as once charged; he ruled Assyria 722–705 B.C., built a new capital at Khorsabad, and erected a magnificent palace there. Shishak I of Egypt invaded Judah about 925 B.C. (1 Kings 14:25–28) as his inscriptions on a temple wall at Luxor, Egypt, attest. Babylonian records demonstrate that

Belshazzar was in charge in Babylon when it fell to the Persians (Daniel 5), even though critics long claimed the account to be in error. Cyrus the Great of Persia did issue a decree permitting the Jews to return to Palestine from captivity in Babylon, as Ezra 1 says. Any visitor to the British Museum in London may see the inscription in the manuscript room. Moreover, the manuscript room also houses the inscription of Sargon II in which he tells of his invasion of Judah (Isaiah 36).

Of course, the testimony of archaeology is incomplete. Thousands of cities of the ancient world still lie under the sands of the Near East. With new information have come new problems of interpretation because in the fragmentary state of our knowledge the new discoveries do not always seem to jibe with biblical accounts. But to date, archaeological discoveries have not proved the Bible to be in error. New historical and archaeological investigations are constantly providing greater support for the historical accuracy of the Old Testament.

WHAT BOOKS BELONG IN THE OLD TESTAMENT?

To ask what books belong in the Old Testament is not a purely academic question. No individual believer can decide what a correct religious teaching is or determine God's instructions for daily living except on the basis of authoritative Scripture. He or she wants to know how the Old Testament was compiled and whether or not all the books should be viewed as mandatory truth. What will we do with the conflicting claims of Protestants and Roman Catholics over the so-called Apocrypha?

The specific and detailed origins of the Old Testament are lost in antiquity, but there seem to be at least four criteria involved in the process of Old Testament formation: inspiration, the writer's official position, human reception, and collection or official ratification. Apparently the Old Testament was formed in a very simple and natural way. God communicated His truth to and through men to whom He imparted a prophetic gift. The recipients recognized them as men of God with a message from the Most High. Their written messages were received as obligatory on the people and were officially accepted by the populace as a whole and by the religious leaders more specifically.

To begin with, the two tablets of the Law (written by God Himself) were placed in the ark of the covenant (Exodus 25:21), the most priceless possession of Israel; and all of Moses' Laws (the first five books of the Old Testament, one fourth of the total) were written in a book (scroll) and kept beside the ark (Deuteronomy 31:24–26). The commands of the Law were binding on Joshua, Moses' successor (Joshua 1:7, 8); and they were enjoined on all the people of Israel in a great ceremony in the vicinity of Shechem soon after Joshua led them into the land (Joshua 8:30–35). In the future, when Israel would set up a kingdom, the king was to have a personal copy of the Law and to live by its precepts (Deuteronomy 17:18–20). Kings were judged according to obedience to the Law (e.g., 2 Kings 18:6). Both Israel and Judah were carried into captivity because of failure to obey it (2 Kings 17:7–23; 18:11, 12; Daniel 9:11–13). Jews who returned from the captivity fully recognized the Law of Moses as binding upon them (Ezra 3:1, 2; Nehemiah 8:1–8; 10:28, 29). The criteria noted above are clearly evident here. God spoke to Moses on the mount and even wrote on two tablets of stone. The priests and the people as a whole received the five books of Moses as God's Word. A copy of the books was kept near the ark and was supposed to be kept by the king. Moses was God's spokesman, accredited by miracles in the court of Pharaoh and in the wilderness and vindicated against those who disputed his divinely appointed leadership by judgment direct from the hand of God (see Numbers 16 and 12:6–8). All this adds up to a public and an official adoption of the five books of Moses as sacred Scripture.

God promised Moses that He would raise up a whole line of prophets after him in Israel, culminating in the person and work of

Jesus Christ (Deuteronomy 18:15–22). The primary function of these men was to proclaim the truth of God; and of course, they would also predict the future. Joshua may qualify as a prophetic successor of Moses. The early Jewish work Ecclesiasticus (composed about 180 B.C.) calls Joshua the "successor of Moses in prophecies." His leadership in Israel was attested by miracles (crossing of the Jordan and fall of the walls of Jericho), and he did predict at least one event that came true (Joshua 6:26; cf. 1 Kings 16:34). In any case, Joshua 24:26 says he "wrote these words in the Book of the Law of God" (NKJV), presumably referring to our book of Joshua. Since he wrote in "the Book of the Law of God," it would appear that he simply added to the already officially recognized writings of Moses. Possibly Samuel the prophet wrote Judges and 1 Samuel down to 25:1, when he died. Presumably the prophets Nathan and Gad took up the account there (1 Chronicles 29:29), and the prophets Abijah and Iddo continued the narrative later (2 Chronicles 9:29). Other prophets apparently contributed to the writing of Kings and Chronicles. Actually the Hebrew Bible calls Joshua, Judges, Samuel, and Kings "the former prophets." Of course, writers of the many books of Old Testament prophecies were men who had official positions as prophets and whose messages were recognized as coming from God. We know less about the poetic books. David (a prophet according to Acts 2:30) wrote about half the Psalms. Other writers of Psalms—Heman, Jeduthun, and Asaph—are also called prophets (1 Chronicles 25:1–5). Presumably Solomon wrote Proverbs, Song of Solomon, and Ecclesiastes; and God spoke to him in visions and dreams like the other prophets.

While we do not have information on how all the Old Testament books were accepted by the Hebrews into their sacred collection (and there is not space here to discuss what we surmise), we do know that by New Testament times the Hebrews recognized as Scripture only our present thirty-nine books. The order in which they placed them was somewhat different from ours, however. After the Law and the prophets, they listed a group of writings that began with the Psalms and ended with 2 Chronicles. Luke 24:44 seems to refer to the entire Old Testament in this arrangement when it speaks of law, prophets, and psalms (which headed the last section of the Hebrew Bible).

CORROBORATION AND DISPUTES

An especially valuable statement on the contents of the Old Testament appears in the writings of Flavius Josephus about A.D. 90. After referring to the contents of the sacred collection (the thirty-nine books we now have), he says no one had dared to add anything to them since the days of King Artaxerxes I of Persia (465–425 B.C.).[9] In other words, nothing had been added since the writing of Malachi around the end of Artaxerxes' reign. The testimony of this learned Jew is important not only for the date of the close of the Old Testament but also in answering the late date that liberal critics assign to such books as Daniel and Ecclesiastes.

It should not be assumed from what has been said that there was no debate among the Hebrews over whether or not some books should be included in the Old Testament. However, this discussion did not reflect any general opposition to any one of the books and did not delay their acceptance as Scripture. Individual Jewish rabbis and their followers expressed these doubts. Questions arose particularly over Esther, Song of Solomon, and Ecclesiastes. Though questioned because it did not mention the name of God, Esther was seen to reflect everywhere the provident hand of God in human affairs. The Song of Solomon was opposed because some passages bordered on the erotic if taken literally. When interpreted allegorically to refer to God's love for Israel, it was no longer questioned. Inclusion of Ecclesiastes was disputed because of alleged pessimism and Epicureanism; but as the author's special technique and purpose became more fully understood, opposition declined.

In more recent centuries there has been a continuing debate between Protestants and Roman Catholics over whether or not the apocryphal books are part of the Old Testament. The fourteen books in question are 1, 2 Esdras, Tobit, Judith, Remainder of Esther, Wisdom of Solomon, Ecclesiasticus, Baruch, Song of the Three Children, History of Susanna, Bel and the Dragon, The Prayer of Manasses, and 1, 2 Maccabees. While these books do help to fill in the gap between the Old and New Testaments, especially as they reflect religious viewpoints and provide some knowledge of the history of the times (notably 1 Maccabees), they have no real claim to being part of authoritative Scripture. They do not claim to be Scripture, were not considered to be so by Jerome, who translated the Latin Vulgate, and were not even officially recognized by the Roman Church until the Council of Trent (1545–63). The Hebrew Old Testament never included them, nor did Josephus or the great Philo of Alexandria (who lived about the time of Christ). The early lists of the Apocrypha disagree considerably in their contents, and none of them have the exact list that the Roman Church approved. Moreover, they abound in historical, geographical, and chronological inaccuracies, teach doctrines at variance with inspired Scripture, and contain folklore, myth, legend, and fiction.[10]

HOW DOES THE OLD TESTAMENT RELATE TO THE NEW TESTAMENT?

The Old and New Testaments are simply component parts of one divine revelation. The Old Testament describes human beings in the first paradise on the old earth; the New Testament concludes with a vision of them in the new heaven and new earth. The Old Testament sees people as fallen from a sinless condition and separated from God; the New Testament views them as restored to favor through the sacrifice of Christ. The Old Testament predicts a coming Redeemer who will rescue humanity from the pit of condemnation; the New Testament reveals the Christ who makes salvation possible. In most of the Old Testament the spotlight focuses on a sacrificial system in which the blood of animals provides a temporary handling of the sin problem; in the New, Christ appears as the One who came to put an end to all sacrifice—to be Himself the supreme sacrifice. In the Old Testament numerous predictions foretell a coming Messiah who will save His people; in the New, scores of passages detail how those prophecies were minutely fulfilled in the person of Jesus Christ, the son of Abraham and the son of David. As St. Augustine said more than 1500 years ago:

> The New is in the Old concealed;
> The Old is in the New revealed.
> The New is in the Old contained;
> The Old is in the New explained.
> The New is in the Old enfolded;
> The Old is in the New unfolded.

Notes

1. Josephus *Contra Apionem* 1.8.
2. Though some of the material of Kings and Chronicles is similar, the differences are considerable. Kings, written before the exile, presents an account of the history of Israel from the days of David to the conquest by Nebuchadnezzar and interweaves the history of the Northern and Southern Kingdoms. Chronicles, completed after the exile, describes the divinely authorized dynasty of David and tells about David, Solomon, and the history of the Southern Kingdom, whose kings all descended from David. It stresses the spiritual foundations of Israel as the covenant people of God.
3. Josephus *Contra Apionem* 1.8.
4. William Henry Green, *General Introduction to the Old Testament: The Text* (New York: Scribner, 1926), p. 179.
5. Robert Dick Wilson, *Scientific Investigation of the Old Testament*, with Revisions by E.J. Young (Chicago: Moody, 1959), pp. 61–62.
6. Green, p. 164.

7. R. Laird Harris, "How Reliable Is the Old Testament Text?" in *Can I Trust the Bible?* ed. Howard F. Vos (Chicago: Moody Press, 1963), p. 130.

8. Ibid., pp. 130–131.

9. Josephus *Contra Apionem* 1.8.

10. For a very helpful discussion of the subject, see Merrill F. Unger, *Introductory Guide to the Old Testament* (Grand Rapids: Zondervan, 1952), chap. 4.

The Early History
of God's People

In the Beginning

Genesis 1–11

GOD does not leave human beings to wonder about the origin of their world or themselves. Nor does He leave them in the dark as to why they have a tendency to do evil and why they die. Furthermore, He has chosen to tell them what lies beyond the grave and whether there is any hope for them in that future world. Moreover, He provides an account of the struggle between the forces of good and evil down through the centuries and of His wonderful care and provision for those who put their trust in Him. Most of this begins to unfold in the early chapters of the Old Testament.

Those who write about the Old Testament commonly divide their discussion into units that cover individual books or groups of books such as law, history, poetry, and prophecy. The approach here is primarily to deal with time periods in the history of Israel, prefaced by some discussion of the early beginnings, and to divide the treatment of the text accordingly. Thus, this chapter deals with Genesis 1–11;

chapter 3 deals with the patriarchs in Genesis 12–50, and so on. In this way the reader can discover how the books of the Old Testament relate to the flow of history or to Hebrew development.

AUTHORSHIP AND DATE OF THE PENTATEUCH

Even though discussion of the Pentateuch (first five books of the Old Testament) is divided into three separate chapters, the same questions of authorship and date concern all five books. Until the nineteenth century almost everyone believed that Moses wrote the first five books of the Old Testament. But with the rise of literary criticism and the dogma of evolution, that changed. Just as scholars doubted that Shakespeare wrote the dramas traditionally attributed to him and that Homer wrote the *Iliad* and the *Odyssey*, so they also doubted that Moses wrote the Pentateuch. And when the teachings of evolution began to make their impact during the latter part of the nineteenth century, the concept of slow development was applied to Scripture. Thus it was taught that the Pentateuch developed gradually; documents and sources were collected and edited until it finally came to its present form during the fifth century B.C.

There is abundant support for the view of Mosaic authorship, however. The Pentateuch itself claims that important parts were written by Moses (e.g., Exodus 24:4, 7; Deuteronomy 31:9, 24–26). Passage after passage in Leviticus and Numbers specifically says that God communicated accompanying information to Moses (Leviticus 1:1; 4:1; 6:1; etc.; Numbers 1:1; 2:1; 4:1, etc.). Internal evidence shows that an eyewitness wrote the Pentateuch. Those parts of the Pentateuch that involve Egypt contain many references that show the author's familiarity with Egypt and contain information hard to obtain in Canaan several centuries after Moses' day, when liberals hold it was written. Egyptian names, Egyptian words borrowed by the writer, Egyptian customs and geography all indicate that the author knew Egypt well.

Internal evidence also shows that the Pentateuch was written in the desert from the vantage point of a people with Egypt behind them and Canaan before them. They worshiped in a tabernacle, not a temple (see Leviticus 14:8, 34; 16:21; Numbers 2:2; Deuteronomy 11:10; 12:9; 15:4, 7; 17:14). The picture one gets is not that of an agricultural people settled in Palestine for almost a thousand years. A common liberal view is that Deuteronomy was composed by Hebrew priests during King Josiah's revival in 621 B.C., but many conditions indicated in Deuteronomy were not true of the seventh century B.C. Directions concerning extermination of Canaanites and the way of dealing with the cities of the land (Deuteronomy 20:1–20), allusion to recent bondage in Egypt (Deuteronomy 23:7), and regulations concerning the choice of a king and his duties (Deuteronomy 17:14–20) hardly have significance for Palestinians of 621 B.C.

Support from Other Quarters

The claims of the Pentateuch to be a revelation of God to Moses are frequently supported in the rest of the Old Testament, intertestamental literature, and the statements of Christ. Several times the Law of Moses is appealed to in Joshua, showing that it was in written form at this early date (e.g., Joshua 1:7, 8; 8:32, 34; 22:5). A few examples will suffice to demonstrate that the rest of the Old Testament follows the example of Joshua and refers to the "law" or "book" of Moses: 1 Kings 2:3; 2 Chronicles 23:18 and 34:14; Ezra 3:2 and 6:18; Nehemiah 8:1–8; Daniel 9:11, 13. The testimony continues during the intertestamental period, notably in Ecclesiasticus 45:3, 5 (written about 180 B.C.) and in Philo (*Life of Moses* 3.39), dating about the time of Christ's birth. These are supported by the eminent Josephus (*Antiquities* 4. 8. 48) who wrote about A.D. 90. All three of these declare for Mosaic authorship of the Pentateuch.

Christ on numerous occasions spoke of the Law of Moses, sometimes of the "book of Moses" (Mark 12:26), and twice of

"Moses and the prophets" (Luke 16:31) or Moses, the prophets, and the psalms (Luke 24:44), obviously making Moses author of the first part of the Old Testament on a par with other major sections. Of course, the early church, the church of later centuries, and the Jews unanimously accepted that view until the rise of destructive higher criticism. The evidence is too compelling to be dismissed lightly by a group of rationalists.

The exact date when Moses wrote individual books of the Pentateuch will never be known, but the latest possible date for completion of all five books of the Pentateuch is the time of Moses' death just before the Hebrews crossed the Jordan and attacked Jericho. The time assigned to his composition is related to the whole problem of the date of the Exodus which is discussed later. The writer concludes that the death of Moses came about 1400 B.C. and that this is, therefore, the latest possible date for writing the Pentateuch.

THE CREATION (Genesis 1–2)

In simple, concise, nontechnical language Moses answers one of the big questions of life: "Where did the earth come from?" Says Moses, "In the beginning God created the heavens and the earth." Then with broad strokes of the pen he proceeds to sketch out six creative days that culminate with a description of the origin of the first human couple, thus answering another of the big questions of life: "Where did human beings come from?" These two chapters are truly a masterpiece, suitable for the plain people of his day and all succeeding ages. Yet they do not close the door on scientific and philosophical investigation, for they state only *that* God created, and do not describe *how*.

Nor does Moses say when creation took place. "In the beginning," at the outset of His creative work, God called into being the heavens and earth; at the end of the process He created human beings. If God did not set dates, we do not need to do so either.

Even such an ultraconservative Bible student as C.I. Scofield, editor of the Scofield Reference Bible, stated on page 3 of his Bible (1909), "The first creative act refers to the dateless past and gives scope for all the geologic ages."

According to the Genesis account, the creative work of God took place on six days and had specific results as follows:

Day 1   Light appeared. Some sort of cosmic light or the sun, moon, and stars are involved. It is, of course, possible that creation of the earth came subsequent to creation of some other parts of this solar system and to other solar systems. In such an event, the light of the sun and stars would exist prior to the earth.

Day 2   The firmament came into existence. This is a mistranslation of a word signifying "expanse," and probably refers to the atmosphere around the earth.

Day 3   Dry land appeared. God gathered the waters into lakes and seas, perhaps by depressing part of the earth's crust and raising other parts. Plant life appeared.

Day 4   The sun, moon, and stars either were created or became visible and began to serve their known functions.

It is important to note that the Hebrew word for "create" used earlier in the chapter does not occur in verse 16. Therefore, the implication is that the sun, moon, and stars did not come into existence at this time, but were assigned their relationship to the earth as twin regulators to establish days, seasons, and years.

Day 5   Marine life and fowl appeared.

Day 6   Land animals and humans crowned the creative work. Three classifications of terrestrial life are listed: cattle (animals capable of domestication), creeping things (reptiles or a variety of short-legged creatures that may appear to crawl), and beasts of the earth (truly wild animals that cannot be domesticated).

The Challenge of the Theory of Evolution

Until the impact of Charles Darwin (*Origin of Species*, 1859; *Descent of Man*, 1871) almost everyone in Western Christendom accepted the biblical account. Since that time the evolutionary hypothesis has been increasingly endorsed and today is held as fact by a great many. In short, this position holds that beginning with self-reproducing chemicals and one-celled forms, there was a slow development over a very long period of time through plant and animal stages until human beings finally appeared on the scene. The process is thought to work by mutation and natural selection. That is to say, living organisms change (mutation) and may pass on those mutations to forms they generate. Those forms best able to adjust to their environment (the "fittest") survive and reproduce; others simply die out. Nature itself determines which are the most fit (natural selection). It is popular to deny that there has been any divine influence on these processes.

Biblical literalists are quick to point out that the dogma of evolution is only a working hypothesis that has not been proved. It leaves a great many unanswered questions or has many loopholes in its argument, a few of which follow:

1. It does not satisfactorily explain the origin of simple life in the universe but usually assumes spontaneous generation of life from chemicals.
2. It fails to account satisfactorily for the origin of the spiritual nature of humanity.
3. The argument of the survival of the fittest does not account for the artistic talents of human beings.
4. There is no evidence for the crossing over from plant to animal life or for moving from one species to another, though many biologists consider the latter probable. To put the matter in another way, there is a lack of sufficient intermediate forms, and scientists are unable to prove genetic continuity among various organisms living and extinct.

5. The anthropological evidence is composite in nature. That is, one must skip from continent to continent to reconstruct the story of human development. For instance, for a segment of anthropological history, one must jump from Java (Java man) to China (Peking man) to Europe (Neanderthal man). The evidence commonly has been arranged according to the theory of development from the simple to the complex.

6. Much of the evidence is very partial—partial skeletons and discovery of skeletons without tools or primitive tools without skeletons. Skeletal reconstruction is conjectural and sometimes open to considerable question.

7. So-called vestigial remains, organs supposedly left over from a previous stage of evolutionary development (e.g., appendix, tonsils) often prove their usefulness, and therefore are no firm evidence for evolution.

Coming to Terms with Modern Science

Although these and many other far more technical questions may be raised about the theory of evolution, no intelligent and informed Bible student will dismiss the accumulating evidences about early ages in the fields of geology, anthropology, biology, and other sciences. One simply must come to terms with some of this information. To do so, some have espoused a "gap" theory. That is, there was an original good creation as described in Genesis 1:1 but between Genesis 1:1 and 1:2 a catastrophe occurred, and expanded ages elapsed, followed by God's recreation as described in chapters 1 and 2. In response to this view, it should be noted that there is no specific statement anywhere in Scripture of a judgment or catastrophe between Genesis 1:1 and 1:2, and there is no justification for translating "and the earth *became* desolate" (v. 2; the verb is normally rendered "was" throughout the Old Testament). Apparently verse 2 merely describes the world as "desolate and uninhabitable," at a stage not yet ready for human occupation.

Others have adopted a "day-age" theory, according to which the days of Genesis 1–2 are thought of not as twenty-four-hour days but as expanded periods of time somewhat corresponding to the geologic ages. A variation of this theory holds that there were literal creative days separated by expanded periods of time.

An important means of coming to terms with contemporary scholarship concerns itself especially with the term "kinds" of Genesis in chapter 1. All of nature is said to reproduce "after its kind," not to cross certain divinely fixed boundaries. No one knows exactly what "kind" should be equated with in our biological classification—genera? families? or something else? In other words, there seems to be some room here for mutation (or change) and even natural (or supernatural) selection. For instance, we may observe that there are many varieties of cats or dogs or cows, and these may have descended from one parent "kind" that existed in Eden or on the ark of Noah. Thus, there may have been mutation from the parent dog and selection to produce the many varieties now known, but dogs always produce dogs—"after their kind." Likewise, the Bible refers to only one human pair, but there are many races and subraces in the world today. Obviously there had to be some changes to produce these anthropological differences, but human beings cannot crossbreed or hybridize with any animals and can only produce human beings—"after their kind." All this adds up to saying that Bible believers may accept a certain amount of variation in nature and, in this way, achieve some degree of a meeting of minds with modern science. But the extent of this change or diversification appears to have fixed limits (within "kinds") according to Scripture and science. The "missing links" are numerous indeed.

Before leaving the subject of creation, it is important to say something about the fact that human beings were created in the image of God (Genesis 1:26, 27; 1 Corinthians 11:7). Apparently this likeness to God involved both a natural and a moral likeness. By nature, man and woman were like God in that they possessed intellect, emotions, and will. Their moral likeness consisted in sinlessness. On the basis of both the moral and natural likeness, man and woman could have fellowship with God. When they sinned, the moral likeness was lost, and fellowship with God was severed. But men and women still possess a natural likeness to God (James 3:9). Would it make a difference in human relations if we recognized that all with whom we come in contact are human beings truly created in the image of God?

The essence of this natural likeness is nowhere clearly described but may be inferred from the early chapters of Genesis. There we see that human beings are distinct from animals and have been given dominion over them and all the rest of creation (Genesis 1:26). To exert this dominion we must exercise intelligence or reasoning power; we have a mind. Moreover, we have the ability to communicate with each other and with God in meaningful speech. Last, like God, we as human beings have the power to create in a host of ways. In all these and no doubt additional ways men and women may be said to possess the image of God.

The Fall and Beginnings of Civilization
(Genesis 3–5)

When God created Adam, He placed him in the beautiful Garden of Eden, located in the vicinity of four rivers. Two of these are not known, but the other two (Tigris, biblical Hiddekel; and Euphrates) are in modern Iraq or ancient Mesopotamia. Presumably, then, the garden was situated somewhere in or near Mesopotamia. Apparently Eden was an unbelievably magnificent spot, hardly the setting for the fall of humanity. This fact argues cogently for the view that improving the human moral and social environment would not necessarily make people good.

Genesis 3 provides an answer to another of the big questions of life: How do we account for the origin of sin and evil in the world? The Genesis record makes it abundantly clear that sin was not a part of God's original creation but came as the result of temptation of the first man and woman, whom God had created with the power of choice. They freely chose to rebel against God at the suggestion of an alien evil spirit. This spirit is not merely some impersonal force but is a powerful supernatural personality in conflict with God. His power is so tremendous that even the archangel Michael did not dare bring a judgment against him (Jude 9). Presumably Satan's own rebellion against God had occurred before the creation of the earth or at least before the creation of humanity.[1]

A Simple Choice with Disastrous Consequences

Satan used as his instrument in the temptation the serpent, apparently a very wonderful creature in its uncursed state. His approach was first to question whether God had not permitted Eve to eat of every tree of the garden. Perhaps he came to Eve with this doubt because she had gotten the prohibition second hand. Adam heard the command direct from God and knew certainly the details of it. Eve got the word from Adam and might have been made to question whether she had heard right. At any rate, Satan was able to concentrate on the prohibition and make her forget all the privileges she enjoyed in the garden. At least that is the implication of her reply; note that she omits "all" or "every" in 3:2 and adds "neither shall you touch it" in 3:3. In the latter case she seems to be saying, "Not only can't we eat fruit of the tree of good and evil, we can't even touch it!" Satan now moves on to declare categorically that God was wrong, that she would not die if she ate. And finally, he asserts that if she ate, she would become as God. Eve's first major mistake was giving audience to Satan. Her second error was consenting to linger and look on that which was forbidden. And she "saw that the tree was good for food," or appealed to the appetite (lust of the flesh, 1 John 2:16), "and that it was pleasant to the eyes" (lust of the eyes, 1 John 2:16), "and a tree to be desired to make one wise" (the pride or vainglory of life, 1 John 2:16). So her temptation was on the same pattern as that with which Satan confronts human beings today and with which he confronted Christ in the wilderness (Matthew 4:1–11). Eve and Adam both ate of the fruit of the tree, and their eyes were opened—but only to see their shame and guilt. Eve was deceived, but Adam sinned knowingly (1 Timothy 2:14); why he did so, we can only speculate. Sometimes questions are raised concerning why the fall of humanity should hang on such an insignificant issue as eating a little fruit. Actually the sin, which really occurred before the first pair partook of the fruit, was not in the eating but in the disobeying and rebelling prior to that act. They chose to believe the word of Satan rather than the word of God and sought to elevate the will of humanity above the will of God. They wished to break the bounds of limitation imposed upon them and to become like God.

Results of the fall were swift in coming. Moral guilt was incurred, and fellowship with God was broken; they could not commune with Him in the garden as before. In fact, He expelled them from their beautiful home. Then He condemned them to exhausting labor to make a living; this toil was made more difficult by a curse on nature that will continue until the end times (Romans 8:20–23). The need to work is often looked upon as a result of the fall, but such is not the case; Adam was very busy before the fall, fulfilling his responsibility to "till" and "care for" (NEB) the garden. Women were condemned to suffering in childbearing. Judgment came upon the serpent, too, for being the instrument of Satan and perhaps for breaking the bounds of divine limitation upon the animal world and "speaking" with man, thus seeking to be equal with man.

Satan uttered a half-truth when he told Eve she would not die. God did not strike her down immediately, but she did die eventually. And in subsequent chapters of Genesis, the effects of sin are vividly portrayed in such events as the murder of Abel (chapter 4); in the "morgue" of chapter 5, where the phrase "and he died" constantly appears; and in the occasion for the flood (chapter 6).

Throughout the rest of the Bible, the pall of sin hangs heavy. Paul observed, in speaking of Adam, that "by one man sin entered into the world, and death by sin" (Roman 5:12). Evidently what Paul had in mind was both physical and spiritual death. Though physical death of the first pair was postponed for a while, spiritual death (separation from God) was not. Fellowship with God was broken, and Adam and Eve were promptly banished from the garden.

The introduction of Romans 5 raises the whole question of the historicity of the fall, and of the other early chapters of Genesis, for that matter. The apostle Paul by inspiration accepts the fall as fact and develops a thesis revolving around two headships: those who by natural generation are under the headship of Adam with its condemnation of sin and death, and those who by supernatural regeneration (new birth) are under the headship of Christ with its accompaniment of spiritual and physical life. Not only did Paul treat the Genesis 3 narrative as history in Romans and in 2 Corinthians 11:3, but Christ also seems to do so in John 8:44. Moreover, the early chapters of Genesis do not appear as poetic myth but are factual prose connected with historical narrative that has been corroborated at many points by archaeological and historical investigation.

Genesis 3 is not all gloom. Verse 15 promises a "seed of woman" who will crush the head of the serpent, that is, destroy him. This is, then, the first Old Testament announcement of the coming Messiah who would eventually judge Satan on the cross.[2]

Beginnings of Civilization

Genesis 4 presents a very telescoped account of the increase of human population on earth and the beginnings of civilization. The narrative centers especially on Adam's sons Abel, Cain, and Seth; but there are hints of numerous progeny of Adam and Eve and their children. Cain and Seth had to get wives from somewhere and certainly must have married sisters. Presumably other unnamed sons of Adam and Eve did likewise (see Genesis 5:4). Enoch built a city (4:17), implying a fair-sized population. Presumably in the youth of human history the marriage of close relatives did not create the problems it would today after the degrading influence of sin has taken its toll over the millennia. Presumably, too, women were capable of bearing more children over a longer period of time, and infant mortality was probably minimal.

Civilization, at least in terms of village life, metallurgy, musical development and so on, reportedly began in the line of Cain (Genesis 4:16–22). But there is no hint of chronology in Genesis 4. Approximately 9500 B.C. at Abu Hureyra on the Euphrates in Syria[3] or the early eighth millennium B.C. at Jericho is as far back as we can now go with village life. But if one grants the extreme destructiveness of the flood, perhaps all the antediluvian civilization was wiped out and known early civilization dates rather to the post-Noahic period.

There are numerous chronological indications in chapters 5 and 11, however, and on the basis of such information many have sought to work out a chronology going all the way back to creation (tight chronology view, which holds that there are no gaps in the biblical genealogies). But the tendency among Bible scholars today is to conclude that biblical genealogies are not designed to be complete but include only representative names in the line of the Redeemer. They hold that there are gaps in the biblical chronology, so we cannot assign dates to our ancestors in the early chapters of Genesis[4]. It would seem, however, that the existence of such gaps would not warrant pushing the origins of humanity back as far as anthropologists commonly do. Even if there are no gaps in biblical chronology, it still is not easy to establish a date for the creation of human beings. There are many variables in the evidence, and the some 200 systems of chronology based on the tight chronology view differ several millennia in their conclusions about a date for the creation of Adam and Eve.

THE FLOOD (Genesis 6–10)

With the passage of time, humanity became so depraved that God determined to destroy all except a righteous remnant and start over in His program to populate the earth. To carry out His plan, He chose Noah, his three sons, and their wives. Noah, a "preacher of righteousness" (2 Peter 2:5), had charge of building a huge boat to protect himself, his family, and the animals from extinction by the predicted flood. While it is not clear how long it took to build the ark (Genesis 6:3 may indicate that it was 120 years), there was time for people to repent of their sins and be saved from God's wrath. Apparently even the workmen employed in construction of the ark did not have any sympathy for Noah's message.

It is not possible to be dogmatic about measurements of the ark. They are given in cubits, and we do not know the exact length of a cubit in earlier times. But during the Hebrew monarchy a cubit was about eighteen inches. Figuring on that basis, we can determine that the ark was 300 cubits (450 feet) long, 50 cubits (75 feet) broad, and 30 cubits (45 feet) high, and had a displacement of some 43,000 tons—much larger than many modern ocean-going ships. Various computations have concluded that there was room enough on the ark's three decks for Noah, his family, the animals, and their provisions. A single pair of the unclean animals and seven pairs each of the clean animals were taken on board. (Evidently the distinction between clean and unclean preceded the Mosaic covenant.) What the ark looked like is difficult to determine from Scripture. Even the nature and placement of the window is debated, but it seems best to conclude that it consisted of an eighteen-inch opening running all the way around the ark under the roof.

A study of the text reveals that human and animal life were shut up in the ark for just over a year (exactly 371 days; cf. Genesis 7:11; 8:13, 14). A casual reading of the biblical account might lead to the conclusion that the flood came simply as a result of rain for forty days and forty nights. But it is nowhere stated that the rain ceased at the end of forty days. Evidently it continued intermittently for another 110 days (Genesis 7:24; 8:2, 4). In addition, Genesis 7:11 (NKJV) states that "the fountains of the great deep were broken up." Exactly what that means is not clear. Often it is interpreted to say that some convulsion of the earth's crust released stores of subterranean waters. But to date geologists have been unable to find evidence of such subterranean reserves or of any general and cataclysmic alteration of the earth's crust that may have eliminated such reservoirs by the collapse of geological structures above them.

How Far and How High?

The extent of the flood is often debated. Those who hold to a local flood observe that all Scripture requires is the flooding of the inhabited earth and that the passages that speak of the earth may just as well be translated "land;" thus eliminating some intimations of universality. They also argue that to cover the highest mountains would require several times as much water as now exists on this planet. Moreover, they conclude that most plant life would have been destroyed by submersion under salt water for a year. Presumably most of the marine life would also have been killed off by the flood, as a result of dilution of salt waters of the oceans or starvation from the disturbance of normal feeding grounds.

Those who argue for a universal flood note that Genesis 7:19 indicates universality in referring to "the whole heaven." Moreover, they conclude that if the flood were local, the area affected by it could be quickly replenished with animal and plant life from adjacent regions and that a large ark and care for the animals would be unnecessary. Furthermore, the highest mountain of the Ararat chain reaches a height of almost 17,000 feet; therefore a tremendous quantity of water would be required to cover it. This water certainly would not stand in a heap somewhere, but would spread over the entire earth because water seeks its own level.[5] And of course a local flood would not have fulfilled the purpose of judging the sinfulness of the entire antediluvian population, unless, of course, all human beings were then living in a limited locale. The fact that there are over 270 flood accounts from all parts of the world is significant support for a universal flood.

When the flood occurred must remain entirely open to question. The chronology date of approximately 2250 B.C. held to in a previous generation cannot be followed, because there is no indication of extensive flooding anywhere in the world at such a late date. Moreover, the so-called flood layers excavated in Mesopotamia can have nothing to do with the Noahic flood because they date to several periods of history widely separated in time. At present there does not seem to be a time in the geological timetable when the flood can be placed with any degree of certainty. That it occurred is corroborated by Peter (2 Peter 2:5; 3:6) and by Christ Himself (Matthew 24:37–39).

Noah's Curse and the Table of Nations

Before leaving the discussion of this section, we must say something about Noah's curse (Genesis 9:25, 26). This is a difficult passage, and little detail appears. One thing is clear, however: the curse was on Canaan, not Ham. We know from history and archaeology who the Canaanites were and something of their degraded moral condition. They were not a black people, and they have disappeared from history. So obviously this curse has nothing to do with a supposed inferiority of black people. Since the Canaanites have long ago become extinct, we conclude that the curse has been completely fulfilled; therefore we have no right to apply it to any modern people. Moreover, the curse does not seem to have involved biological or intellectual inferiority, but concerned primarily a religious or moral degradation.

After the flood, the sons of Noah had the responsibility of repopulating the earth. Chapter 10 summarizes the geographical distribution of their descendants. This is often called the Table of Nations. Certainly the chapter hints at the passage of a very long period of time and suggests areas to which various families migrated. Japheth and his sons settled in an area stretching across Eurasia from the Black and Caspian seas to Spain. The Hamites went down into Africa and later spread west along the Mediterranean coastland. Shem and his descendants occupied the area north of the Persian Gulf. Naturally, a considerable ethnic, linguistic, and cultural mixture of the various peoples took place.

THE CONFUSION OF TONGUES (Genesis 11)

The evolutionist holds that the languages of the earth originated by a process of development, as romance languages developed from Latin. Scripture declares, however, that at a specific time in history, God broke into the affairs of humanity and in an act of judgment deliberately originated a number of languages.

A reverent and intelligent Bible student may well believe that both the biblical and developmental viewpoints concerning the origin of language are true. At Babel, God did establish parent languages of the earth; from those, currently known languages developed. No one can deny that new languages have come into being in historic times. Certainly Latin does not have a history as ancient as Egyptian, nor Spanish and French a history as ancient as Akkadian.

An Attempt to Explain as Myth

As a result of the destructive higher criticism of the last century, the view has become prevalent that the Bible is full of myth and folklore. The story of the tower of Babel is classified as a myth—a story that must have been invented at some time in Hebrew history to account for the diversity of language. According to those who hold such a view, this myth developed in connection with the ziggurats or stage towers in Mesopotamia. These ziggurats, over thirty of which are known to exist, were composed of successively smaller stages, or stories of sun-dried or burnt brick, on the top of which was constructed a temple. The ziggurat most commonly associated with the origin of the Hebrew myth is the one at Babylon, some 295 feet high and originally consisting of seven stages, with a temple on the topmost level. The view would be, then, that someone saw this ziggurat and composed a myth about the origin of languages; finally, this myth found its way into the book of Genesis.

We must ask, however, whether the account in Genesis 11 can be accounted for so simply. In Genesis 9:1, God specifically told Noah and his sons, "Be fruitful and multiply, and fill the earth" (NKJV). In direct disobedience, their descendants were concerned lest they be scattered over the earth. In pride they sought to build a city and tower as a rallying point and as a symbol or memorial to their greatness. God could not condone this. Genesis does not say that they intended to enter heaven by means of this tower or that they intended to use it for worship purposes. The Hebrew simply calls it a *migdal* ("tower"), which could be used for defense or a number of other purposes; there is no indication that the builders planned to erect a temple on it so the structure could serve as a "link between earth and heaven" as the ziggurats did. Moreover, the Genesis narrative implies that such towers had not been built before and that this would, therefore, be something unique in the experience of humanity.

The ziggurats of Mesopotamia, on the other hand, were built for the express purpose of worshiping a local deity, not as an evidence of disobedience to him. Furthermore, the larger ziggurats came about as a result of slow development over a period of millennia. The earliest consisted only of a clay brick platform with a temple on it; a stage tower of several stages did not appear until the third millennium B.C., long after the diffusion of languages.[6] So if we assign any credence to the Genesis narrative at all, there can hardly be any connection between the Tower of Babel and the ziggurat at Babylon or anywhere else. Moreover, we should take into account the fact that the inhabitants of Mesopotamia came from the mountains to the east, and the ziggurats may merely have been an effort on the part of these people to construct a manmade mountain in the plains so they might be nearer to their gods. In their original homes they built high places in the mountains. Having moved to the plains, they were forced to build mountains before they could establish their high places in them.

In 1876 George Smith of the British Museum published a mutilated Assyrian tablet that seems to reflect the account of Genesis 11. This tablet indicates that the hearts of some of the people were evil and that during the night the gods destroyed the work on the ziggurat that the men had done during the day. The account also mentions divine confounding of speech and scattering of the people abroad.[7] Possibly we have here evidence of a tradition of the origin of languages in Mesopotamian literature, a tradition that harks back to an actual historical event. If so, there is no good reason for denying that in Genesis 11 we have another form of that tradition; we may reverently believe that in Genesis 11 we have the purer form, preserved by God Himself.

Notes

1. There is no necessary conflict between this statement and Genesis 1:31. In the latter the focus of attention is on earth; no reference is made to the condition of angelic beings at that time.

2. For a detailed discussion of this verse, see H.C. Leupold, *Exposition of Genesis* (Grand Rapids: Baker Book House, 1942), pp. 163–70.

3. A. N. T. Moore, et al. Village on the Euphrates (Oxford: Oxford University Press, 2000), p. 104.

4. For a discussion of this issue, see Oswald T. Allis, *The Five Books of Moses* (Philadelphia: Presbyterian & Reformed, 1943), pp. 261–64; Gleason Archer, *Survey of Old Testament Introduction*, 2nd rev. ed. (Chicago: Moody, 1973), pp. 185–89; Merrill F. Unger, *Introductory*

Guide to the Old Testament (Grand Rapids: Zondervan, 1951), pp. 192–94; and B.B. Warfield, *Studies in Theology* (New York: Oxford U. Press, 1932), pp. 235–58.

5. It should be noted that a flood covering the earth to the height of Ararat would require about three times as much water as exists on the earth today. Covering the earth to the height of the Himalayas would require eight times as much water as now exists on earth. At the present stage of scientific investigation, it is impossible to say where that much water could have come from or where it went after the flood. Of course, God could have put it there and taken it away again, but there is no statement of miraculous action of this sort in the Genesis narrative.

6. Andre Parrot, *The Tower of Babel* (New York: Philosophical Library, 1955), pp. 22, 26–43.

7. George Smith, *The Chaldean Accounts of Genesis* (London: Sampson, Lew, Marston, Searle, and Rivington, 1876), pp. 160ff.

༺᯽༻

3

Fathers in Israel: Abraham, Isaac, Jacob, and Joseph

Genesis 11–50

T HE patriarchs were a group of men (Abraham, Isaac, Jacob, and his sons) who inaugurated the Hebrew ethnic and religious development and controlled Hebrew affairs for over two centuries. They are called *patriarchs* because they were fathers not only to their immediate family but also to the extended family of the Hebrews, over which they exercised a fatherly kind of control. As such, they ruled and judged the Hebrews, looked after their best interests, and led them in worship.

Abraham, as the first of this group and ancestor of the rest, holds a special place in all three great monotheistic faiths of the world. He is, of course, progenitor of the Jews through Sarah and of the Arabs (largely Muslim) through Hagar. And he holds a special place in Christianity as an example of justification by faith and as the ancestor of Christ, through whom all Christians obtain their salvation.

ABRAHAM (Genesis 11:10–25:10)

God called Abraham out of Ur, a wealthy, populous, and sophisticated pagan center of southern Mesopotamia (modern Iraq), to follow Him wherever He directed. The path led to Canaan or Palestine, which was at that time a cultural backwater. Even before Abraham left Mesopotamia, God made with him the famous Abrahamic covenant, which promised him a land, a posterity, and a special divine favor ("I will bless them that bless you, and curse him that curses you"), and which pledged that he would be a channel of blessing to the entire world ("In you shall all families of the earth be blessed?" See Genesis 12:1–3). In Genesis 13:14–18, God confirmed this unconditional covenant, promising him this new land *forever*, along with innumerable descendants. Subsequently, in Genesis 15:1–21, God again confirmed the Abrahamic covenant but added the significant prediction that the guarantee of Canaan in perpetuity did not mean they would always occupy the land in every generation. He also spelled out the limits of the Promised Land (from the river of Egypt to the Euphrates, some 500 to 600 miles in extent), a territory far in excess of Canaan or Palestine (about 150 miles from Dan to Beersheba).

A final confirmation of the covenant to Abraham appears in Genesis 17:6–8. It again guarantees the land of Canaan to Abraham's posterity and injects the added note that kings (foregleam of the Davidic line) would arise in his line. (It is important to add to the Abrahamic covenant the Davidic covenant. See discussion under DAVID in chapter 8, noting 2 Samuel 7.) Passages dealing with the Abrahamic covenant are some of the most important in the Old Testament, for they are the basis for ultimate Jewish possession of the eastern end of the Mediterranean, God's guarantee of special favor and protection of the Jews through the millennia (which prevented their extinction in spite of their sins and the violent opposition of their enemies), and the appearance of the Messiah to provide spiritual blessing for all humanity.

A Man of Generosity and of Weaknesses

Scripture generally portrays Abraham as a man of faith and magnanimity. After entering Canaan, he found that one plot of land would not support the numerous flocks and herds of both himself and his nephew Lot; so he offered Lot the best lands of the area, and he moved off to more marginal territory. Subsequently, he rescued Lot after he was carried off in an invasion of Canaan and pled for him with God when God determined to destroy Sodom and the cities of the plain (the account of which is not hard to believe even from a purely naturalistic standpoint when one knows something of the combustible nature of materials in the area). Abraham's faith and spiritual maturity are frequently expressed in his building of altars and sacrificing on them, and especially in his obedience to God's command to sacrifice his only son on Mount Moriah (see Genesis 22). In commenting on this event, the book of Hebrews says Abraham's faith was so great he even believed that God could raise his son from the dead (Hebrews 11:19).

Although Scripture elevates Abraham to an extremely high position, it does not gloss over his weaknesses: his lapse of faith when he went down into Egypt (Genesis 12:10–13:1), and his doubts about God's providing him with a natural heir, which led to his taking the slave girl Hagar to wife, followed by the birth of Ishmael, progenitor of the Arabs (Genesis 16).[1] The Bible is always careful to present the unvarnished truth about even the most remarkable of the giants of faith. But Abraham's lapses must be viewed against the backdrop of his willingness to sacrifice his only beloved son, demonstrating his supreme faith and devotion to God and picturing the act of God the Father in sacrificing His only Son for the sins of the world.

ISAAC (Genesis 25:11–28:5; 35:27–29)

Isaac is somewhat obscured by the more eventful lives of his father and his son. He grew up in the shadow of a godly father and in the memory of his offering on Mount Moriah. He seems to have been a very devout man, and God confirmed to him the covenant made with Abraham (Genesis 26:3–5). To Isaac and Rebekah were born two sons (Jacob and Esau), and the most dramatic event of his later life was his mistake in identifying his sons and bestowing his blessing on the younger of them (Genesis 27). To a modern Westerner, this passage is puzzling. Why was not the mistake rectified, we ask? The answer is that what Isaac was doing involved something of the modern equivalent of making out his will. Scripture indicates and archaeological discoveries confirm that oral blessings (wills) were irrevocable in patriarchal society. Esau recognized this fact and did not ask Isaac to change his will, but merely asked for some sort of additional blessing (see Jacob's blessings in Genesis 48–49).

JACOB (Genesis 28:5–36)

Jacob (meaning "supplanter") truly lived up to his name, as he first persuaded his brother Esau to sell his birthright and then deceived his father and stole the oral blessing. But when Jacob went to the home of his mother's brother Laban in search of a wife, he more than met his match in craftiness. Ultimately he worked for Laban fourteen years for his wives Leah and Rachel and six years for the flocks and herds obtained from Laban.

Periodically, Bible students ask how or why God should bless such a scoundrel as Jacob, seeming even to reward his evil ways. By way of answer, we must first reckon with the fact that God calls followers not because of what they are but for what they may become by His grace. No one deserves the blessings of God. Second, God had made an unconditional covenant with Abraham and confirmed it to Isaac; this involved working through the natural descendants of Isaac, that is, Jacob. Third, however dimly, Jacob apparently had some appreciation of the spiritual blessings of God's covenant. On the way to Laban's home in northern Mesopotamia, he stopped at Bethel, sacred as a shrine of his grandfather Abraham. There God revealed Himself to Jacob and confirmed the Abrahamic covenant to him, without any indication that He approved of all his actions (Genesis 28). Fourth, Jacob was exiled from home for his deception of Isaac and endured many maturing situations during the twenty years in exile. Fifth, a chastened man, he met God in a spiritually revolutionizing way along the banks of the Jabbok River on the journey home (Genesis 32). Then God changed his name to Israel ("fighter for God"). So God did not reward evil with good, but pursued Jacob over the years until he came to the end of himself and acknowledged God's preeminence in his life.

Jacob's or Israel's sons became the ancestors of the twelve tribes of Israel. The names of these sons and Jacob's inspired predictions concerning their future appear in Genesis 49. Since Jacob adopted Joseph's two sons (Ephraim and Manasseh) as equal to his other sons (Genesis 48:5), there were technically thirteen tribes, but only twelve are uniformly reckoned (e.g., Exodus 24:4; Joshua 4:2). In such reckonings Ephraim and Manasseh are included together as the tribe of Joseph (Numbers 26:28; Joshua 17:14–18). Levi, the priestly tribe, was supposed to be supported by the others when the Israelites settled down in Canaan after the conquest and did not, therefore, receive an allotment of land. Joseph, whose two sons Ephraim and Manasseh received separate assignments in the Promised Land, took the place of Levi.

JOSEPH (Genesis 37–50)

Son of Jacob's favorite wife (Rachel), Joseph incurred the wrath and jealousy of his brothers because of his dreams and his father's favoritism. The "coat of many colours" (KJV) or "richly ornamented robe" (NIV) was not just a fabric of beauty but was the kind of long, flowing garment that an overseer or a superior would wear and, therefore, expressed the father's thought that Joseph should have preeminence over his brothers and would one day be his father's principal heir. Their hatred led to a decision to kill Joseph, but a change of plan resulted in his sale into slavery in Egypt. There, as a slave in the house of Potiphar, he rose to a place of remarkable trust but was thrown in prison through a false accusation of Potiphar's wife. While in prison, he again rose to a supervisory position. And ultimately, because of his wise interpretation of the king's dreams, he was elevated to the equivalent of prime minister. In this office he had the capacity to make special provision for his brothers when they came to Egypt during the famine to buy grain, and could influence the king to invite them into the land to live. The area assigned to them was Goshen, a grassland good for sheep pasture in the eastern Delta region. It is clear that Joseph viewed Israelite residence in Egypt as temporary, for before he died he made his relatives promise to bring his body with them when they left Egypt and returned to the Promised Land.

NOTE

1. The latter answers another of the big questions of the latter twentieth century: What is the origin and explanation of the Arab-Jewish conflict? And, of course, the Abrahamic covenant certifies who will ultimately control Palestine.

⊱≼✠≽⊰

4

Up from Slavery:
Moses and the Exodus

Exodus 1–15

THERE are about 350 silent years between Genesis and Exodus. Genesis ends with the Israelites recently arrived in Egypt. Exodus opens with events that anticipate their leaving. The total stay was 430 years (Exodus 12:40, 41). Scripture says little about those centuries except that the Hebrews multiplied greatly, and it implies that they were prosperous. In fact, they did so well that apparently the Egyptians grew both jealous and fearful of their power and wealth and determined to curb further expansion. This they sought to do, first, by trying to work the Hebrews to death. When that approach failed, the Egyptian king ordered all Hebrew males killed at birth.

Of course, God could not permit the extinction of the people He had promised to bless and protect; so He began to raise up a deliverer in the person of Moses. Rescuing him from a watery grave in the Nile, God led in his adoption into the ruling family, which gave Moses access to the knowledge and culture of Egypt. At the age of forty, Moses chose to identify himself with his people and their cause and fled to the Sinai Peninsula (Acts 7:23). There he married into one of the tribes descended from Abraham and spent another forty years (Acts 7:30). Those were not years of marking time, because he was becoming familiar with an area where for forty years he was to lead the children of Israel. In the solitude of the desert he came to know God with an intimacy that made him the great leader of his people in days ahead.

In the burning-bush meeting with God (Exodus 3–4), Moses was understandably reluctant to return to Egypt to tangle with the Pharaoh and win release of the Hebrews. Not only was he very uncertain that the Hebrews would accept him as their leader, but also he had a healthy respect for the power of Pharaoh and the Egyptian Empire. Moses had firsthand knowledge of that power, which was the greatest in the world at that time (with the possible exception of Shang China—an empire he could not have known). God provided Moses with three miracles, to assure him of God's call and help, to accredit him before the Hebrew elders, and to persuade Pharaoh to accept Moses' request. They were the rod that became a serpent, the leprous hand, and the water that turned to blood. God also provided Moses with Aaron as his spokesman and companion.

PERPLEXING QUESTIONS ANSWERED

There are two moral or ethical questions in this conversation between Moses and God that periodically bother Bible students. First, in Exodus 3:22 (see also 11:2), the King James Version unfortunately makes reference to Hebrew "borrowing" of gold and silver from the Egyptians when, of course, they never expected to return it. How could God bless a subterfuge? The problem is solved when we discover that the translation should be literally "ask" (so the NKJV and RSV), apparently as a gift.

The second problem arises in Exodus 4:21 when God said he would harden Pharaoh's heart so he would refuse to let the Hebrews go. It is often objected that it is not fair for God to harden a man's heart and then punish him for his rebelliousness. Moreover, this hardening is also often connected with salvation; and it is asserted that it is not fair for God to send a person to perdition if God hardens that person's heart against the truth. By the way of answer, it should be made clear that the issue here is one of public policy—whether or not the Hebrews shall go free—and not salvation as such. Furthermore, a study of Exodus 4–14 will show that Pharaoh, as a wicked man, hardened his own heart seven times before God is said to have hardened it once and that ultimately Pharaoh hardened his own heart a total of ten times, and God hardened it ten times. Perhaps this illustrates the truth that when people willfully turn their backs on God, ultimately He may in judgment confirm them in their wayward state (see Romans 1:24, 26–28).

In Moses' contest with Pharaoh, he smote Egypt with ten plagues at the command of God:

1. water turned to blood
2. frogs
3. lice (word uncertain, perhaps gnats, sand fleas, or mosquitoes)
4. flies (flies is supplied in the English text; the reference to swarms may be to a mixture of irritating insects)
5. murrain of beasts (a severe and deadly epidemic not otherwise identified)
6. boils on man and beast (inflamed painful boils or abscesses)
7. hail
8. locusts
9. darkness
10. death of firstborn.

It is often argued that these plagues were in line with terrible natural catastrophes that hit ancient Egypt periodically and should, therefore, not be viewed as especially miraculous. While many of them did partially follow the orderly working of nature's laws, they were far more than that. There was an unparalleled intensity of these calamities. They occurred in an ascending order of intensity and effect. From several of them, the Hebrews of the land of Goshen were immune. The plagues came and went according to a precise, divine timetable (e.g., Exodus 8:23).

Finally, they had as their purpose discrediting the gods of Egypt and exalting the most high God of heaven (Exodus 12:12). The plagues clearly discredited specific gods of Egypt (e.g., the Nile was worshiped as Hapi, plague 1; the frog, worshiped as Heqt, plague 2; the bull, worshiped as Ptah, plague 5; the sun, worshiped as Amon-Re, Aton, etc., plague 9). While we cannot be certain, the whole series of plagues must have spread out over most of a year.

Just before the last plague, in the same night that the death angel invaded the homes of all Egypt, the Israelites made the Passover sacrifice, according to divine instructions. This involved slaying a lamb for each household, unless the household was too small. This lamb without blemish prefigures the person and sacrifice of Christ, whose blood was to be shed for the sins of all. The fact that the blood was to be placed on the doorposts of each house illustrates the truth that Christ's blood must be appropriated for one to be released from the penalty of sin. Anyone who was careless about applying the blood to the doorpost or who opposed this divine provision came under the judgment of God.

After the death of the firstborn throughout Egypt, the Pharaoh and the people begged the Hebrews to leave lest they all be slain. The Hebrews had been making preparations to go for some time and were now ready even though the task had been immense. There were 600,000 men over twenty years of age, plus women and children, for a total of some 2,500,000. In addition, there were flocks and herds and personal belongings.

LOCATING THE EXODUS IN TIME AND SPACE

When the Exodus occurred has occasioned considerable debate. The simplest place to begin on this question is with 1 Kings 6:1. This verse states that the Exodus took place 480 years before the dedication of Solomon's temple, which took place in the fourth year of his reign. If one accepts the chronology of E.R. Thiele,[1] which begins Solomon's reign in 970 B.C., the dedication of the temple would have been in 967 B.C. (his fourth year). By adding 480 years to that date, one gets 1447 B.C. for the date of the Exodus. Other scholars give slightly different dates for Solomon's reign, so an approximate date of 1440 B.C. for the Exodus and a date of 1400 B.C. for the conquest under Joshua would be good round numbers to suggest. Some, for a variety of reasons, would prefer to date the Exodus around 1275 B.C. There do not seem to be any insurmountable objections to the early date, however.[2]

Numerous questions have also been raised about the route of the Exodus. There is no debate over the fact that the Hebrews took a circuitous route through the Sinai Peninsula instead of the direct road along the Mediterranean into Palestine. While they might have traversed the latter in a couple of weeks, God observed that they might not be able to handle the military demands of this route (Exodus 13:17). Exactly where they went as they traveled east from Goshen is a matter of considerable discussion. Part of the problem relates to the meaning of the term *yam sûph* (translated "Red Sea" in the King James and other versions) and part to the difficulty or impossibility of identifying several of the sites connected with the Exodus narrative (for example, the three place names of Exodus 14:2 cannot be identified with any degree of certainty). Some have argued that *yam sûph* should be translated "Sea of Reeds" and have sought to relate it to a lake or lakes now part of the Suez Canal system. Such a position cannot be effectively supported, however. The Greek translation of the Old Testament, Acts 7:36, and Hebrews 11:29 understands *yam sûph* to refer to the Red Sea. Moreover, Exodus 14:27 and 15:5, 8, 10 seem to require something more than one of the lakes of the Suez region. Furthermore, it has been observed that *yam sûph* in Exodus 10:19 would seemingly have to be more than marshy lakes of the Suez region; the Gulf of Suez is large enough to destroy the hordes of locusts and is properly placed for a northwest wind to blow the locusts into its waters. Certainly in Numbers 14:25 *yam sûph* is the Red Sea. Perhaps it is best, then, to conclude that the Hebrews journeyed southward to the west of the present canal system and crossed the Red Sea just south of the modern port of Suez.

In recent years Doron Nof, professor of oceanography at Florida State University, and Nathan Paldor, an expert in atmospheric sciences at Hebrew University in Jerusalem, have produced a study that shows how strong winds in the region of the north end of the Red Sea (see Exodus 14:21) could have lowered the water level and allowed the Israelites to cross. They also identify an undersea ridge that could have provided a temporary bridge for the Israelites to pass over.[3] These scholars were not trying to "prove" the accuracy of the Exodus narrative but merely sought to discover whether this crossing was scientifically plausible.

Notes

1. E.R. Thiele, *The Mysterious Numbers of the Hebrew Kings*, rev. ed. (Grand Rapids: Zondervan, 1983).

2. See Howard F. Vos, *An Introduction to Bible Archaeology* (Chicago: Moody, 1983), pp. 55–60 for a fuller discussion of the issue.

3. See John N. Wilford, "Oceanographers Say Winds May Have Parted the Waters," *New York Times*, March 15, 1992, p. 12; Doron Nof and Nathan Paldor, "Are There Oceanographic Explanations for the Israelites' Crossing of the Red Sea?" *Bulletin of the American Meteorological Society*, March, 1992, pp. 305–14.

Power in the Desert: The Wilderness Wanderings

Exodus 15—Deuteronomy 34

TO modern Americans used to the quick fixes of a Six Day War (1967), a Grenada invasion (1983), Operation Desert Storm (1991), or the breathtaking speed of German unification (1990), the wilderness wanderings of Israel may seem painfully slow, unnecessary, and inefficient. But those wanderings were not merely an unimportant interlude in the history of Israel; God was molding a nation out of a rag-tag horde of Egyptian slaves, and He was giving those people the basic religious institutions designed to mold and characterize them. At Sinai, Moses delivered to Israel the Law, the pattern of the tabernacle (which later became the pattern for the temple) and orders for its operation, detailed instructions for the priesthood and the sacrificial system, and some commands concerning the later development of kingship. Moreover, through miracle after miracle, God demonstrated His mighty power and prepared His people for the challenge of the conquest and settlement of Canaan. If we accept the early date of the Exodus, the period of wandering (c. 1440–1400) extended long enough for the Egyptian control of Canaan to slip so badly (during the Amarna Age) that Israelites would not be forced to do battle with their former masters during the conquest.

JOURNEY TO SINAI (Exodus 15:22–19:1)

The period of the wanderings was truly a remarkable time. God demonstrated His presence with the Hebrews by a pillar of cloud that hovered over them by day and by a pillar of fire by night. He provided food enough for all in the form of manna for forty years (Exodus 16:35), a substance that appeared like frost on the ground six mornings a week. (On the sixth day they were to gather a double portion so there would be something for the Sabbath.) Periodically, God provided water by miraculous means; and He arranged that clothes did not wear out, presumably even growing as a person matured.

Unfortunately, even the presence and power of God did not inspire sufficient faith to help them meet each new test. After the marvelous deliverance through the plagues and opening of the Red Sea, they murmured at Marah for lack of water (Exodus 15:24). After the miracle of sweetening the water at Marah, they murmured because of lack of food (Exodus 16:2). After provision of water and food, and in spite of God's evident presence with them in the cloud, the congregation again murmured when the need for water became critical. In fact, they were so furious with Moses that they were about to stone him (Exodus 17:3, 4). And there were to be repeated occasions of murmuring later in the wanderings (Numbers 14:2; 16:41; Deuteronomy 1:27). At length, at the end of six weeks, the company of Hebrews reached Mount Sinai. Along the way they had prevailed over the Amalekites in battle and had met Moses' father-in-law, Jethro, who gave some sound advice on administration.

AT SINAI (Exodus 19:2—Numbers 10:10)

The Law (Exodus 19:2–24:18)

For a year the Israelites camped in the vicinity of Mount Sinai at the southern tip of the Sinai Peninsula. Soon after they arrived, God gave them the Decalogue, or Ten Commandments. This He did audibly in a voice like trumpet tones (Exodus 19:16; 20:18, 22) so all the company could hear and so they would have no doubt about His commandments to them. The law was given not as a means of spiritual life to the "called out" people, but as a means by which they would become a "peculiar treasure" and a "kingdom of priests" (Exodus 19:5, 6). The commandments are repeated with only slight variations in Deuteronomy 5:16–18.

- The first commandment prohibits worshiping anything before God.
- The second declares God's spirituality and forbids making any material likeness of God.
- The third safeguards God's name and deity.
- The fourth demands that the Sabbath be observed as a day set apart unto God.
- The fifth obligates children to honor their parents as they do God and to assume responsibility for them.
- The sixth forbids murder and should be translated, "Thou shalt not murder," rather than, "Thou shalt not kill." Scripture authorizes capital punishment in such passages as Exodus 21 and probably Romans 13; and while it encourages peace, it does not outlaw warfare.
- The seventh requires sexual purity. While designed to protect the sanctity of marriage, it was applied by Jesus to all sexual immorality—thought as well as deed (Matthew 5:27, 28).

- The eighth stands for the rights of property.
- The ninth prohibits lying and unfounded evidence in general.
- The tenth forbids harboring evil desire for that which belongs to one's neighbor.

After enunciating the principles of the Decalogue, God proceeded in the next three chapters to deal with relations between masters and servants, injuries to persons, property rights, crimes against humanity, the land and the Sabbath, the institution of the feasts of unleavened bread and harvest and first fruits, and instructions concerning conquest of the land. After this giving of the law, the people responded with the commitment, "All the words which the LORD hath said will we do" (Exodus 24:3).

The Tabernacle (Exodus 24–27, 30–31, 35–40)

Not only does the Exodus narrative declare that God communicated instructions to Moses concerning building the tabernacle, but Acts 7:44 and Hebrews 8:5 supply New Testament confirmation of the fact. The tabernacle or tent was to be a sanctuary where God would especially dwell (Exodus 25:8). This does not mean, of course, that God ceased to be everywhere present; it signifies only that people might especially meet Him there.

Measurements connected with the tabernacle are given in cubits, approximately eighteen inches in length. Surrounding the tabernacle was a court with a 450-foot perimeter (150 feet by 75 feet), delimited by a linen curtain hung on bronze pillars (7½ feet high, spaced 7½ feet apart) with silver hooks. This court could be entered only on the east. The eastern half of the court was for the worshipers; in it stood the bronze altar (7½ feet square and 4½ feet high) made of acacia and shittim wood covered with bronze. Beyond the altar stood a bronze laver in which the priests washed in preparation for ministry at the altar or tabernacle. In the western half of the court stood the tabernacle—45 feet long and 15 feet wide. It was divided into two parts; the holy place on the east (30 feet long) could be entered by the priests, but the holy of holies (15 by 15 feet) was accessible only to the high priest on the Day of Atonement. The tabernacle was made of forty-eight planks (20 on a side and 8 on the west end) of acacia wood covered with gold and held together with bars inserted into silver sockets. The structure was covered with a curtain of linen in blue, purple, and scarlet. Protecting this was first a covering of goats' hair, another of rams' skin, and a third of goatskins. Linen veils closed the entrances into the holy place and the holy of holies.

Three pieces of furniture stood in the holy place: the table for the bread of the Presence on the north side, the golden lampstand on the south side, and the altar of incense before the veil that separated the holy place from the holy of holies. The table (about 36 inches long by 18 inches wide by 27 inches high) was made of acacia wood and covered with gold, and had on it twelve cakes of unleavened bread, representing the twelve tribes of Israel. The golden lampstand was made of pure gold and had seven branches. Its seven lamps the priests were to fill with oil each evening. The altar of incense was made of acacia wood covered with gold and was three feet high and one and one-half feet square. In the holy of holies was located the ark of the covenant. This was covered with gold inside and out and measured three feet, nine inches long; with a depth and breadth of two feet, three inches. In it were kept the two tablets on which the Ten Commandments were written, a pot of manna, and Aaron's rod that budded. Its cover was called the mercy seat and represented the presence of God. Two cherubim of gold stood on the lid facing each other, with wings outstretched above the mercy seat. The furniture was made with rings and staves so the priests could carry it.

The Symbolism of Things to Come

There is tremendous symbolism in the tabernacle. Some would construe every detail of the structure to be symbolic. While it is hard to defend such an extreme position, even a minimal symbolism is magnificent indeed. To appreciate the symbolism, it is necessary to look first at worship in the sanctuary. The tabernacle or presence of God was approached after sacrifice on the burnt altar, which required shedding of blood. A priest had to be cleansed in the laver before ministry. The incense on the altar of incense was set afire with a coal from the altar of burnt offering. The high priest on the Day of Atonement sprinkled blood from the altar of burnt offering on the mercy seat for the sins of the nation of Israel.

Offerings on the brazen altar point to the death of Christ, who offered Himself without spot to God (Hebrews 9:14). The altar of incense pictures Christ as the believer's Intercessor, who intercedes on the basis of His shed blood (Hebrews 7:25). The bronze laver is symbolic of spiritual cleansing or washing of water by the Word available to believers (Hebrews 10:22; 1 John 1:9). Worshipers need to be cleansed constantly from defilement. The lampstand may point to Christ as the light of the world (John 8:12; 9:5). The bread on the table (the bread of the Presence) looked forward to Christ as the bread of life, nourisher of the believer (John 6:35–58), and apparently denoted God's presence with His people as sustainer. The curtain that blocked the believer's direct access to God in the holy of holies was torn from top to bottom when Christ died (Matthew 27:51), and now through Him all may go directly to God. Believers have access to God by virtue of Christ's redemptive work; He Himself said, "I am the door: if anyone enters by me, he shall be saved" (John 10:9, NKJV).

The tremendous amount of gold, silver, copper, and fabric required to build the tabernacle was generously contributed by the Hebrews (Exodus 35:21–36:7) and gives some indication of the wealth they had been able to amass while in captivity or had received from the Egyptians as they left. The magnificence of the tabernacle demonstrates the quality craftsmanship of the Hebrews. Presumably they had been trained in metallurgy and many other crafts by Egyptian taskmasters. Admittedly, the biblical account speaks of divine help in doing the work of construction (Exodus 31:1–6; 35:25,

26), but this probably involved a heightening of natural talents and learned skills. This generation of skilled workers died in the wilderness, and presumably they were not able to train their sons and daughters to do as well, for Palestinian excavations of the period of the judges and monarchy do not reveal a very high level of artistic skill among the Hebrews. Once constructed, the tabernacle continued for some four hundred years to be the center for Israel's worship. It remained in use until construction of Solomon's temple; what happened to it then Scripture does not indicate.

The Priesthood (Exodus 28–29)

For orderly ministration and worship, God now established a priesthood. (In earlier centuries a head of a household apparently represented his family before God.) Aaron was to serve as high priest, and his sons were to assist him. The primary function of the priests was to represent human beings before God. Especially they officiated in making the prescribed offerings to God, which served the function of temporarily meeting God's righteous demands of sacrifice for sin. (Such repeated sacrifices looked forward to the perfect and complete sacrifice of Christ on the cross, Hebrews 7:27; 9:11–28.) They also had the responsibility of instructing the laity in the law of God and the job of caring for the tabernacle.

The priests wore a long white linen coat with a girdle or belt that had blue, purple, and scarlet worked into it. They wore a plain cap and linen breeches under the coat.

The high priest's garments consisted of a robe, a coat, an ephod, a girdle, a breastplate, and a mitre. Over a white linen coat he wore a blue robe extending below the knees. Around the bottom of it were attached decorative pomegranates and golden bells. Over the robe he wore an ephod, consisting of two pieces of linen cloth joined with shoulder straps, on each of which was engraved the names of six tribes of Israel. A belt held it together around the waist. The breastplate was suspended by gold chains from the shoulder straps of the ephod and was tied to the waistband with blue lace. It was a pouch nine inches square, on which were mounted twelve precious stones engraved with names of the twelve tribes. The Urim and Thummim (meaning "lights" and "perfections") were kept inside the breastplate. Exactly what they were or how they were used in determining God's will is not spelled out. On the headdress or turban (mitre) of the high priest was a gold plate inscribed with the words "Holiness to the LORD," which served as a reminder of the absolute purity of God's nature.

The Broken Covenant (Exodus 32–34)

How lightly the Hebrews had accepted the legal covenant (Exodus 24:3) is proved by events of chapter 32. Impatient at Moses' extended absence, the people demanded new gods which they could see. Even Aaron, the high priest, who had witnessed most intimately God's mighty works on the Egyptians, was carried away with the popular demand and supervised casting a golden calf and building an altar before it. The bovine worship of Egypt evidently had a strong grip on the Hebrews. The fact that they turned to Egyptian worship patterns so readily on this occasion indicates that paganism must have made deep inroads among them while in captivity. This whole scene demonstrates the inability of the law to make people good and their inability to keep the law in their own strength.

Moses met God's announcement of intention to destroy the Israelites for their apostasy with a prayer of intercession based largely on the Abrahamic covenant. Thereupon, God changed His course of action and determined instead to execute judgment on those who presumably were the worst offenders. Symbolic of the fact that the people had already broken the law, Moses smashed the tablets on which the Ten Commandments were written. Subsequently, God gave the Decalogue to Moses again and once more enjoined the Sabbaths and feasts upon Israel. The degree of

Israel's repentance is seen in the generosity of their offerings for construction of the tabernacle (Exodus 35:21–36:7).

Legal and Priestly Order (Leviticus 1:1–27:34)

The casual reader of Leviticus is often turned off by the immense amount of detail concerning feasts and sacrifices and regulations of life in ancient Israel. But when it comes to Scripture, it is important to stop just casually looking and start to "see." True sight or perception will sometimes involve the use of a pencil and even some tabulation. It soon becomes evident that the key word of Leviticus is "holy," which appears at least eighty-seven times; and a second key word is "atonement," which occurs at least forty-five times. It seems clear, then, that what Leviticus is trying to say is that God is an infinitely holy God and that sinful human beings can approach the infinitely holy God of the universe only on the basis of sacrifice through shedding of blood. This is a book for the people of God, showing how God is to be approached and worshiped. The book insists on holiness of body as well as soul. It makes clear that there is to be order and dignity in the worship of God, for He is a majestic, sovereign, and infinitely holy being. Since He is sovereign and holy and unapproachable by sinful human beings, God must take the initiative in establishing any kind of contact with them; and He has the right to prescribe the nature of that contact. Therefore, it is not surprising that no other book in the Bible contains so many direct messages from God as this one.

- "The Lord spoke," "said," or "commanded" occurs fifty-six times.
- "I am the Lord," occurs twenty-one times.
- "I am the Lord your God," occurs twenty-one times.

It is easy in looking for Old Testament applications to the modern believer to neglect the basic meaning the Old Testament had for worshipers of the pre-Christian era. The sacrificial system (Leviticus 1:1–7:38) was for them a means of approach to God. Since the system was God-given, they could come to God by this means with the assurance that they would be received. The system of offerings involved numerous significant principles. For instance, offerings were commonly substitutionary, in one's stead (e.g., Leviticus 1:4; 3:2; 4:4); offerings were to be of highest quality—the best one had to offer (e.g., Leviticus 1:3; 2:1); sacrifices were to be accompanied by a true penitence and uprightness of life (see Isaiah 1:11–24).

For the modern believer, each of the five offerings presented represents a distinctive aspect of the one offering of Jesus Christ. The burnt offering signified the offerer's complete consecration to God, since the entire sacrifice was to be consumed. This offering may be in view in the appeal of Romans 12:1. The burnt offering pictures Christ offering Himself spotless to God (Hebrews 9:11–14; 10:5–10). The peace offering involved maintenance of communion between the worshiper and God; it could be a thank offering, a payment of a vow, or an expression of love for God. As our peace offering, Christ made it possible for the sinner to be reconciled with God; He made peace (Colossians 1:20). The sin offering was for sins of ignorance, righteous acts inadvertently omitted, or for specific sins of the type not representing open defiance of God (Leviticus 5:1–13; Numbers 15:27–31). This offering pictures Christ as the bearer of the sins of His people ("made sin for us" 2 Corinthians 5:21). Infringement upon the rights of a person or his property or failure to make required offerings to God necessitated the trespass offering. This offering seems to emphasize the price of sin or the harmful effects of sin and looks forward to Christ as the one who bore the injury of sin. (Isaiah 53:10 should be translated, "You shall make his soul a trespass offering" and clearly speaks of Christ.) The meal or grain offering is the only offering that did not involve shedding of blood. It consisted of products of the soil, signifying dedication of one's substance or wealth to God. This offering is taken by some to refer to Christ's perfect humanity, and when involving the offering of first fruits (Leviticus 2:14) is thought to prefigure Christ's resurrection (1 Corinthians 15:20–23).

Leviticus 8–10 describes the inauguration of the priesthood and involves their call (8:1–5), cleansing (8:6), clothing (8:7–13), atonement (8:14–29), anointing (8:30), food (8:31–36), ministry (9:1–24), and failure (10:1–20).

A Call and Guidelines for Holiness

If the key word of Leviticus is "holy" or "holiness," then the book may be looked upon as a manual of holiness, and as such sets forth the holiness required of God's people. A holy people must have pure food (11:1–47), pure bodies (12:1–14:32), pure homes (14:33–57), pure habits (15:1–33), pure worship (17:1–9), pure morals (18:1–30), and pure customs (19:1–22:33). Failure to follow the holy demands of God would result in captivity and dispersion among the nations, but the unconditional Abrahamic covenant remained in force and would guarantee future blessing for Israelites in the Promised Land (chapter 26).

Among the divinely appointed institutions described or alluded to in Leviticus are several special days or feasts or seasons. These may be found primarily in chapters 16 and 23 through 26.

1. **Sabbath**—the seventh day, a day of rest and one devoted to God.
2. **Feast of Passover and unleavened bread**—the fourteenth day of the first month of the religious year (approximately April), reminded the Israelites of God's miraculous intervention in redeeming them from bondage in Egypt. It was followed on the fifteenth and twenty-first by days of holy convocation. During the week between those days, the Israelites were to eat unleavened bread (Feast of Unleavened Bread). The lamb slain on Passover looked forward to "Christ our passover, sacrificed for us" (1 Corinthians 5:7).

3. **Harvest or first fruits**—probably the day after the first day of the Feast of Unleavened Bread and thus the sixteenth day of the first month. The offering of the first fruits of the land (from barley harvest) was to be brought to the priest. This prefigures the resurrection of Christ as first fruits from the dead (1 Corinthians 15:23; Romans 8:29).

4. **Pentecost or Feast of Weeks**—fifty days after feast of first fruits and thus after the wheat harvest. It was a day of rest, on which a special meal offering was presented, perhaps signifying that daily food came from the hand of God. It looked forward to the formation of the Church on Pentecost (Acts 2), which was fifty days after the resurrection.

5. **Feast of Trumpets**—first day of the seventh month (approximately October), ushering in the civil year. It was a day of rest and holy convocation with special offerings being made to God.

6. **Day of Atonement**—tenth day of the seventh month, the most solemn day in the whole year. It was a day of fasting and holy convocation, when the high priest entered the holy of holies to make atonement for the sins of the nation. It looked forward to the once-for-all sacrifice of Christ (Hebrews 9:12).

7. **Feast of Tabernacles**—a seven-day period at the end of the harvest season (fifteenth day of Tishri, approximately October) when the Israelites lived in tents. Daily burnt offerings were made, and the first and eighth days (day after its conclusion) were days of rest and holy convocation.

8. **Sabbatical year**—every seventh year, designated as a year of rest for the land. Fields were left unseeded; vineyards were left unpruned.

9. **Year of Jubilee**—the fiftieth year after seven observances of the sabbatical year. Again the land was to stand idle. Hebrew slaves were freed, and family inheritances were restored to those who had lost them.

Preparation for Continuing the Journey to Canaan (Numbers 1:1–10:10)

The opening chapters of Numbers describe preparations for leaving Mount Sinai and marching to Canaan. The Hebrews had camped for about a year. Probably the organization for march developed earlier had been largely forgotten. Besides, a new element had now been introduced: a worship center, the tabernacle. And they would be facing hostile people; they had to be ready for war.

To that end, God commanded a military census to discover what manpower was available and to organize the forces under specifically named division commanders. The number of fighting men over age twenty was 603,550 (Numbers 1:46), giving a total of some 2,500,000 Israelites. Numerous scholars have raised questions about corruption of the Hebrew text at this point and have suggested drastic reduction of the census figures, but it seems best to take the tally at face value. Other passages indicate the same total (Exodus 12:37; Numbers 11:21). Even a small contingent of, say, 50,000 Israelites would have taxed the resources of the Sinai beyond their limits; so the need for supernatural provision cannot by reduction of the total be eliminated, as many would like to do. Moreover, a few thousand Hebrews would have been no challenge to Pharaoh. His statement was, "The people of Israel are more and mightier than we" (Exodus 1:9, NKJV). While it is not necessary to take his statement literally, it must indicate hundreds of thousands or even millions of Hebrews.[1]

Such a large number of people would require detailed instructions for making and breaking camp, for order of march, and for hygienic precautions. The specifics need not detain us here except to say that at the center of the camp stood the tabernacle, flanked on the east by Judah, Issachar, and Zebulun; on the north by Dan, Asher, and Naphtali; on the west by Ephraim, Manasseh, and Benjamin; and on the south by Reuben, Simeon, and Gad. The signal to march was blown on silver trumpets, and a cloud signifying divine presence moved before them en route. As they marched, six wagons, drawn by twelve oxen, bore curtains and boards of the tabernacle. The furniture was equipped with rings and staves so the Levites could carry it. Before the Israelites left Sinai, they celebrated the Passover, marking their first anniversary of departure from Egypt.

JOURNEY TO CANAAN
(Numbers 10:11—Deuteronomy 34:12)

The Lost Generation (Numbers 10:11–22:1)

Soon after the Hebrews left Mount Sinai, a spirit of rebelliousness arose in the camp. Ultimately, even Moses' closest associates were infected. First, the people complained over lack of variety of food and demanded meat. God promised them flesh for a whole month (Numbers 11:20). Numbers 11:31–35 has several unfortunate translations. What the English should convey is that quail flew about three feet above the ground so the Hebrews could knock them down and collect them. Then they spread them around the camp—a means of preserving food by sun-drying. And before they had finished eating the quail (v. 33), that is, before the month was over, a plague broke out among them. Though this is viewed as divine punishment for their rebelliousness, the plague could have come from spoiled meat.

Second, Miriam (Moses' sister) and Aaron rebelled against Moses' leadership and suffered divine punishment (chapter 12). Third, the whole company of Israelites rebelled against the Lord. As the tribes came to Kadesh-barnea near the southern border of Canaan, they sent twelve men to spy out the land at divine command. The spies brought back a glowing report of the land, but struck fear into the hearts of the people with their description of the impossibility of conquering the inhabitants. Joshua and Caleb filed a minority report, however, and urged trust in God to deliver the land to them. But the people ignored their plea, rebelled against God, and called for a new captain to lead them back to Egypt. In judgment, God declared that this generation would wander in the wilderness for forty years until all the adults had died, except Joshua and Caleb, who had been faithful to Him. Fourth, the Israelites went out to do battle against the Amalekites and Canaanites in disobedience to God's command and were soundly defeated (Numbers 14:41–45).

Fifth, Korah, Dathan, and Abiram persuaded fellow Levites and others to rebel against the divinely ordained leadership of Moses and Aaron. Dathan and Abiram, as descendants of Reuben, eldest son of Jacob, sought to displace the political leadership of Moses. Korah, with supporting Levites, contested the priestly leadership of Aaron and his family. At the height of the rebellion, the earth opened and swallowed up the three ringleaders and their households, and fire destroyed the 250 false priests (chapter 16). In Numbers 16:32, "all the men" might better be translated "everything." That the sons of Korah did not perish with him is clear from Numbers 26:11. Apparently they were adult sons who did not share the ambition of their father. Important descendants of Korah included Samuel, the great prophet and judge. Many in Israel violently opposed Moses for this destruction of the mutineers, blaming him for their deaths. God then sent a plague among the people that took 14,700 lives (Numbers 16:49). It is dangerous to defy God's clearly revealed will and purposes.

After about thirty-eight years of wandering in the desert, probably not far from Kadesh-barnea, the Hebrews returned to that site. There Miriam died (Numbers 20:1), and Moses in a fit of rage and disobedience smote a rock twice to bring forth water for the Hebrews. His sin especially involved refusal to point away from himself and to bring full recognition to God's power in meeting the needs of the people. As punishment, he was denied permission to enter the Promised Land. At length, preparations were made to journey to Canaan. When the Edomites refused the Hebrews permission to go through their territory, they went around Edom to the south. Before doing so, however, they suffered the loss of Aaron, and Eleazar his son became high priest. En route they defeated Canaanites under the leadership of Arad and rebelled once more against God. This time He sent venomous serpents among them, causing many to die. Divinely ordained relief came in the form of a bronze serpent. Those who obeyed the word of God and looked in faith were healed. Jesus later saw this as a fitting symbol of His death on the cross; anyone who in faith likewise turned to Him would have eternal life (John 3:14). Subsequently, God gave victories over Amorites and Bashan.

Throughout this discussion attention has focused on the absolute holiness and absolute obedience God demands of His people, and the judgment that can be expected to fall on the disobedient. Just as severe public punishment descended on the wayward at the beginning of Israel's corporate existence, so it fell on the church during its earliest days (Acts 5:1–11). Such public acts of divine denunciation of sin should give pause to the twenty-first century church, caught up in the moral laxity of western civilization. God's demand for holiness has not changed.

Preparations for Entering Canaan (Numbers 22:1–36:13)

At length, the children of Israel pitched camp in the plains of Moab, ready to enter the Promised Land. Terrified, Balak, the king of Moab, engaged a Mesopotamian prophet by the name of Balaam to curse Israel. This he refused to do and bestowed blessing instead. Finally, however, he gave evil counsel that resulted in many Israelites being dragged into immorality and idolatry. Hence, another of God's purifying judgments came. This was followed by a census, in part to determine the military capabilities of Israel. Therefore, only the adult males were counted, for a total of 601,730 (Numbers 26:51), slightly less than the previous total of 603,550 (see Numbers 1:46). The reduction may be accounted for by the frequent rebellions and massive judgments of God during the wilderness wandering. The new census also provided a means of more equitable division of the land they were about to enter (Numbers 26:52–65).

The imminence of Moses' death and the reason for it were then announced, and commands were given for choosing Joshua as the next leader of the host. Not only was he a man of natural ability, but he also received divine endowment (chapter 27). Numbers 28 and 29 review in outline the whole ritual year with its feasts and festivals and add details about quantities of offerings. Reuben, Gad, and the half-tribe of Manasseh requested permission to settle in the rich grazing lands of Transjordan and reluctantly were allowed to do so on the condition that they join the rest of the Israelites in conquering Canaan before settling down. Since the Levites were not entitled to a tribal inheritance, they were granted forty-eight cities among the inheritance of the other tribes and six of their cities were set apart as cities of refuge or asylum for manslayers to prevent the starting of blood feuds.

Moses' Valedictory (Deuteronomy 1:1–34:12)

In a sense, the book of Deuteronomy is Moses' valedictory. He was soon to "graduate." A new leader was about to take over. With eager anticipation the Israelites stood at the edge of the Promised Land, for which they had waited so long. For his part, Moses yearned earnestly for the welfare of the mass of covenant people spread before him. This generation had not been present at the Red Sea or at Sinai, and needed to be reminded of God's power, watchcare, and requirements. Deuteronomy means "second law," and may be viewed as a restatement of the law, but it is not merely a restatement. It consists primarily of Moses' parting speeches, in which he seeks to urge God's people to follow divine dictates. Gleason Archer finds at least five special emphases in Moses' teaching.

1. God is one, is unique, and is a spirit being.
2. God's relationship to His covenant people is one of love rather than legalism, and for the believer the basic requirement is love for God.

3. Israel's greatest peril is viewed as idolatry, which they are to resist stoutly.
4. Israelites are to live as holy people.
5. Faithfulness to the covenant will result in a reward of material blessing.[2]

The second point is especially crucial for the modern reader. Many stumble over the extensive legal requirements of the Mosaic code and erroneously conclude that salvation during most of the Old Testament period was by works (see especially 6:5; 10:12; 11:1, 13, 22; 13:3; 19:9; 30:6, 16, 20).

Apparently the addresses in the book of Deuteronomy were first delivered orally and later written down (compare Deuteronomy 1:3 with 31:24–26).

Chapters 1:1–4:43 are a review of Israel's failure and successes. Moses zeroed in on the failure at Kadesh-barnea and the resultant thirty-eight years of wandering, but also alluded to a new period of faith and advance that had brought them to the threshold of the Promised Land. Chapter 4 is a fervent plea for obedience to God and avoidance of the mistakes of the past. Chapters 4:43 through 28:68 review the moral, civil, and ceremonial law. In chapter 5 appears a restatement of the Ten Commandments. Chapter 7 contains a command to separate themselves from sin and to destroy the idolatry and idolaters of the land of Canaan. This theme occurs again in chapter 12. Evidence from archaeological discoveries of how degraded the idolatry of Palestine was in that period indicates that it was a case of either destroying or being destroyed. Concluding this long discourse is instruction to hold a ceremony on Mounts Ebal and Gerizim, overlooking the city of Shechem in central Palestine. This event, held on entrance into the land, was to dramatize Israel's covenant responsibilities (see Deuteronomy 27–28). Chapters 29 and 30 introduce the Palestinian covenant. This covenant governs the nation's life in Palestine and relates obedience to God as a condition to possession of the land in a given generation. In fact, it predicts expulsion from the land for Israel's future apostasy, a later restoration to the land, and Israel's subsequent national conversion. This covenant is not to be confused with the Abrahamic covenant, which is unconditional and guarantees ultimate possession of the Promised Land in perpetuity.

As Moses was about to surrender the reins to Joshua, he delivered his last words of advice to all Israel, Joshua, the priests, and Levites in chapter 31. Then he sang a remarkable song of praise to God for His care of His chosen people and uttered a prophetic blessing that specifically singled out each of the tribes of Israel by name (Deuteronomy 32–33). Finally, from the top of Mount Nebo he was permitted to view the Promised Land from which his sin had excluded him. Though he was 120 years of age, his natural strength was unabated and his eye undimmed (34:7). God buried him somewhere in the lonely mountains, and his grave remained unknown so people could not make a shrine of it. But he was destined to enter the Promised Land, because some 1400 years later he appeared on the Mount of Transfiguration with the Lord of glory (Matthew 17:1–8; Mark 9:2–8; Luke 9:27–36)!

Notes

1. For a useful summary on the question, see Gleason Archer, *A Survey of Old Testament Introduction*, rev. ed. (Chicago: Moody, 1973), pp. 234–37.

2. *Ibid.*, pp. 252–53.

"The Lord God Is with You": The Conquest of the Promised Land

Joshua 1–24

F AITHFUL Joshua had the privilege of leading the Hebrews into the Promised Land. For his task he had spiritual preparation in such experiences as accompanying Moses up Mount Sinai (Exodus 24:13), military preparation in fighting the Amalekites (Exodus 17:8–16) and serving as one of the twelve who spied out the land (Numbers 13:8, 16, 17), and general leadership preparation in frequent association with Moses during the wilderness wanderings. Some have concluded that Joshua was around eighty when he became captain of Israel's hosts, and that he commanded them for about thirty years. At any rate, he died at the age of 110 (Joshua 24:29). Without question, Joshua is the main character of the book that bears his name. That he also wrote nearly the entire book is also commonly held. Brief portions, such as the account of Joshua's death, are thought to have been written by Eleazar the priest, or his son Phinehas.

No doubt, almost immediately after Moses' death, God ordered Joshua to take command of the Israelite host. Then God charged him to go over Jordan, to be strong, to divide the land of Palestine among the people, and to be faithful to the Law (Joshua 1:1–8), These were commands with a promise, "The LORD your God is with you wherever you go" (1:9, NASB). And the people readily accepted Joshua's leadership (1:16–18).

ENTRANCE INTO THE PROMISED LAND (Joshua 2:1–5:15)

Preparatory to entering the Promised Land, Joshua sent spies to Jericho. Protected by Rahab the harlot,[1] they came back with a report very different from the one received at Kadesh-barnea. This time, instead of the Hebrews being fearful, it was the occupants of the land who quaked. Terror struck them as reports of God's help for the Hebrews rolled in from the wilderness.

Apparently the very next day after the spies returned, Joshua moved the people to the edge of Jordan and prepared them to cross over. God now promised to part the waters of Jordan before them as He had the Red Sea. The Jordan is not a very wide river opposite Jericho, but in the spring (when the Hebrews crossed, 3:15) it could be formidable. This was especially true in earlier days before much of the water from the Jordan River system has been used for irrigation. When the priests carried the ark to water's edge, the streambed became dry. In fact, the waters were stopped up as far away as Adam and Zareten, some twenty miles north of where the Jordan flows into the Dead Sea. Possibly an earthquake triggered a landslide that blocked the Jordan waters (Judges 5:4; Psalm 114:3, 4). Similar water stoppages resulting from landslides are known to have occurred in A.D. 1267 and A.D. 1927, but they are certainly very rare indeed. God often uses natural means to accomplish His purposes; in such a case the miracle would consist not in the method but the timing of the stopping of the waters. When the Israelites crossed the river and camped in the land, humanly produced food became available to them; and manna ceased to appear.

CONQUEST OF THE LAND (Joshua 6:1–12:24)

It is not the purpose of Scripture to provide a complete history of anything. But as far as Scripture goes, it is an accurate record of what happened. Certainly the account of Joshua's warfare is incomplete. It describes a thrust into the middle of Palestine around Jericho and Ai, a drive in a southerly direction to defeat the Amorite league, and a northern campaign against Hazor and other towns. Nothing is even intimated of the pacification of the Shechem area where the Hebrews assembled to hear the reading of the Law (Joshua 8:30–35). Not only is the history of Joshua incomplete, but it is also very much telescoped. Major military action must have required some six years. Caleb was about seventy-nine when the conquest began and eighty-five after the last great battle with Jabin, king of Hazor (14:7, 10). Moreover, when the main conquest was completed, much remained unconquered. Notable among the towns still in enemy hands was Jerusalem. Individual tribes were left with the responsibility of mopping up resistance in the areas assigned to them.

God Intervenes and Also Judges Sin

The Joshua account is more than a mere history of wars. It is, first of all, an account of the faithfulness of God and His intervention on behalf of His people. At Jericho, they did not attack; they merely followed divine orders and watched the defenses collapse. At Gibeon, hailstones killed more Amorites than did Israelite soldiers, and God provided a unique day to aid them in the struggle (Joshua 10). Many have assumed in the past that the sun shone for a whole extra day and that the earth ceased to rotate on its axis for that length of time; thus God threw the laws of nature out of kilter. Such a view seems entirely

unnecessary. Joshua led his army in a forced night march from Gilgal
to Gibeon, some twenty-five miles uphill. He then apparently made a
surprise attack as the moon was still visible and the sun was rising.
Joshua faced the prospect of his nearly exhausted men having to fight
under a hot, cloudless sky and sought relief for them. God could have
provided local darkness (and apparently did in connection with the
violent hail storm) without interfering with the movement of the earth.
The word translated "stand still" (10:12, NKJV) could better be translated "be dumb" or "desist," that is, "be darkened." It seems to make
much more sense to talk about "Joshua's long night" than "Joshua's
long day." And there is no need for insistence on God's tampering
with the natural laws of the universe. God also intervened on behalf of
His people in the northern campaign (Joshua 11), giving a magnificent victory over the superior chariotry of King Jabin of Hazor.

The Joshua account is, second, a severe indictment of sin.
Again and again God commanded the total extermination of
pagan people for their sinfulness. One should not sit in judgment
on Israel for their bloodthirsty, vindictive ways; they acted on
divine orders. The reason for God's condemnation is explicit and
implicit: explicit in Deuteronomy 7:15; implicit in such passages
as Genesis 15:16 and Deuteronomy 20:17. One may question that
these ancient enemies of Israel were as evil as the Bible claims they
were. But even a superficial glance at Canaanite religion alone ably
demonstrates the iniquity of these peoples. Base sex worship was
prevalent and religious prostitution even enjoined; human sacrifice was common; and it was a frequent practice among them—in
an effort to placate their gods—to kill young children and bury
them in the foundations of a house or public building at the time
of construction. The following verse may refer to the latter fact:
"In his days Hiel of Bethel built Jericho. He laid its foundation
with Abiram his firstborn, and with his youngest son Segub he set
up its gates, according to the word of the LORD, which he had spoken by Joshua the son of Nun" (1 Kings 16:34, NKJV; cf. Joshua
6:26). Archaeological and historical study relative to these peoples

demonstrates the justice of God in His dealings with them. Presumably it was a case of either destroying these very corrupt tribes or being destroyed by them.

Not only does God condemn sin in the lives of pagans, He also judges it among believers. When the sin of Achan infected the Israelite camp (Joshua 7), defeat occurred, and the whole campaign stopped dead in its tracks until the sin was rooted out.

The Joshua account is illustrative, in the third place, of the warfare of the spirit. Hebrews 3 and 4 indicate that just as the Hebrews failed to enter into the Promised Land and rest from their wanderings because of their unbelief, so today those who remain in unbelief fail to enter into God's promised spiritual and psychological rest. Moreover, the Christian life is a warfare and is successful only with the proper armor and vigilance (see Ephesians 6:11–17; 2 Timothy 2:3, 4).

DIVISION OF THE LAND (Joshua 13:1–22:34)

In spite of the fact that Israel had been fighting Palestinian peoples for several years and had conquered much, there were important areas still to be occupied—notable among them the Philistine territory along the Mediterranean coast (Joshua 13:1–7). Generally speaking, the Hebrews were destined for a very long time to be confined to the hill country of Galilee, Samaria, and Judea and thus to become farmers and sheepherders. Moreover, within the land already subjugated, Canaanite or Amorite strongholds held out (e.g., Jerusalem). Yet for all practical purposes the conquest was complete, and God commanded Joshua to divide the land west of the Jordan among the nine and one-half tribes (13:7). The land east of the Jordan, Moses had already assigned (Numbers 32–33): the northern part to the half tribe of Manasseh, the central part to Gad, and the southern to Reuben.

What the very detailed geographical references in these chapters reduce to is this. Simeon occupied territory west of the southern part of the Dead Sea, Judah west of the northern part of the Dead Sea. The northern border of Judah lay approximately on a line extending west from the northern shore of the Dead Sea. Just above that, Benjamin occupied a tract extending from the Jordan into central Palestine, and Dan lay just west of Benjamin. Ephraim had the southern part of Samaria; and the half-tribe of Manasseh, the northern part. From the southwest corner of the Sea of Galilee extended the territory of Issachar, and west of them lay Zebulun. To the west and north of the Sea of Galilee, Naphtali had its holdings; and west of them Asher occupied the Carmel range and points north. Shortly afterward the Danites moved north of the Sea of Galilee and subjugated that region. Of course, the Levites had no tribal allotment, but received towns distributed throughout the holdings of the other tribes. Shiloh (about 30 miles north of Jerusalem) was established as the religious center of Israel, and the tabernacle was located there (Joshua 18:1).

Joshua's Farewell Address (Joshua 23–24)

Before Joshua died, he called Israel together at Shechem and pled with them to continue loyal to God and His covenant and exhorted them to complete the conquest of the land. Apparently up to this point (perhaps fifteen or more years after the division of the land), they had not been so zealous as they should have been in military activity. The leaders assured Joshua that they would serve God faithfully, and the people apparently did until the older generation died, and a new generation arose that knew little of God's miraculous acts on behalf of His people.

Note

1. It is interesting that Rahab was destined to be in the line of the Lord Jesus (Matthew 1:5), demonstrating how fully He humbled Himself in the incarnation and how fully the grace of God can overcome sin and ennoble the sinner. Furthermore, the inclusion of the Gentile blood of Rahab and later of Ruth the Moabitess (Ruth 4:13–21; cf. Matthew 1:5) in the line of the Messiah implies the universality of His redemption.

7

"Everyone Did What Was Right in His Own Eyes": The Judges

Judges, Ruth, 1 Samuel 1–8

THE period of the judges appears to be a rather confused time, both to people of early Hebrew history and to modern students of Bible times. At least, it was a period when there was no political unity; and warfare broke out as Hebrews tried to complete their occupation of the land or as the Canaanites tried to reassert themselves. Twice, the inspired writer said, "In those days there was no king in Israel; everyone did what was right in his own eyes" (Judges 17:6; 21:25, NKJV). Who that writer may have been is not certain. Evidently he wrote after the monarchy had been established and presumably early in the monarchy period. The prophet Samuel is a good candidate, but we cannot be certain of his authorship.

The judges were divinely enlisted leaders who ruled over Israel when the nation was a loose confederacy. They were at the same time judges, civil functionaries, and military leaders. The book of Judges is a sad book that tells of human proneness to wander from God and the results of spiritual decline. Actually it pictures a series of recurring cycles: apostasy from God, punishment in the form of oppression by neighboring tribes, cry to God for relief, redemption or release from bondage, and a period of rest from oppression. One must not conclude that the book depicts only gloom, however. Of the 410 years referred to in the book, during only some one hundred years of that time are the people said to have been in sin. So it is also a book of faithfulness to God, and it is a book of God's grace in watchcare and restoration.

CHRONOLOGY OF THE JUDGES

The chronology of the judges presents some very real problems. Adding up all the years of oppression and rest recorded in the book yields a total of 410 years. The book of Acts gives a total of 450 years from the days of Joshua to Samuel (Acts 13:20). Apparently the difference is to be accounted for by the forty years of Eli's ministry (1 Samuel 4:18). Even if one puts the date of the Exodus at about 1440 B.C., there is not room in the chronology for a 410-year period of the judges; it is over one hundred years too long. This conclusion is arrived at as follows. Saul apparently began to rule about 1050 B.C. To that date must be added 40 years for Eli's judgeship, 410 years of history recorded in the book of Judges, 30 years of Joshua's leadership, and 40 years of wandering in the wilderness, plus an unknown number of years for Samuel's leadership. The total would push the date back to before 1570 B.C.—much earlier than an Exodus of 1440 B.C. The usual conclusion, then, is that some of the judges ruled at the same time, which was possible because they did not always govern the entire land. For instance, Deborah and Barak exercised power in northern Palestine; Samson, in southwest Palestine; and Jephthah, on the eastern frontier.

Merrill F. Unger worked out a chronology of the judges as follows (all dates approximate): oppression by Mesopotamia (1361–1353 B.C.); deliverance under Othniel and forty-year rest (1353–1313); oppression by Moabites (1313–1295); deliverance under Ehud and eighty-year rest (1295–1215); oppression by Canaanites (1215–1195); deliverance under Deborah and Barak and forty-year rest (1195–1155); oppression by Midianites (1155–1148); deliverance under Gideon and forty-year rest (1148–1108); Abimelech at Shechem (1108–1105); oppression by Ammonites (though eighteen years locally, it presumably afflicted all Israel only about one year, c. 1105 B.C.); deliverance under Jephthah (1105–1099); Philistine oppression (1099–1059); judgeship of Samson (1085–1065).[1] It will be noted that Unger omitted the judgeships of Tola and Jair, which presumably had only local influence and overlapped with Ammonite and Philistine oppression. He also omitted the judgeships of Ibzan, Elon, and Abdon, likewise presumably local in significance and partially overlapping the period of Philistine domination. No chronology of the judges can be accepted with any degree of finality, but perhaps Unger's attempt will serve as a useful approximation.

The Judges

Oppressor	Years of Oppression	Judge	Length of Judgeship or Rest	Scripture Reference
Mesopotamia	8	Othniel	40	3:8–11
Moabites				
Ammonites	18	Ehud	80	3:12–30
Amalekites				
Philistines	?	Shamgar	?	3:31; cf. 5:6
Canaanites	20	Deborah and Barak	40	4:1–5:31

(Continued)

The Judges (Continued)				
Oppressor	Years of Oppression	Judge	Length of Judgeship or Rest	Scripture Reference
Midianites	7	Gideon	40	6:1–8:28
		Abimelech (usurper)	3	8:29–9:57
		Tola	23	10:1, 2
		Jair	22	10:3–5
Ammonites	18	Jephthah	6	10:6–12:7
		Ibzan	7	12:8–10
		Elon	10	12:11, 12
		Abdon	8	12:13–15
Philistines	40	Samson	20	13:1–16:31
		Eli	40	1 Samuel 1:1–4:18
		Samuel	?	I Samuel 7:3ff.

VALUE OF THE BOOK OF JUDGES

The book of Judges provides an important historical link between the conquest of Palestine and beginnings of the monarchy. Without it, our understanding of later Hebrew developments would be much less clear. The book demonstrates by means of numerous examples the principle laid down in the earlier Old Testament books that obedience to the law meant life and peace, while disobedience resulted in oppression and death. Further, the book shows that God was always ready to forgive His penitent people, and it indicates the degree to which the Hebrews had already departed from the high moral and ethical demands of the law. In its vivid portrayal of the weakness and confusion of a period when every man did that which was right in his own eyes, the book prepares the way for the single superior authority of kingship.

THE LEADING JUDGES

Othniel, A Deliverer from Judah

A very definite philosophy of history appears in Judges: the Israelites suffered national oppression not because they experienced economic, political or military weakness, but because they turned their backs on God and served idols. The first oppression came at the hands of Chushanrishathaim, who apparently ruled a principality in northern Mesopotamia. Whether he was a Hittite or Aramaic prince is unimportant. The fact is, he exercised power over the Israelites from a considerable distance for a period of eight years. Othniel, nephew of Caleb, who had distinguished himself as a warrior during the conquest and who for his valor had won the hand of Caleb's daughter, rallied his people and defeated and drove out the invaders, giving the land rest for eighty years. Apparently the oppression was extensive (though perhaps not including all the Hebrew tribes), because Othniel was from Judah in the south. It is said of Othniel, as well as the other judges, "The LORD raised up a deliverer . . . the Spirit of the LORD came upon him" (Judges 3:9, 10, NKJV).

Ehud, A Deliverer from Benjamin

Again the biblical philosophy of history comes clear. God strengthened the Moabites against Israel because of their sin (Judges 3:12). So the Moabites, joined by Ammonites and Amalekites, moved west of the Jordan and set up headquarters in the vicinity of Jericho, oppressing the Israelites for eighteen years. At length, in answer to Hebrew petitions, God raised up Ehud, a Benjamite, to deliver his people. One year, when Ehud brought the annual tribute to King Eglon of Moab, he won a private audience with the king and assassinated him. Quickly Ehud sounded the war cry in the nearby hills of Ephraim and pulled together a force of Israelites. The leaderless occupation forces decided to retreat across the Jordan. When they got to the fords of the Jordan, however, they found the Israelites waiting for them, and a massacre ensued which won an eighty-year period of rest for the Hebrews. Probably contributing to peace in the area of Palestine is the fact that the thirteenth century was the era of the great Ramses II and other strong kings of the Egyptian Nineteenth Dynasty. During those days it was not wise for tribes of Palestine and Syria to build up their power and thus invite Egyptian retaliation.

Deborah and Barak, Deliverance by a Woman

The spotlight next focuses on northern Palestine where a second King Jabin of Hazor (not to be confused with the one Joshua defeated) led a Canaanite confederacy. Evidently the earlier Hebrew victory over Jabin I had not been complete, and Hazor had regained sufficient power to oppress the northern tribes of Israel for twenty years. This time the deliverer was a woman, apparently a very outstanding person, because Western Asia in the second millennium B.C. was truly a man's world. Not only did Deborah lead Israel to military victory with the help of Barak, but also she served as a prophetess and judge long before her military ventures. Barak collected an army of ten thousand from the northern tribes of Zebulun and Naphtali and met Jabin's famed corps of nine hundred chariots in the Valley of Megiddo near the Kishon River. God brought a sudden storm over the area, and flash floods mired the chariots, destroying the excellent Canaanite advantage and giving the victory to the Hebrews. Sisera, captain of the host, fled and finally met his death at the hands of a Kenite woman, Jael, as he slept in her tent. Thereafter, Israel enjoyed forty years of peace.

Gideon, A Deliverer Who Made Sure God Got the Glory

The fourth oppression occurred at the hands of Midianites, Amalekites, and other camel-riding peoples of the East. Apparently they made annual raids across the Jordan into the good grain-growing areas of Israel, especially the plain of Esdraelon. As the people cringed in caves and mountain strongholds and cried for relief, God sent a deliverer in the person of Gideon. When enemy forces gathered in the Valley of Esdraelon, Gideon assembled an army of 32,000 from Manasseh, Asher, Zebulun, and Naphtali (northern tribes affected by the incursion) to do battle with an estimated 135,000 enemy. The tribes involved probably could not have fielded such a large army; presumably the 135,000 were bands of marauders who invaded for the annual plundering expedition. By the use of a fleece twice exposed, Gideon determined that God had, indeed, called him to deliver Israel (Judges 6:36–40). But God reserved to Himself the glory of victory. So first He reduced the number by commanding that all the fearful should be sent home; 22,000 went, showing the discouragement of Israel. Then He eliminated another 9,700 by testing their battle readiness at the springs of Harod, at the northern foot of Mount Gilboa. Only 300 stood the test, keeping one hand on their swords while lapping water with the other. These Gideon divided into three companies and made a surprise attack in the blackness of a moonless Palestinian night. As the 300 ran down the slopes of Mount Moreh near the eastern end of the plain of Megiddo, they blew trumpets, smashed jars revealing torches, and shouted the battle cry, "The sword of the Lord and of Gideon." The enemy fled in panic across the Jordan, thinking a great host pursued them. Probably each of the 300 was thought to be a platoon commander, who carried a torch to give direction to his men and to provide a rallying point for them. Gideon called the people of Ephraim to marshal forces and cut off the enemy's escape at the Jordan. The Israelites won a preliminary victory at the Jordan and a complete victory east of the

Jordan. The Israelites then begged Gideon to become their king. This he refused to do: "I will not rule over you. . . . the LORD shall rule over you." While Gideon lived the country had rest for forty years. After his death, the people turned openly to the worship of Baal.

Abimelech, A Renegade Who Claimed Kingship

Abimelech, a son of Gideon by a concubine in Shechem, was not so reticent as his father about claiming the kingship. A renegade of the first order, he succeeded in having himself proclaimed king in Shechem, but how much support he enjoyed in Israel is not clear. He killed all but one of his seventy brothers because they were potential rivals. Finally, after three years of treachery and bloodshed, even the Shechemites tired of him. Although he put down a revolt there, he was not so successful at the nearby town of Thebez, where a woman dropped a millstone on his head. To avoid the shame of being killed by a woman, he ordered his armorbearer to kill him. Thus ended the civil war.

Jephthah and a Foolish Vow

On the eastern frontier, the Ammonites now asserted themselves, oppressing Israel for eighteen years. To the rescue came Jephthah, son of a harlot and a Gileadite named Gilead. Because of his illegitimacy his half brothers had thrown him out of the household, and he had gone to live in an area north of Gilead, where he demonstrated his military ability. When Jephthah's family was in serious trouble, they sent for him to lead them in war against the Ammonites. This he promised to do if he could retain his leadership after the war was over. Then, enabled by God, he proceeded to raise an army from Manasseh and Gilead and to win a decisive victory over the Ammonites.

But before he went into battle, he vowed to God that if victorious, he would offer as a burnt offering whatever came forth from the doors of his house to meet him upon his return. After the victory his only child, a daughter, rushed out to meet him as he came back home. There has been endless discussion in biblical literature over this ill-considered vow. Some argue that Jephthah was a rather wild man, living on the fringes of Israelite religious influence in an area where pagans would have practiced human sacrifice. He had made a vow, and one would expect him to keep it. Others argue just as cogently that human sacrifice was an abomination to God, and it is inconceivable that any God-fearing person could have committed such a crime. They say his daughter was allowed two months to bewail her virginity, not her loss of life (Judges 11:37, 38); and the implication is that she became a virgin devoted to the service of God at the central sanctuary (cf. Exodus 38:8; 1 Samuel 2:22; Luke 2:36, 37). The real pain for Jephthah, then, was termination of his line. Leon Wood observes that if he did literally sacrifice his daughter, the place of sacrifice would have been the tabernacle, and no priest would have been willing to officiate. He also notes that the latter part of Judges 11:31 may be translated "shall surely be the LORD's, or I will offer it up for a burnt-offering"—the first part indicating what Jephthah would have done if a human being had met him and the latter if an animal.[2]

Samson, Deliverer of Great Strength and Great Weakness

The Philistines, who Scripture says oppressed the Israelites for forty years before Samson began to deliver them from bondage, brought on the last great oppression. Actually the bondage would not cease until David's conquests established the Hebrew kingdom or empire. Samson's judgeship is distinct from the others in that his birth was announced, his Nazarite way of life enjoined, and his relief for Israel came not from leading armies of his fellow citizens. He was born of Danite parentage and lived on the border between Philistia and Israel. As part of his Nazarite vow, his hair was never to be cut. It is common to picture Samson as a huge man with great muscles, but there is no hint in Scripture of anything unusual about his physique. In fact, his strength was such a puzzle to the Philistines that they tried every ruse to learn his secret. If he had been an unusual physical phenomenon, they would not have had any question about the matter. The truth is, Samson was a rather normal human being who was an example to both Israelites and Philistines of the ability of God to empower an individual.

Probably the stories of Samson's feats of strength are only selected accounts of his many acts of physical prowess. And it may be argued that many of his actions (e.g., releasing three hundred foxes with burning firebrands to destroy Philistine crops) were not merely a result of fits of anger but calculated efforts to destroy the power of the Philistines. For twenty years he judged Israel, per-haps at Hebron; and during those years his life apparently was generally exemplary. Presumably it was near the end of his min-istry that he became involved with the harlot at Gaza and with Delilah. He was to pay dearly for his sin—first with the loss of his eyesight and later with his life. But his dying moment was destined to be his greatest triumph. His prayer for the restoration of God's power was answered, and he pulled down the temple of Dagon with tremendous loss of Philistine life and of his own. While he had failed to deliver Israel from the Philistines, he had restrained them temporarily and kept his people from being completely uprooted or enslaved. In spite of his weakness, he won a place among the heroes of faith (Hebrews 11:32). The grace of God appears in the life of Samson as in that of David later on. After a fall comes restoration to divine favor, although the sin itself is not without its consequences.

Eli, A Break in the Line of Warrior Deliverers

Evidently, Ammonite oppression in the east and the judgeships of Jephthah and his successors were at least partially contemporary with Philistine domination in the west and the activities of Samson.

Evidently, also, the lives and ministries of Eli and Samuel overlapped that of Samson; and all three of them were concerned with the Philistine threat. Eli was the high priest who presided at the tabernacle at Shiloh. In this capacity he led and ruled the Hebrews for forty years. Scripture also calls him a judge (1 Samuel 4:18); thus his listing here. He was not really a warrior and deliverer as the other judges were. Eli was pious and patriotic, but his great fault lay in his indulgent treatment of his sons. They were so evil that they brought reproach upon God, upon their father, and upon themselves. Ultimately they died under the judgment of God. Conditions were destined to get worse for Israel before they got better. The Israelites fought a preliminary battle against the Philistines at Aphek (New Testament Antipatris, Acts 23:31; just northeast of modern Tel Aviv) with the loss of four thousand men. Fearful that their cause would be completely lost, they brought the ark from Shiloh and sought to use it as a kind of "good-luck charm"; they evidently had little appreciation of the presence and power of God with them. The Philistines determined to fight harder than ever and utterly swept the field, killing thirty thousand Israelites (including Eli's two sons) and capturing the ark. When Eli heard the news, he fell and broke his neck and died.

Samuel, Dedicated to God

Samuel then became the spiritual leader of Israel. He had been in preparation for this moment all his life. Dedicated to God from birth by a godly mother, he had come to live at the sanctuary at Shiloh at an early age. Before the catastrophe at Aphek, his reputation had been firmly established in all Israel from Dan to Beersheba (1 Samuel 3:20). Actually Samuel is called a prophet (1 Samuel 3:20) and a judge (1 Samuel 7:15–17), and acted as priest (1 Samuel 9:12, 13; 13:8–13). He took over at a most difficult time in Israelite history After Aphek, the Philistines moved into Israelite territory, destroying Shiloh itself and eliminating what little Hebrew metal industry still existed. Their goal was to make the Hebrews completely dependent upon them.

There is about a twenty-year silence in the biblical narrative (except for the account of the wanderings of the ark), with almost nothing said about either Samuel or Hebrew difficulties (1 Samuel 7:2). When the curtain goes up again (perhaps around 1060 B.C.), Samuel is at Mizpah, calling the people to repentance and revival. Spiritual restoration is followed by military and political restoration. The Israelites win a great victory over the Philistines at Mizpah and recover territory lost to the Philistines earlier. A new level of national stability is achieved (1 Samuel 7:13–17). Of course, all this upturn of events did not just happen. No doubt Samuel had been extremely busy trying to pull things together in the face of almost insurmountable odds. Evidently he had moved the tabernacle to Nob where it appeared later (see 1 Samuel 21:1–9). Apparently, too, he had established training schools for young prophets (I Samuel 10:5–12; 19:19–24) in an effort to expand spiritual influence in the realm. And certainly some of the judicial and religious activity mentioned in 1 Samuel 7:16, 17 must have gone on during the silent years.[3]

Unfortunately, Samuel's sons were not much better than Eli's; and as Samuel grew older, the people became restless about the future. Moreover, they wanted a king like the other nations so they could establish the kind of central power necessary to meet such national emergencies as the Philistine threat. Samuel took the request as a lack of appreciation for all his hard work, a sort of vote of no confidence. But God made it clear that the opposition was really to the divine plan of theocracy. God granted the Hebrews' wish but warned them of the disadvantages of kingship (I Samuel 8:9–21). The concept of kingship was not new to Israel. It had been hinted at in Genesis 49:10 and Numbers 24:17 and Moses had made some very clear statements about it in Deuteronomy 17:14–20. Moreover, the people had begged Gideon to become king, and some had actually followed the usurper King Abimelech of Shechem for a while.

REPRESENTATIVE STORIES FROM THE
PERIOD OF THE JUDGES (Judges 17–21)

Representative narratives from the period of the judges occur in the last chapters of judges and the book of Ruth and give some idea of what life was like in this difficult period. The first story (Judges 17–18) tells how Micah, an Ephraimite, established his own private shrine, complete with graven images, and employed an itinerant Levite to be his priest. It recounts, too, how most of the Danites, forsook their allotted territory and moved north of the Sea of Galilee, stealing Micah's shrine and priest on the way. This narrative is reported to illustrate that during the period "everyone did what was right in his own eyes" (Judges 17:6, NKJV). How true that was: a private shrine was established in competition with the main shrine at Shiloh; graven images were used in worship in clear violation of the Mosaic Law; a Levite illegally entered into a private religious arrangement; the Danites moved where they did not belong and set up a false tribal worship.

The first story reveals religious and political confusion during the period of the judges. The second (Judges 19–21) reveals moral decline. A Levite and his concubine had an experience in Gibeah of Benjamin somewhat reminiscent of Sodom in Lot's day (Genesis 19). Presumably the whole tribe was infected with sodomy or other sexual looseness, because they refused to surrender the wrongdoers. So civil war followed, which almost obliterated the tribe of Benjamin.

A Promise of Hope in a Desolate Time

Of far different character is the story of Ruth. Ruth 1:1 states that events narrated in the book took place during the days of the judges. Details of the last verses of Ruth 4 indicate that Ruth was the great-grandmother of David, and this book must have been written during his reign, possibly by Samuel. If David began to rule about 1010 B.C. at the age of thirty, his birth must be placed about 1040 B.C., and the story of Ruth occurred during the latter part of the twelfth century. The narrative provides a glimpse into ordinary events in the lives of common people during the days of the judges. An Israelite family— Elimelech, Naomi, and their two sons—went to Moab during a famine in Judah. There the father and his sons all died, leaving the mother and two Moabite daughters-in-law, Ruth and Orpah, behind. Naomi then determined to return to Bethlehem in Israel and took Ruth with her. At Bethlehem, Ruth gleaned barley in the field of a wealthy relative of Elimelech, Boaz, who then married her. To this union was born Obed; to Obed, Jesse; to Jesse, David.

This little book, then, provides a partial lineage of David and thus of Christ, who was in the line of David. It shows that there was Gentile blood in that line, a fact that has profound implications when we consider that He was to be a Savior for all mankind. The book shows, too, that Gentiles could be joined to the common-wealth of Israel on condition of faith in God; the true faith knows no national or racial boundaries. The special teaching in the book, however, concerns the kinsman-redeemer, which harks back to Leviticus 25:25–48 and looks forward to the ministry of Christ. The kinsman-redeemer had the privilege of redeeming either an inheritance or a person. The idea was to restore inheritance to a family that had lost it and also to raise up an heir to enjoy the inheritance. In this case, Boaz would not gain possession of the land himself but would hold it in trust for Ruth's son, who would then inherit the estate of Mahlon. For one to be a redeemer he had to be a blood relative, had to have the wealth or means to redeem, and be willing to redeem. All these things are true of Christ, our Redeemer. By assuming human flesh at the incarnation, He became related to humankind; He had infinite holiness that could be reckoned over to our account (the means to redeem); and He came willingly to pay our sin-debt by offering Himself as the spotless lamb of God for the sins of the world. Thus He became our Kinsman-Redeemer.

Notes

1. Merrill F. Unger, *Archaeology and the Old Testament* (Grand Rapids: Zondervan, c. 1954), pp. 182–87. Leon Wood seems to hold to somewhat similar dates in Leon Wood, *A Survey of Israel's History* (Grand Rapids: Zondervan, 1970), pp. 212–29.

2. Wood, pp. 223–24.

3. Who wrote 1 Samuel is not certainly known. Possibly Samuel wrote the first part down to his death in chapter 25, and Gad or Nathan may have brought the book to its present form near the end of David's reign. Possibly, too, Nathan and Gad are responsible for writing 2 Samuel.

8

The Clamor for a King: Saul, David, and Solomon

1 & 2 Samuel, 1 Kings 1–11, 1 Chronicles, 2 Chronicles 1–9

ISRAEL asked for a king and got one. The first king was Saul, who ruled for forty years (Acts 13:21); the second was David, who likewise ruled for forty years (2 Samuel 5:5); the third was Solomon, who also ruled for forty years (1 Kings 11:42). This span of about 120 years is commonly called the united monarchy because these men ruled over all Israel. It is followed by the period of divided monarchy when there were two kingdoms, Israel and Judah. An exact chronology is hard to set, but one of the finest chronological studies ever done on a segment of Scripture is E.R. Thiele's *The Mysterious Numbers of the Hebrew Kings*. Thiele puts the division of the kingdom at 931 B.C. Working backward, then, the dates of Solomon would be 970–931; David, 1010–970; and Saul, 1050–1010 B.C. This is the chronology followed here.

SAUL (1 Samuel 9–31; 1 Chronicles 10)

The people asked for a king like the other nations around them. God granted them a king, but not one like those of the surrounding nations. The Hebrew king was to be a man of God's own choice. In his public and private life he should follow God's dictates, and he was not to intrude into the affairs of the priesthood; God had His own appointed leaders there. Above all, he must not slip into the ways of idolatry but rather was to exert all the influence of his office to keep his people on God-honoring paths. If a Hebrew king failed in one or more of these respects, he ran the risk of being deposed by God, of having his line brought to an end, or even of bringing his people into captivity to a foreign power. All this must be kept in mind when studying the reigns of Saul, David, Solomon, or the kings of the divided monarchy.

Saul began well. He was endowed with a kingly appearance and was head and shoulders taller than almost any other Israelite (1 Samuel 10:23). He came from the small tribe of Benjamin and so was not a party to tribal jealousy, as would have been the case if he were from the leading tribes of Ephraim or Judah. He was God's choice and enjoyed confirming signs, among which was the Spirit of God coming upon him when he joined the company of prophets (1 Samuel 10:1–10). When Samuel presented him to the people at Mizpah, they received him, and a kind of "palace guard" joined him (10:26). But Saul was still an unknown to the people; there was no capital city; and strongly separatist tendencies existed among the tribes. An opportunity soon presented itself for Saul to win general public approval, however. The Ammonites advanced on the eastern frontier and threatened Jabesh-gilead, which sent to Saul for help. Saul answered their call by sending a general appeal to the tribes. A total of 30,000 came from Judah and 300,000 from the other tribes. From the many who appeared, Saul selected a fighting force and won a crushing victory. The Israelites now accepted him as king, and Samuel crowned him at Gilgal. Subsequently, he had the good sense to avoid heavy tax burdens or radical changes in the Hebrew pattern of life. He established his capital at his hometown of Gibeah, three miles north of Jerusalem, and built a fortress-palace there.

The First Mistakes

But Saul had ruled for only about two years when he began to show signs of slipping from God's way. At Gilgal he grew impatient waiting for Samuel to come to offer a sacrifice, and he did it himself. Soon afterward, Samuel appeared and rebuked Saul, declaring that God would ultimately rend the kingdom from him for his sin of intruding into the priestly office (13:13, 14). However, God was not through with Saul's administration. Soon thereafter, He gave Saul a great victory over the Philistines and, subsequently, over the Moabites, Ammonites, and Edomites east of the Jordan and Zobah to the north of Damascus. These successes show Saul to have been a much more effective military leader than is commonly recognized; and they were no doubt foundational to the later establishment of David's empire. Presumably for some twenty years Saul was on reasonably good behavior.[1] Then Samuel commissioned him to fulfill God's curse against the Amalekites (Exodus 17:14; Deuteronomy 25:17–19) and destroy them utterly. When Saul only partially obeyed, Samuel broke with him and never saw him again as long as he lived. Soon after, God commanded Samuel secretly to anoint David king. Bereft of divine approval on his administration and of the support of Samuel, Saul began to show signs of depression. In an effort to lift him from these moods, his advisors sought for a court musician and settled on David, son of Jesse.

David's lyre was effective at times in restoring Saul to a better frame of mind, but the king passed increasingly through alternating moods of depression, rage, and normalcy. Seemingly this mental condition was brought on by a frustration derangement: God was against him; David's star constantly rose as Saul's set; Saul's son Jonathan had placed himself on David's side; Saul lived under the realization that his days were numbered; and Samuel's counsel was no longer available.

The Rise of a Rival

David's rise to prominence was tremendously spurred by his victory over Goliath and the accompanying defeat of the Philistines. The king made David commander of the army, and with his continuing successes the young man built a great reputation throughout the land and was more highly thought of than Saul himself. Soon the king in fits of rage began to make attempts on David's life. David ducked the spears Saul hurled at him in the palace. Then he experienced deliverance at Gibeah by the help of his wife (Saul's daughter) Michal (1 Samuel 19:1–17); at Ramah by the help of the Spirit (19:18–24); at Gibeah by the help of Jonathan (20:1–42); at Keilah by the help of Abiathar (23:7–13); at Maon by the help of the Philistines (23:15–29); at Engedi (24:1–22); at Hachilah (26:1–25); and finally, by the death of Saul at the hand of the Philistines.

The Philistines had been a threat to the Hebrews throughout Saul's reign. Declining in ability to manage the kingdom and unable to locate an equally capable replacement for David as commander of the forces, the king found it impossible to prevent Philistine inroads into Hebrew territory. At length they moved in force through the Valley of Esdraelon and camped at Shunem, a few miles south of which, at Mount Gilboa, the Israelites took up battle stations. Terrified at the outcome and unable to get counsel from God (1 Samuel 28:6), Saul searched out a spiritistic medium in an effort to communicate with the dead Samuel (1 Samuel 28:7–25). This act not only violated a Mosaic prohibition, but Saul's own earlier command (Leviticus 20:27; 1 Samuel 28:9). What happened to the medium caused her complete loss of composure. Instead of some sort of contact with an impersonating demon, she experienced a supernatural appearance of the prophet Samuel himself, who bypassed her and spoke directly to Saul, predicting utter defeat for Israel and the death of Saul and his sons. The prediction came true the following day. Utterly crushed, the Israelites fled from many of their towns to escape the victorious Philistines, who now moved into Israelite territory in force.

Saul's Downfall and David's Struggle

Thus, he who began well ended disastrously. Saul left his land in worse condition than he had found it—at least as far as the Philistine threat was concerned. Probably the effects of his earlier victories east of the Jordan were largely dissipated. The country was as disunited as it had been forty years earlier. The people who wanted a king like other nations had gotten one too much like the others. God wanted the king to be different. Because he was not, God deposed him and sought for another "after his own heart."

That man was David, anointed by Samuel but on the run to escape Saul's designs on his life. More than once his whole cause seemed lost, but he continued doggedly; more than once he had opportunity to take the life of his enemy, but he determined not to do so. On two occasions, however, David's difficulties proved too much for him, and in frustration he sought refuge among the enemies of Israel. The first of these occurrences took place soon after his flight from the court of Saul. At that time it seemed that the place of refuge he could reach most quickly was the court of Achish, king of Gath. When he arrived there, the king called attention to the Hebrew warrior's victories over the Philistines, and David in fear feigned madness (1 Samuel 21). The second occasion of David's flight to Gath came after he had been pursued by Saul for an extended period of time, and his will to resist was worn down. This time his circumstances were different. He had several hundred men with their families under his leadership and provision for them was difficult indeed. Apparently he and his men accepted mercenary status in the Philistine armed forces, a fact that obligated them to participate in the great battle that destroyed Saul and his son. On that occasion, David's contingent was saved from fighting the Israelites by fear on the part of some Philistines that he might defect. While David lived at Ziklag in southern Philistine territory (for about eighteen months), he carried on military action against tribes traditionally enemies of Israel and shared the booty with Judean towns, thus keeping his political fences mended in preparation for the day when he should be king.

DAVID (2 Samuel 1–24; 1 Kings 1:1–38; 1 Chronicles 11–29)

That day was not long in coming. When David and his men returned to Ziklag from the conclave that prepared for the battle of Mount Gilboa, they discovered their homes burned and their families gone. A punitive expedition against the Amalekites, who were responsible, recovered everything, with much booty besides. Soon after David and his men returned to Ziklag, word came of the Israelite defeat and the death of Saul. Following a period of mourning, David by divine guidance took his entire company to Hebron, where he was declared king over Judah (2 Samuel 2:14). It was natural that the tribe of Judah should take such a step because David's home was Bethlehem of Judah; his campaigning as captain of Saul's army had been largely on the edge of Judah, so he was better known there than in the north; and he had been sending gifts to Judean cities for some time.

The other tribes elevated a son of Saul, Ishbosheth, to the throne at the new capital of Mahanaim. This town, east of the Jordan, was safe from the Philistines, who now controlled much of the west bank of Jordan. As time passed, periodic armed clashes occurred between Israel and Judah. The cause of Ishbosheth gradually weakened, and ultimately both the Israelite commander-in-chief and the king were assassinated. Then armed contingents, or their representatives, from all over Israel came to Hebron to beg

David to become their king (see 1 Chronicles 12:23–40). Apparently some hard bargaining occurred, and understandings were reached that led to the establishment of a more fully integrated state than Saul had ruled. So "David made a league with them" and "they anointed David king over Israel" (2 Samuel 5:3). He had begun to reign in Hebron seven and one-half years earlier at the age of thirty, and was destined to reign another thirty-three years over all Israel from Jerusalem (2 Samuel 5:4, 5).

Jerusalem Becomes the Capital

Apparently the Philistines did not interfere with David's rule in Judah; they may even have considered him a vassal. The rest of Israel west of the Jordan was largely under their control. But when David became king of all Israel, they clearly recognized his rising threat and mounted an attack. While it is difficult to sort out the exact order of events from Scripture, they probably attacked before he captured Jerusalem. At any rate, near the beginning of his reign, he fought two major contests with the Philistines and so completely defeated them that they never again posed a major threat to Israel. Also near the beginning of his reign, he sought a new, more-centrally located capital. Jerusalem was in many ways ideal. Its location was fairly central, its water supply adequate, and its defense capability excellent. Moreover, it was in neither Judah nor Ephraim and so was not involved in any jealousies between large tribes. Finally, its capture removed a Canaanite stronghold from the midst of Israelite territory. Joab was awarded command of the armed forces for his success in taking Jerusalem from the Jebusites.

Then David sought to make Jerusalem the religious as well as the political capital. For several decades the ark had been separated from the tabernacle. David made arrangements to bring the ark to Jerusalem, and installed it there in a tabernacle, amid great rejoicing and offering of sacrifices. Though he planned to build a proper house for God in the capital later in his reign, God made it clear that David's son, who would be a man of peace, should build it instead (1 Chronicles 28:2–6). Though David spoke about building a house for God, God declared that He would establish David's house. In fact, He unconditionally promised David a house or line forever, a throne forever, and a kingdom forever (2 Samuel 7; 1 Chronicles 17). This prediction could be fulfilled only in the person of David's greater Son, the Lord Jesus Christ, who will reign on Mount Zion during the millennial kingdom and forever in the New Jerusalem. David submitted in humble gratitude to the wishes of God and collected large quantities of material for future construction of the temple. Though David could not build the temple, he did give careful attention to organization of the priesthood, liturgy, and music of the tabernacle, and thus of temple worship (1 Chronicles 24–25). The titles of the Psalms ascribe seventy-three of them to David. From his youth he had been both a musician and a devout person. David was a poet of the heart, a universal poet. His hymns of praise and confession run the whole gamut of human experience and are loved and sung in palaces and hovels all over the earth. Scripture calls him the "sweet psalmist of Israel" (2 Samuel 23:1).

David's Empire

In 2 Samuel 8, 10–12, and 1 Chronicles 18–20, reference is made to the numerous wars of David and his building of an empire. There is no evidence that he was a conscious imperialist, but apparently he responded to military situations as they arose. First, he fought with Moab to the east of the Dead Sea and dealt harshly with it, making it a vassal state. What the provocation was, Scripture does not indicate. On one occasion he left his father and mother under protection of the king of Moab (1 Samuel 22:3, 4), and there is a Jewish tradition that they were cruelly slain there, but no evidence exists of any connection between such a tragedy and this conquest. Next, he made Edom a vassal state, and in this way controlled territory all the way to the Gulf of Aqaba. He also fought against Damascus, Zobah, and Hamath. Zobah and Damascus; also apparently became vassal states; David stationed troops in Damascus. How much control he had over Hamath (which extended to the Euphrates) is not certain. Following a war with Ammon to the south and east of Gilead, he annexed that territory to his kingdom. At an early date he established good relations and possibly an alliance with Tyre. So his territory and/or sphere of influence extended all the way from the border of Egypt (about fifty miles south of Gaza) and the Gulf of Aqaba in the south to a point near the Euphrates in the north and from the Mediterranean to the Arabian Desert.

David may well have been the strongest ruler in the contemporary world. By this time the Minoan, Mycenaean, Hittite, Old Babylonian, and Egyptian powers were down or utterly destroyed. A power vacuum in the Middle East would have permitted an even greater empire if David had wanted to build it. The only places to rival David's power were India and China. The former, in its Vedic Age, was not united and had a multiplicity of states ruled by relatively independent princes. The latter was in the Chou period, when emperors were increasingly weak and checkmated by numerous feudal lords, much the same as kings of Western Europe were during the Middle Ages.

David's Sins

Scripture records two major sins of David. The first was committing adultery with Bathsheba and the subsequent murder of Uriah her husband (2 Samuel 11–12). God severely reprimanded David through Nathan the prophet, who predicted that the child of the adultery would die and that the sword would never depart from his house. The child died soon after birth. Fulfillment of the prophecy of strife in David's household is abundantly evident in the troubles of the last years of his life.

David's second great sin involved a census-taking (2 Samuel 24; 1 Chronicles 21). What makes the act so sinful Scripture does not reveal, but it must have been serious. Wood observes, "Even cold-hearted Joab urged the king to refrain in the action, and the degree of God's displeasure is indicated by the severity of the punishment inflicted as a result. The real sin may have concerned intended imposition of high taxes, and possibly even conscript labor."[2] At any rate, Gad the prophet presented David with three kinds of divine punishment, from which he must pick one. David chose "three days of pestilence," which resulted in the death of seventy thousand people. The plague stopped just north of Jerusalem, at the threshing floor of Araunah the Jebusite. In gratitude and repentance, David bought the floor and oxen from Araunah and offered sacrifices to God. This threshing floor has special significance as the traditional spot on the hill of Moriah where Abraham offered Isaac and as the place where Solomon later built the temple.

The Succession Problem

Like other oriental monarchs, David fell into the practice of keeping a harem. Scripture names eight wives and twenty-one children and refers to other wives and concubines. Such a situation opened the door to all sorts of evils, not the least of which were the inability of a king to exercise proper parental supervision, the rise of harem squabbles, and the question of succession to the throne. At the time of Solomon's birth, Bathsheba, the child's mother, was David's favorite; and Solomon was, at least privately, designated as heir to the throne; but he was far down in the list of heirs. While David was king in Hebron, six sons were born to him. The first was Amnon, later killed by Absalom; the second was Chileab, unheard of in later life, who presumably died young; the third was Absalom, and the fourth Adonijah (see 2 Samuel 3:2–5). It is the third and fourth sons who particularly figured in the succession squabble.

Absalom, a very handsome and clever young man with a considerable amount of leadership ability and a flair for public relations, decided to try for the throne (2 Samuel 15:18). Making a special effort to win the hearts of the people and laying his plans well, he pulled together a force at Hebron and had himself anointed king. Then he marched on Jerusalem. David had no choice but to flee. He went to Mahanaim, which had served as capital of Israel while David ruled at Hebron. In a hard-fought battle, David's men won a decisive victory, and Joab himself killed Absalom, contrary to orders, bringing the rebellion to an end. On the heels of Absalom's revolt, Sheba, a Benjamite, led a secession movement of the northern tribes. This was quickly stamped out (2 Samuel 19–20).

Probably two or three years later, David's fourth son, Adonijah, made an attempt to seize the throne. If the law of the firstborn had been strictly followed, he would have been heir to the throne. Adonijah's support was formidable, and included Joab and the high priest Abiathar. Plans were made for an anointing ceremony at the spring En-rogel southeast of Jerusalem. News of the affair leaked out, and Nathan the prophet and Bathsheba took the lead in reporting the situation and persuading David to announce for Solomon. This he did, and plans proceeded immediately for the anointing of Solomon at the spring Gihon east of Jerusalem. The cheering at Solomon's ceremony could be heard at Adonijah's gathering just over a little ridge about two-fifths of a mile away. Adonijah's following melted away, and Adonijah submitted to Solomon, averting civil war (1 Kings 1:1–2:9; 1 Chronicles 22:6–23:1; 28–29).

David in Retrospect

Without doubt, David was Israel's greatest king. Jerusalem came to be known as the city of David. Christ was to be born in the line of David and will some day rule on David's throne. In fact, David is called a "man after God's own heart" (1 Samuel 13:14; Acts 13:22; see also 2 Chronicles 8:14, "man of God"), perhaps the strongest word of approval God ever spoke concerning a man. Exactly what this means is open to interpretation. Certainly it does not mean that he was perfect, nor even that he never committed a major sin. He was a man with feet of clay, and he broke many of the commandments, being guilty among other things of adultery and murder. (It may be observed that one of the strongest arguments for inspiration of Scripture is the way in which the weaknesses and follies of its best men are recorded with utmost frankness.)

If David's private life was not always exemplary, in what sense can he be described as a "man after God's own heart"? Possibly the answer is twofold: in his attitude toward sin and in his public policy. Though David sinned, when he was confronted with the error of his way, his heart broke in penitence. Observe how he bared his heart before God in Psalm 51 (NKJV): "Have mercy upon me, O God . . . cleanse me from my sin. For I acknowledge my transgressions, And my sin is always before me. . . . Wash me, and I shall be whiter than snow . . . Create in me a clean heart, O God, And renew a steadfast spirit within me. . . . Restore to me the joy of Your salvation. . . . A broken and a contrite heart—These, O God, You will not despise." Generally David's public policy honored God. For example, he refused to take the life of Saul or to reward those who did because Saul was "God's anointed," and God would punish him in due time. He gave proper honor to the sanctuary of God and organized the worship and service of the Levites and sought to build the temple. In general, the principles by which he lived ring clear from his charge to Solomon before his death: to walk in God's ways, to keep God's commandments, to serve God with a perfect heart and a willing mind (1 Kings 2:3–4; 1 Chronicles 28:9).

SOLOMON (1 Kings 1:39–11:43; 2 Chronicles 1–9)

David was a man of war and a builder of empire. Solomon was a man of peace and builder of palaces and cities and fortifications and the temple. But before he could start his building activities, he had to consolidate his power. How much real opposition he had is questionable, but there were problems left from the latter days of David's reign. Adonijah apparently was still a threat to the crown and was liquidated, along with the somewhat unscrupulous Joab and David's opponent Shimei. Abiathar the high priest suffered expulsion from office for his complicity in the Adonijah coronation. After this minimal action, Solomon seems to have been firmly entrenched as head of state.

The Foundation of Solomon's Glory

Apparently much impressed by the spiritual testimony left by David and greatly desiring God's blessing on his rule, Solomon, near the beginning of his reign, made a great sacrifice to God at Gibeon. God met him there and in effect said, "Make a wish, and it will come true." Instead of asking for the things sovereigns usually want (wealth, power, fame, etc.), Solomon asked for wisdom. God was so pleased with this request that He granted it and promised riches and honor as well. Since the wisdom of Solomon is so proverbial, it may be useful to note what it was. Solomon requested, "Give to Your servant an understanding heart to judge Your people" (I Kings 3:9, NKJV), and the writer of 1 Kings relates a test case of two women who were arguing over which was the real mother of an infant (3:16–28).[3] Evidently the wisdom sought and granted primarily concerned administrative or judicial decisions, and we should not conclude that it necessarily extended to all things. For instance, it may be seriously questioned whether a truly wise man would have tried to maintain a harem of seven hundred wives and three hundred concubines (1 Kings 11:3), for it would have been impossible physically or financially. Moreover, his numerous children would not have enjoyed proper parental attention; and the many foreign deities these women brought into the very center of Israelite affairs threatened to undermine the true faith. Perhaps his wisdom did not include a very complete understanding of fiscal matters either, because he tried to do more than the economy would allow and left the state in serious financial straits.

But Solomon, like us, may have had greater wisdom than he sometimes displayed. Often we allow our greed or pride to subvert our wisdom. Possession of wisdom does not necessarily mean that we will have the courage or restraint or perseverance to pursue a wise course of action. Having said this, however, we have to infer that the book of Proverbs and other biblical and non-biblical references do indicate that Solomon's wisdom was far-reaching. First Kings 4 is an especially important statement on this subject. It describes his administrative skill and his intellectual achievements. He is credited with three thousand proverbs, a thousand and five songs, and many scientific studies, such as botanical and zoological classification (vv. 29–34). The fame of his wisdom spread abroad and many foreigners came to hear his wisdom for themselves. The visit of the Queen of Sheba is a case in point (1 Kings 10).

Probably soon after consolidating his position at court, Solomon began to fortify his kingdom: Hazor in the north; Megiddo, overlooking the Valley of Esdraelon; Gezer, Beth-horon, and Baalath, guarding Jerusalem from the west; and Tadmor, either Palmyra 175 miles northeast of Damascus, or a site south of the Dead Sea (1 Kings 9:15, 17, 18) in the east. But that was only the beginning of Solomon's building activity. He outfitted cities for his chariot corps (fourteen hundred chariots) and cavalry units (twelve thousand horses; 1 Kings 9:19; 10:26). Moreover, with the help of the Phoenicians he built a seaport at Ezion-geber adjacent to modern Eilat on the Gulf of Aqaba (an arm of the Red Sea) and built a fleet to use the port. He greatly enlarged Jerusalem by enclosing the temple area to the north of David's city and the southwestern hill now known as Zion.

The Glory of Solomon's Temple

But Solomon's greatest building project was the temple. Begun in his fourth year (967 B.C.), it was built on the site of Araunah's threshing floor and took seven years to complete. Just twice the size of the tabernacle, it was built on the same basic plan. It measured ninety feet long and thirty feet wide. The holy place occupied two-thirds of the interior and the holy of holies the rest. Thus the holy of holies was a cube, thirty feet on a side and thirty feet high. In it, of course, stood the ark made at Sinai. This was flanked by huge cherubim with a fifteen-foot wingspan. The temple walls and floor were of stone, the floor covered with cypress and the walls covered with cedar and overlaid with gold. Across the front of the holy place extended a porch thirty feet long and fifteen feet deep, on which stood two bronze pillars twenty-four feet high. Around the temple on the two sides and back were constructed chambers for storage purposes.

In the holy place were the altar of incense, ten golden lamp-stands, and ten tables for the bread of the Presence. In front of the holy place extended the court of the priests—one hundred fifty feet wide and three hundred feet long. Here stood the bronze altar of burnt offering (thirty feet square and fifteen feet high) and a great laver shaped like a bowl (7½ feet high and 15 feet in diameter). This rested on twelve bronze oxen, three facing in each direction. In addition, there were ten smaller lavers for washing various parts of the sacrifices. Beyond the court of the priests lay the outer court, three hundred feet wide and six hundred feet long.

Thirty thousand Israelites worked in one-month shifts, preparing the wood for the temple in the forests of Lebanon, and 150,000 aliens living in Israel worked as burden-bearers and stonecutters. Phoenician craftsmen supplied the technical skill for this and for most of Solomon's other construction, including his seaport and navy. The celebration of dedication lasted two weeks and involved the sacrifice of 22,000 oxen and 120,000 sheep (2 Chronicles 7:4–10). It was accompanied by the descent of the "cloud" of God's glory upon the structure and a second appearance of God to Solomon. Thus auspiciously began the history of the famous structure that was to last until the Babylonians destroyed it in 586 B.C.

The Magnificence of Wealth and Spiritual Decline

In addition to the temple, Solomon also built a palace at Jerusalem. On the grounds were government offices, living quarters for the daughter of Pharaoh, and Solomon's private residence. It is difficult to know how to interpret the Hebrew of 1 Kings 7:1–12, whether to consider this construction as one great edifice or distinct but closely connected buildings. Perhaps the latter is preferable, and the complex would then include the hall of the cedars of Lebanon (presumably an armory, 1 Kings 10:16, 17; Isaiah 22:8), connected by a colonnade seventy-five feet long and thirty feet wide, to a throne room containing a gold and ivory throne approached by six steps (1 Kings 10:18, 19). Adjacent to the throne room stood Solomon's private residence; nearby was a separate house for the daughter of the Pharaoh of Egypt, with whom Solomon had made an alliance (1 Kings 3:1).

Scripture is replete with references to the wealth and ostentation of Solomon. Some of this was made possible by saddling the Hebrews with a heavy burden of taxation, part by gifts and tribute from foreign peoples (1 Kings 10:24, 25), and part by trading activities. Solomon had an alliance with Hiram, king of Tyre, which involved much more than a supply of cedar from the forests of Lebanon. Phoenician sailors served regularly in Solomon's fleet, which ranged the Red Sea and probably the Indian Ocean. Luxury goods were no doubt brought north from Ezion-geber to Phoenician ports and from the east through Damascus to Phoenician ports, as well as south to Israel. The Phoenicians transshipped many of these commodities all over the Mediterranean world. It has been suggested that the Queen of Sheba (Sabeans in South Arabia, area of modern Yemen) would not have come twelve hundred miles on camelback through dangerous territory with rich gifts for Solomon merely to bask in his wisdom; perhaps he was too effectively moving in on her sphere of economic influence (1 Kings 10:1–13; 2 Chronicles 9:1–12). Or possibly she sought a commercial alliance with him.

There are evidences of decline in Solomon's latter days. His foreign wives began to turn his heart away from God, and he even built places of worship for many foreign deities (1 Kings 11:7–8), thus incurring the wrath of God. Jeroboam, the son of Nebat, later to become Jeroboam I of the Northern Kingdom, began to entertain ideas of revolt and fled to Egypt to escape Solomon's wrath (1 Kings 11:26–40). Meanwhile, Hadad of Edom (1 Kings 11:14–22) and Rezon of Damascus (1 Kings 11:23–25) were apparently loosening the apron strings of the empire and achieving a considerable amount of independence for their areas. Solomon began well and sought mightily to honor God, especially in building the magnificent temple. But foreign wives and their idolatry proved to be his downfall, and before he died, God informed him that for this reason He would rend the kingdom at his death and give most of it to someone other than his son. But for David's sake, God would keep Judah and Jerusalem in the hands of the Davidic line (1 Kings 11:9–13).

Notes

1. The time lapse is concluded as follows: Saul's first great sin occurred a couple of years into his reign, about 1048–1047 B.C. Shortly after his second great sin David was anointed king. David was thirty at the time of Saul's death in 1010 B.C. If he were 15–20 at the time of his anointing, the date of the battle against the Amalekites must have been 1030–1025 B.C. So about twenty years elapsed between his two great sins (c. 1048–1027 B.C.).

2. Leon Wood, *A Survey of Israel's History*, p. 278.

3. Who wrote 1, 2 Kings is not certainly known, but Jewish tradition concludes that it was Jeremiah.

Chaos under the Kings: The Divided Kingdom

1 Kings 12–22, 2 Kings, 2 Chronicles 10–36

AFTER the death of Solomon, Western Asia and the Mediterranean were destined to be very different from what they had been in the earlier period. During the days of Saul, David, and Solomon, there had been a political vacuum in the area into which the Hebrews and Phoenicians could move. By 900 B.C. the Hebrew kingdom was divided into two warring segments. Egypt and Assyria were on the rise. During subsequent centuries, the Assyrians would reach their peak and decline, the Neo-Babylonian or Chaldean power would do the same, and the Persians would establish their empire. In the west, a new arrangement of city states would rise in Greece, political stirrings would occur in Rome, and Phoenicians would plant numerous colonies in Europe and North Africa.

The twenty rulers in Israel and the twenty in Judah presented in the books of Kings and 2 Chronicles involve a welter of detail that is extremely hard to keep straight.[1] Perhaps the best way to handle the material is first to present a chart of the rulers and then to

discuss developments in the kingdoms of Israel and Judah by looking briefly at the individual royal administrations. The following
chart is adapted from E. R. Thiele, *The Mysterious Numbers of the
Hebrew Kings*. Occasionally dates overlap; in such cases there were
periods of coregency.

RULERS OF THE DIVIDED KINGDOM

Jeroboam I	930–909	Rehoboam	931–913
Nadab	909–908	Abijam	913–910
Baasha	908–886	Asa	910–869
Elah	886–885		
Zimri	885		
Tibni	885–880		
Omri	885–874	Jehoshaphat	873–848
Ahab	874–853		
Ahaziah	853–852	Jehoram	853–841
Jehoram	852–841	Ahaziah	841
Jehu	841–814	Athaliah	841–835
Jehoahaz	814–798	Joash	835–796
Jehoash	798–782	Amaziah	796–767
Jeroboam II	793–753	Azariah (Uzziah)	792–740
Zachariah	753–752	Jotham	750–732
Shallum	752		
Menahem	752–742		
Pekahiah	742–740		
Pekah	752–732	Ahaz	735–715
Hoshea	732–723/22	Hezekiah	715–686
		Manasseh	696–642
		Amon	642–640
		Josiah	640–609
		Jehoahaz	609
		Jehoiakim	609–597
		Jehoiachin	597
		Zedekiah	597–586

THE NORTHERN KINGDOM (1 Kings 12–22; 2 Kings 1–17)

The separate existence of Israel or the Northern Kingdom was not a new development. After Saul's death the north had gone its own way while David ruled in Hebron, and David had extended his rule over the northern tribes only after tough negotiations (2 Samuel 5:1–3). Some thirty years later, Israel had briefly supported Sheba in a revolt against David. But now, under the leadership of Jeroboam, the division was to become permanent. Ahijah had predicted it, and God had informed Solomon that it would occur because of his idolatry. With the death of Solomon, Jeroboam had returned to Israel from exile in Egypt; and when Rehoboam went to Shechem to be crowned by all the tribes, Jeroboam led the opposition forces in demanding a reduction of taxes. Upon Rehoboam's refusal to exercise leniency, the northern tribes split off and crowned Jeroboam king. When Rehoboam gathered a force of 180,000 to force reunification, a prophet of God stopped him and the rupture became final.

Jeroboam and Nadab (1 Kings 12:25–14:20)

Jeroboam had the responsibility of setting up the government of the Northern Kingdom. He established his capital first at Shechem and later at Tirzah. In order to prevent continuing contacts with Judah and ultimate reunification of the two states, he felt he had to set up a new worship; so he built shrines at Dan in the north and Bethel in the south for the new calf worship. Presumably he knew he could not succeed in persuading the people to worship calves as gods and may have intended that God be thought of as invisibly riding on the calves. Several peoples of Western Asia represented their deities as standing or sitting on the backs of animals. At any rate, God condemned the false worship and informed Jeroboam that his son would be assassinated in office and his line wiped out. Jeroboam suffered loss of territory too; Damascus and

Moab became independent. His son, Nadab (1 Kings 15:25–31), ruled for only two years before Baasha killed him and the other members of Jeroboam's household. Nadab is said to have continued in the sin of his father (in maintaining the calf worship), as did all other rulers of Israel who followed.

Baasha and Elah (1 Kings 15:32–16:20; 2 Chronicles 16:1–6)

Baasha succeeded Nadab. Baasha's twenty-four-year administration was characterized by warfare against Judah. When he began to enjoy some degree of success in ventures against the Southern Kingdom, Asa of Judah persuaded Syria to invade Israel. Because Baasha continued in the way of Jeroboam religiously, his line was also condemned, and his son Elah ruled only two years before being assassinated.

Zimri and Tibni, Omri (1 Kings 16:11–38)

Zimri assassinated Elah, and during his seven days of rule managed to wipe out the house of Baasha. Omri, commander of the armed forces under Elah, then declared himself king and killed Zimri, but had to compete with another contender, Tibni, who managed to rule over a part of the Northern Kingdom for four years.

Omri established a dynasty that was to last through three additional kings (Ahab, Ahaziah, Jehoram). He was a powerful ruler, and for some time to come Assyrian rulers called Israel "the land of Omri." He built the permanent capital of the Northern Kingdom on the excellent site of Samaria, an easily defended hill three to four hundred feet high, surrounded by a prosperous agricultural region. After he achieved internal stability, Omri began to look outward, conquering Moab and possibly making an alliance with King Ethbaal of Tyre. At the least, he married his son Ahab to Jezebel, daughter of Ethbaal.

Ahab, the Most Sinful of All (1 Kings 16:28–22:40)

King Ahab is one of the best-known figures of the Old Testament. This is true in part because his wife was Jezebel and in part because the prophet Elijah so dramatically opposed him. Since Scripture is always primarily interested in moral and spiritual issues, attention during Ahab's reign focuses on the introduction of Baal worship. Baal worship was not new to Israel. It had crept in from the north during the latter days of the judges, and Samuel had fought it then; but under David and Solomon it had apparently almost disappeared. Now, however, Ahab and Jezebel promoted worship of this idol and even persecuted followers of God. Worse than Jeroboam's calf worship, this was open, blatant polytheism with its accompanying licentious worship, including religious prostitution. Thus, Ahab earned the reputation of being the most sinful of all Israel's kings. The great opponent of Ahab and Jezebel was the prophet Elijah, who appeared suddenly from Gilead and predicted a drought, which lasted for over three years. After that, he arranged the famous contest with the prophets of Baal on Mount Carmel (1 Kings 18), which brought acknowledgment of God by the people and death to many prophets of Baal. Subsequently, Elijah predicted the destruction of Ahab's line for his murder of Naboth and seizure of Naboth's vineyard (1 Kings 21:1–29). Scripture presents Ahab as more than merely an ungodly king; he was a powerful military man. In two major campaigns he worsted the Syrians, showing them leniency because of the threat of rising Assyrian power. However, Scripture does not allude to Ahab's biggest battle of all—participation in a coalition that sought to stop Shalmaneser III of Assyria (at Qarqar) from expanding his empire into Syria and Palestine. For the great battle of Qarqar in 853 B.C. Ahab furnished two thousand chariots and ten thousand soldiers, according to Assyrian records. Apparently the coalition stopped the Assyrians for the moment. Ahab's ability to field two thousand chariots shows something of the wealth and power of the Northern Kingdom. It should be remembered that Solomon kept only fourteen hundred chariots. Ahab's building activity is also ignored in Scripture. How widespread it was we cannot say, but excavations show that it extended at least to Samaria, Hazor, and Megiddo.

Ahaziah (2 Kings 1:2–18)

Ahab's son, Ahaziah, succeeded to the throne when his father was killed in a third war against the Syrians. During his short reign of a year or two, Ahaziah was unable to resubjugate the Moabites, saw his joint naval expedition with Judah down on the Gulf of Aqaba end in failure (2 Chronicles 20:35–37), suffered the condemnation of Elijah, and finally died of a fall. About this time, the ministry of Elijah came to an end, and God swept him to heaven in a whirlwind. Elisha continued the ministry of his spiritual father.

Jehoram (2 Kings 3:1–9:26)

A second son of Ahab and Jezebel, Jehoram, now took the throne for twelve years. At the beginning of his reign he fought a major war with Moab; in spite of initial successes, he ultimately failed to resubjugate the Moabites. Jehoram's reign was marked by frequent relations (mostly unfriendly) with the Aramean kingdom of Damascus. Elisha was at the height of his ministry during the reign of Jehoram and performed numerous miracles. For instance, he provided water when the combined armies of Israel, Judah, and Edom were about to die of thirst during the attack on Moab; he healed Naaman, captain of the forces of Syria, of his leprosy; and temporarily blinded the Syrian soldiers who came to capture him.

Jehoram faced several fierce Syrian attacks, one of which was successful in laying siege to Samaria itself, and a second resulting in the wounding of Jehoram. While Jehoram lay recuperating at Jezreel, the usurper Jehu (anointed at the command of Elisha) attacked, killing not only the king of Israel but the visiting king of Judah (Ahaziah) as well.

Jehu (2 Kings 9:11–10:36)

Jehu became God's agent for punishing the house of Omri and destroying Baal worship in Israel. Actually, Jehu was no friend of God and seems to have exterminated Baalism to a large degree because of the strong link between religion and state. That is, if he would eliminate the Omri dynasty, he must destroy the religious system that formed one of its important bases of support. The blood purge of the outgoing dynasty was swift and complete, It began with Jezebel and extended understandably to the seventy "sons" or male "descendants" of the house of Ahab, forty-two relatives of Ahaziah, all the court officials of Jezreel and Samaria, and the prophets and priests of Baal. Jehu was doomed to a very troubled reign. Apparently he did not enjoy full support of the populace and no doubt suffered because he had killed too many of the individuals who knew how to make the machinery of government work. According to an Assyrian inscription, Shalmaneser III of Assyria forced him to pay tribute. Hazael of Damascus defeated him and took Bashan and Gilead. He got no help from Phoenicia or Judah because of his attacks on Ahab's house and Baalism. The Phoenicians were devotees of Baal. Jezebel had been a Tyrian princess, and a daughter of Ahab and Jezebel (Athabah) had become queen of Judah and continued to rule there after the death of her husband.

Jehoahaz and Jehoash (2 Kings 13:1–14:6)

Jehu's son, Jehoahaz, capitulated to the armed might of Hazael of Syria, and ultimately found his armed forces reduced to ten thousand foot soldiers, ten chariots, and fifty in the cavalry corps. Finally, in desperation, Jehoahaz turned to God for help and in his last days enjoyed some relief because of the death of Hazael and Assyrian pressure on the Syrians. His son Jehoash began the restoration of Israel's power. Receiving Elisha's deathbed promise of victory over the Syrians, Jehoash went on to recover all the territory lost to Hazael earlier and also to enjoy a decisive victory over Judah, even breaking down part of the wall of Jerusalem.

Jeroboam II (2 Kings 14:23–29)

Jeroboam II (son of Jehoash) was the outstanding king of the Northern Kingdom. Scripture focuses on Jeroboam's evil ways but observes that in spite of them God brought relief to Israel and expanded her borders in his days. As a matter of fact, Israel under his leadership was able to expand her borders northward approximately as far as David and Solomon had done and to enjoy an accompanying economic prosperity. All this was possible in part because the Assyrians greatly weakened Syria and then became so preoccupied with their own internal affairs for some decades that they were no threat to the westland. Jeroboam's son, Zachariah (2 Kings 15:8–12), proved to be either incompetent or to have too many enemies. At any rate, he was assassinated after only six months. But Shallum (2 Kings 15:13–15), his assassin, lasted only one month and was in turn killed by Menahem.

Menahem and Pekahiah (2 Kings 15:16–26)

Menahem was more successful, but by now the Assyrian Empire was expanding again. Pul (2 Kings 15:19), otherwise known as Tiglath-pileser III (744–727 B.C.), campaigned in Syria and Palestine in the last days of Menahem and put the nation to tribute. By laying a heavy tax on his people in order to pay the sum exacted by Pul, Menahem retained his throne, and the Assyrians let Israel alone. Menahem's son Pekahiah (2 Kings 15:23–26) continued the policies of his father but apparently was opposed by those who favored revolt against Assyria. After two years of rule, Pekah assassinated Pekahiah and began to rule.

Pekah (2 Kings 15:27–31)

Pekah presumably ruled for several years over a portion of Transjordan before the coup that gave him control over the entire state. During the eight years when he ruled all Israel, he cooperated with Syria in an effort to establish an alliance against Assyria. Ahaz of Judah refused to go along with that. Of course, there was no sufficient power in the west to stand against Assyria, which advanced and brought an end to the kingdom of Damascus in 732 B.C. A revolt placed Hoshea on the throne in the same year.

Hoshea (2 Kings 17:1–6)

Evidently coming to the throne with the approval of Tiglath-pileser of Assyria, Hoshea was powerless to change Israel's tributary status. When the Assyrian ruler died in 727 B.C., Hoshea entertained heady ideas of revolt, hoping the new king, Shalmaneser V, would not be able to maintain the power of his predecessor. He was wrong. Shalmaneser began a three-year siege of Samaria in 725 B.C., and the Assyrian army took the city either in the last days of Shalmaneser or the early days of his successor, Sargon II. At any rate, Sargon (721–705 B.C.) claimed the victory and certainly did the mopping up after the battle. His records state that he carried off 27,290 captives into Assyria. Numerous non-Jews were resettled in the Northern Kingdom, leading to the halfbreed population and mixed religious situation that existed there in post-exilic and New Testament times. For two centuries God's faithful prophets had been warning the kings and the people of Israel that their idolatry and other sins would bring judgment at the hand of God. They had refused to listen.

THE SOUTHERN KINGDOM (1 Kings 14:21–15:24; 22:41–50; 2 Kings 8:16–29; 11–25; 2 Chronicles 10–36)

The history of the Southern Kingdom, or Judah, was destined to be quite different from that of the Northern Kingdom. The temple was there, and so were many Levites. Soon after the division of the kingdom, numerous Levites and others who refused to compromise with the paganism of the north came south, strengthening the spiritual element in the state. Since only Judah and Benjamin made up the Southern Kingdom, it enjoyed greater political unity than did the north. All the kings were of the Davidic dynasty instead of being from several dynasties. Eight of her kings were good to excellent, whereas none of the northern kings were classified as good. Because of this better record, God permitted the kingdom about one hundred more years of existence than the north enjoyed. But in spite of its advantages, Judah also slipped into idolatry and ultimately went into captivity for her sins.

Rehoboam (1 Kings 14:21–31; 2 Chronicles 10–12)

Rehoboam started well. During the first three years of his rule, he led the kingdom in the ways of righteousness. But then a rapid decline set in, and high places and groves began to appear everywhere. In punishment, God sent against the land a massive Egyptian invasion under the leadership of Shishak (Sheshonk I, 945–924 B.C.). Coming probably in the year 926 B.C., this invasion not only wrought havoc in Judah, but also involved the Northern Kingdom, as Shishak's inscriptions show. When God made it clear to Rehoboam that this punishment had come because of idolatry (2 Chronicles 12:5), the king and many of the leaders of the country confessed their sins and God moderated the attack. Subsequently, Rehoboam fortified at least fifteen cities to the south and west of Jerusalem to prevent a recurrence of Egyptian inroads. Rehoboam was also involved in warfare with Jeroboam all during his reign, but the struggle must have consisted of border skirmishes rather than major pitched battles because at the beginning of the kingdom God forbade a major effort to resubjugate Israel (2 Chronicles 11:1–4), and Rehoboam had obeyed.

Abijam (1 Kings 15:1–8; 2 Chronicles 13)

During his brief three-year reign, Abijam (or Abijah) continued the warlike policies of his father and enjoyed considerable success in taking Israelite border towns. Also, as his father had done, he fell into idolatry. In fact, conditions were so bad that God would have brought an end to Abijam's line if it had not been for His covenant with David.

Asa (1 Kings 15:9–24; 2 Chronicles 14–16)

Abijam's son, Asa, began his forty-one-year reign well. He launched a reform program and destroyed many of the foreign altars and idols that had infested the land during the days of his father. Moreover, Asa built up his army and defenses. All his efforts were not enough, however, to meet the mighty Egyptian onslaught that came during his fourteenth or fifteenth year (c. 896 B.C.). When the Ethiopian Zerah, apparently commander under Osorkon I (924–889 B.C.), invaded the land, his force was so overwhelming that Asa ran to God for help. Winning a great victory, he listened to the appeals of the prophet Azariah and launched a major religious reform throughout Judah. But strangely, soon afterward he suffered a spiritual relapse. In the face of an attack by Baasha of the Northern Kingdom, he robbed the temple treasury and sent a gift to Benhadad in Syria, with a plea for an attack on the Northern Kingdom. Though this move was very successful, the prophet Hanani criticized the king for failure to depend on God and for making an unholy alliance. Angered, the king threw Hanani into prison and from then on Asa does not appear to have been very faithful to God. When seized with illness near the end of his life, he put his trust in physicians and sought no help from God.

Jehoshaphat (1 Kings 22:41–50; 2 Chronicles 17–20)

Apparently Asa's disease was so crippling that he made his son Jehoshaphat coregent during his last three years. Jehoshaphat went on to rule another twenty-two years on his own after his father died. A good king, like his father before him, he instituted reforms near the beginning of his reign and gave orders to the Levites to teach the law, an indication that they had become lax in their duties. When Jehoshaphat was faced with a combined attack of Moab, Ammon, and Edom (2 Chronicles 20:1–30), he called for a time of fasting and prayer and was rewarded with a great victory. He also improved and expanded legal services in the kingdom. In spite of his good points, Jehoshaphat failed miserably in making an alliance with the house of Omri. This involved marriage of the crown prince, Jehoram, to Ahab's daughter Athaliah, and subsequently introduced Baal worship in Judah. Moreover, it linked Jehoshaphat in joint ventures with three Israelite kings. When he joined Ahab in war against Syria, Ahab lost his life in the venture, and Jehoshaphat nearly did. Jehoshaphat built a commercial fleet in Judah's port of Ezion-geber with the help of Ahaziah of Israel, and the fleet was wrecked. Then Jehoshaphat allied himself with another son of Ahab, Jehoram, in a war against Moab, and nearly perished for lack of water during the struggle, which ultimately turned out to be a defeat for Israel.

Jehoram (2 Kings 8:16–24; 2 Chronicles 21)

Jehoram ruled for four years as coregent with his father, and then went on to rule alone for eight years. His reign contrasted markedly to his father's. No doubt under the influence of his wife Athaliah, daughter of Ahab and Jezebel, he restored the idolatry that Jehoshaphat had destroyed. He also murdered his six brothers, endured two successful revolts by Edom and Libnah, and experienced a humiliating invasion by Philistines and Arabians, who even carried off Jehoram's wives and all his sons except Ahaziah (2 Chronicles 21:14). Either Athaliah was not among the wives carried off or she was ransomed, because she served as advisor to her son Ahaziah and ruled subsequently in her own right. When Jehoram died of a terrible intestinal disease, he was so disliked that no one regretted his passing.

Ahaziah (2 Kings 8:25–29; 9:27–29; 2 Chronicles 22:1–9)

The only remaining son of Jehoram, Ahaziah, ruled Judah for less than a year. Under the domination of his mother (Athaliah) and influenced by the example of his father, he promoted Baal worship and allied himself with his mother's brother Jehoram of Israel in war against Syria. Jehoram was wounded in the struggle; and when Ahaziah went to visit Jehoram at Jezreel, Jehu usurped the throne and killed both Jehoram and Ahaziah.

Athaliah (2 Kings 11:1–16; 2 Chronicles 22:10–23:15)

Athaliah was cruel and ambitious like Jezebel, her mother. After the death of her son, she decided to seize the throne for herself, and killed her grandchildren so there would be no pretenders to the throne. But she was not completely successful. One of Ahaziah's sons, the infant Joash, was rescued and hidden for six years. Then Jehoida, the high priest, laid careful plans to crown Joash. When he did so, Athaliah fled and was caught and executed.

Joash (2 Kings 12; 2 Chronicles 23:16–24:27)

Joash had a good record in his early years, thanks largely to the counsel of Jehoiada, the high priest. He destroyed the temple of Baal in Jerusalem, and fully reinstituted Mosaic offerings in the temple. A religious revival broke out in the land, and needed repairs were made in the temple. But after the death of Jehoiada, Joash lapsed into idolatry. So far did he slip that he even had Jehoiada's own son, Zechariah, stoned to death for rebuking his sinful actions (2 Chronicles 24:20–22). But God does not condone sin in high or low places; later that same year Hazael of Damascus marched through the country on a devastating campaign and spared Jerusalem only after Joash paid in tribute every bit of treasure he could find. Finally, Joash's policies became so unpopular that he was assassinated.

Amaziah (2 Kings 14:1–20; 2 Chronicles 25)

The son of Joash, Amaziah, ruled for twenty-nine years, only about five as sole ruler and the rest as coregent with his son, Uzziah. Like Joash, his father, Amaziah started well and enjoyed the blessing of God. Greatly interested in regaining use of the port of Ezion-geber, he launched a very successful war against Edom. But he made the great mistake of bringing back Edom's false gods and worshiping them. For this a prophet of God forecast the king's destruction. Defeat came to him at the hands of Israel, and apparently Amaziah was taken as a prisoner of war and remained in captivity until the death of the Israelite king Jehoash (2 Kings 14:13, 17). Finally, he was released and ultimately died at the hands of an assassin. This action did not affect the continuity of the Davidic line because Uzziah (Azariah) had already been ruler of Judah in fact for some years.

Uzziah (2 Kings 14:21–22; 15:1–7; 2 Chronicles 26)

Uzziah, also known as Azariah, was a very good king whose success related directly to his dependence on God (2 Chronicles 26:5, 7). He ruled for a total of fifty-two years and thus was second only to Manasseh in length of reign among the kings of Israel and Judah. He was sole ruler for only seventeen years, however, serving as coregent with Amaziah at the beginning and with Jothan at the end of his reign. When Uzziah came to the throne, Judah lay almost flattened by the power of Israel. But gradually he asserted independent power and built up the walls of Jerusalem, improved the fortifications of the city, regrouped the army, and equipped it with superior weapons. As he became strong at home, he was soon in a position to expand. He subdued the Philistines to the west, strengthened his hold on Edom to the south, and extended his rule over the Ammonites. Good relations apparently existed with Jeroboam II in Israel, who was also powerful, wealthy, and expansionistic. Between them, the two Hebrew kings controlled approximately the equivalent of David's empire. This was possible because Assyria was somewhat in decline at the time. Unfortunately, at the height of his power, Uzziah forgot the real source of his strength, and in the face of opposition by eighty priests insisted on going into the holy place and burning incense. For this act of sacrilege, God smote Uzziah with leprosy, and he could no longer go into the temple at all and could not even enjoy ordinary social privileges. His son Jotham became coregent during the years 750–740 B.C.

Jotham (2 Kings 15:32–38; 2 Chronicles 27)

During much of his reign, Jotham merely carried out the policies of Uzziah, including the building of fortifications. He is classed as a good king, and enjoyed the favor of God. He put down an Ammonite revolt, the only serious internal threat to the realm. The power of Assyria was rising again, but Jotham refused to join Rezin of Damascus and Pekah of Israel in an alliance to oppose the great Tiglath-pileser III of Assyria. Isaiah and Micah prophesied in Judah during this time, and as is evidenced by their words, continuing prosperity had made its inroads. Judah had settled into a complacent type of secularism; sacrifices continued at the temple, but there was no real religious vitality.

Ahaz (2 Kings 16; 2 Chronicles 28)

Ahaz endured the combined wrath of Rezin and Pekah, who tried to force him to abandon his pro-Assyrian policy and join them against Tiglath-pileser III. Unable to withstand the combined attack, he sent a gift to the Assyrian ruler and begged his help. Tiglath-pileser was only too glad to respond. But before Rezin and Pekah were forced to go back home, they inflicted great destruction on Judah and killed some 120,000 people. Their 200,000 captives were soon released, however. Shortly thereafter, Ahaz drifted into religious apostasy: he made images to Baal and worshiped in high places. For his sins he began to experience military reverses at the hand of the Edomites and Philistines. Meanwhile, Tiglath-pileser was successful against Judah's enemies; he destroyed the kingdom of Syria and annexed it along with part of the kingdom of Israel (732 B.C.).

Hezekiah (2 Kings 18–20; 2 Chronicles 29–32; Isaiah 36–39)

Hezekiah was one of Judah's very best kings. He worked hard to destroy idols, high places, altars, and other trappings of idolatry, and is said to have conducted himself as David his father (2 Chronicles 29:2). There was plenty of need for reform after the evil influence of Ahaz. Hezekiah was anti-Assyrian in his foreign policy, but that did not become evident as long as the powerful Sargon II lived. When Sargon died in 705 B.C., Hezekiah apparently decided that his son Sennacherib would be an easier target. Hezekiah joined a coalition of western Asiatic powers against Assyria. Busy elsewhere for about four years, Sennacherib did not mount a major western offensive until 701 B.C. At that time he crushed the power of Tyre, moved south against the Philistines and defeated them, and then invaded Judah. About this time, an Egyptian army came north against Assyria, and Sennacherib had to dispose of that before he could proceed with his Judean campaign. Also about this time, or possibly a little earlier, Hezekiah was afflicted with a severe illness that appeared terminal. Concerned not only for himself but also for his people who might be leaderless at such a crucial time, Hezekiah prayed for healing and received a grant of fifteen years of additional life. Sennacherib marched almost irresistibly into Judah and took Lachish after a siege. (A whole wall of pictorial inscription in his palace describes the event; this is now in the British Museum in London.) After conquering forty-six towns of Judah, he encamped around Jerusalem. God gave assurance of His help through Isaiah, the court prophet, and brought an end to Sennacherib's invasion by destroying most of his army with some sort of plague. Predictably Sennacherib did not mention the defeat in his records; the best he could do was claim to have shut up Hezekiah "like a bird in a cage" in his capital city, Jerusalem. (The inscription is in the British Museum in London.) Since Jerusalem was a major objective, he would have made much of its conquest if he had achieved it. After Sennacherib returned to Assyria, Hezekiah was evidently very prosperous and very successful in his administration (2 Chronicles 32:27–29), no doubt doing much to rehabilitate the state.

Manasseh (2 Kings 21:1–18; 2 Chronicles 33:1–20)

Manasseh did not follow in the steps of his father, but became one of the very worst kings of Judah. During the first eleven of his fifty-five years of reign (longest of any king of Israel or Judah), he was coregent with Hezekiah and must have been kept on a tight leash. But after Hezekiah's death, Manasseh established altars of Baal throughout the land and even set up an image of a Canaanite deity in the temple. He killed many who opposed his idolatry, perhaps even the prophet Isaiah, as tradition indicates. The prophets warned Manasseh about his evil ways, but he paid no attention. Finally, the Assyrians invaded Judah and carried Manasseh captive to Babylon. There the Judean had a real change of heart and subsequently was allowed to return to Jerusalem. The Assyrians even permitted him to rebuild his fortifications to protect the realm against Egypt. On return home, Manasseh sought to abolish the idolatry for which he had earlier been responsible, but evidently he was not extremely successful.

Amon (2 Kings 21:19–26; 2 Chronicles 33:21–25)

Amon ruled only two years and reverted to the idolatry of his father's earlier years. Some of his servants banded together and assassinated him.

Josiah (2 Kings 22:1–23:30; 2 Chronicles 34–35)

The eight-year-old son of Amon, Josiah, next became king. He must have had excellent advisors from the onset. By the time of his sixteenth year, he began of his own accord "to seek after the God of David" (2 Chronicles 34:3). Subsequently, he launched a major program to cleanse the entire kingdom of idolatry and even extended his efforts to the Northern Kingdom, now only loosely under Assyrian control. Assyria was rapidly declining and about to fall, so Judah had nothing further to fear from that quarter. Babylon was on the rise. Finally, in 609 B.C., after the fall of Nineveh (612), Pharaoh Necho of Egypt marched north through Palestine to aid remaining Assyrian forces. Anti-Assyrian Josiah tried to stop Necho at Megiddo and lost his life in the process. During Josiah's reign, Jeremiah began his ministry. Zephaniah, certainly, and Nahum and Habakkuk, probably, also prophesied during his reign.

Jehoahaz, Jehoiakim, Jehoiachin, Zedekiah (2 Kings 23:31–25:21; 2 Chronicles 36:1–21)

Three sons of Josiah subsequently ruled Judah. Jehoahaz (2 Kings 23:31–33; 2 Chronicles 36:1–3) lasted for only three months, apparently because Necho (who now dominated Palestine) did not think him to be sufficiently cooperative. Necho appointed a second son, Jehoiakim (2 Kings 23:34–24:7; 2 Chronicles 36:4–8), king later in 609 B.C., but he was not able to control the situation for long. In 605, Nebuchadnezzar sent Necho fleeing back to Egypt and moved into Syria and Palestine, where he demanded numerous hostages— including Daniel and his friends—to guarantee Hebrew submission. In 597, Nebuchadnezzar again entered Judah, this time to put down a revolt led by Jehoiakim. Before Nebuchadnezzar arrived, Jehoiakim, died, and his son Jehoiachin (2 Kings 24:8–16; 2 Chronicles 36:9, 10) was left to face the Babylonians. Victorious, the Babylonians carried off much booty and thousands of leading citizens, including Ezekiel and the king. Nebuchadnezzar put Zedekiah (2 Kings 24:17–25:21; 2 Chronicles 36:11–21; Jeremiah 39:1–10), Jehoiachin's uncle and third son of Josiah, on the throne. Zedekiah seems to have been generally inept, and was never well-received by his people. Constantly urged to rebel against Babylon, he finally decided to do so. Nebuchadnezzar laid siege to Jerusalem in January of 588. During the following year; when Pharaoh Hophra of Egypt invaded Palestine to aid the Hebrews, he forced a temporary lifting of the siege. But Nebuchadnezzar dispatched Hophra and reimposed the siege of Jerusalem, taking the city in July, 586. About a month later he destroyed the city and the temple and carried off the upper classes from the capital and its environs. The judgment of God had finally fallen on the Jews for their idolatrous ways.

NOTE

1. Tradition considers Ezra the author of Chronicles sometime late in the fifth century B.C. While that view cannot be proved conclusively, there are no strong arguments against it.

10

God Remembers His People: Captivity and Restoration

2 Chronicles 36, Ezra, Esther, Nehemiah

G OD is the God of the second chance, and the third, the fourth, the fifth chance, and more. Though we utterly fail Him again and again, He gives new opportunities to return to Him and serve Him once more. Furthermore, we may confidently rejoice with the Psalmist, "the Lord is my shepherd" (Psalm 23:1). That means He has His eye on me even when I am wandering all over the pasture. If I am wounded or get caught in the brambles, He will dress my wound or free me from my entrapment. As with us, so with the ancient Hebrews, in wrath God remembered mercy. Though He punished the Hebrews for their idolatry by sending them into captivity in Mesopotamia, He followed them there with His hand of protection and blessing. And ultimately He brought them once more to Canaan. In His providence, He also raised Daniel from slavery to an office equivalent to prime minister in Babylon. Presumably Daniel was in a position to make things a little easier for the second group of exiles when Nebuchadnezzar carried off Ezekiel and others in 597 B.C. Probably he was also able to cushion the sufferings of those whom the Babylonians enslaved at the fall of Jerusalem in 586 B.C. Daniel held high office under the Persians too, and possibly had a hand in facilitating the return of the exiles in the early days of Cyrus' reign over Babylon. Daniel was still going strong in Cyrus' third year (Daniel 1:21; 10:1).

THE REMNANT RETURNS

As Jeremiah had predicted (Jeremiah 25:11), the period of captivity was about seventy years in length. At the end of that time, God stirred up Cyrus to make a decree that the Jews might return to their homeland. He even sent with them numerous valuable items that Nebuchadnezzar had taken from the temple.

The decree came in the first year of Cyrus (in his rule over Babylon, Ezra 1:1). Since Cyrus entered Babylon at the end of October, 539 B.C., the decree was probably issued during 538, and the captives may have made the journey to Jerusalem in 537. Obviously the span from 586 to 537 B.C. is not seventy years. Various ways of computing the number are suggested. For instance, one may figure it from the first deportation of Hebrew captives in 605 to 537 or 536, almost seventy years. Or one could figure from the time the temple was destroyed in 586 to the time it was rededicated in 515, a full seventy years.

Although Cyrus benefited the Jews by helping them return home and although Isaiah called him God's "anointed" (evidently to accomplish divine purposes, Isaiah 45:1), he was no worshiper of the God of heaven. Apparently he was a very humane man and a wise administrator. He permitted all the peoples captured and deported by the Assyrians and Babylonians to return to their homes. In this way he eliminated numerous sources of disaffection and gained an immense amount of good will. By no means did all

Jews accept Cyrus' offer. About fifty thousand made up the first contingent under the leadership of Sheshbazzar, who evidently passed off the scene early and was replaced by Zerubbabel. Zerubbabel as governor and Joshua (Jeshua) as high priest (Ezra 2–3) carried the real burden of leading the repatriates back to Jerusalem and laying the foundations of the second temple.

When people of the land (Samaritans and others) desired to join with the Jews in rebuilding the temple, the Jews refused the offer, not wishing to get mixed up with any false religion. After this the Samaritans became openly hostile, first engaging in guerrilla tactics and then hiring lobbyists at the Persian court to work against Jewish interests. Presumably this was possible because Daniel was no longer living. These men were able to frustrate the progress of rebuilding the city of Jerusalem and the temple for some fifteen years. The opposition of those in the land is understandable because the newcomers threatened their control of the land and their economic position.

But finally, in the second year of the Persian king Darius I (520 B.C.), the prophets Haggai and Zechariah began their ministry and encouraged completion of the temple (Ezra 5:1; Haggai 1:1; Zechariah 1:1). As construction progressed, again non-Jewish inhabitants of Judea opposed the work. This time the builders referred to Cyrus' decree authorizing rebuilding of the temple, and a copy of the decree was found. The temple was finally completed in the spring of 515 B.C. (sixth year of Darius, Ezra 6:15). Ezra chapter 6 ends in 515 B.C., and chapter 7 refers to events in the seventh year of Artaxerxes (458 B.C.); so there is a gap of fifty-seven years between the two. During this period of silence occurs the story of Esther.

ESTHER: FOR SUCH A TIME AS THIS

The story of Esther begins in the third year of Ahasuerus (Xerxes), in 483 B.C. (Esther 1:3), and recounts a most dramatic chapter in Persian Jewry. Impetuous Xerxes, who had been drinking heavily during a great feast at his winter palace in Shushan (ancient Susa, about 150 miles north of the Persian Gulf), commanded Queen Vashti to come in. Why he wanted her to appear is not clear. Presumably it was not to make a lewd display before the assembled throng, as is frequently asserted; apparently she was to come fully dressed, "wearing her royal crown" (Esther 1:11). When Vashti refused to come to the banquet (for reasons that are not explained), Ahasuerus, in a fit of rage, decided to depose her and look for a new queen.

The search ultimately produced Esther, a beautiful Jewess. But the king did not make his final selection until his seventh year (479–78), probably just after his disastrous defeat at the hands of the Greeks. In the early days of Esther's reign, her uncle Mordecai discovered a plot against Xerxes and reported it to the king, but he was not rewarded immediately.

The main events of the book occurred during Xerxes' twelfth year (Esther 3:7; probably 474 B.C.). At that time, Haman was the king's chief officer, and Mordecai refused to bow to him as the king had commanded. He explained that he took this course of action because he was a Jew (3:4); what that reason involved cannot now be determined with certainty. Haman recognized the religious nature of Mordecai's position and persuaded Xerxes to issue orders for the killing of all Jews. Hearing the order, Mordecai prevailed upon Esther to approach the king to obtain protection for her people. Gaining an audience with Xerxes, Esther invited him and Haman to a banquet at which the king promised to grant some great request that Esther evidently wished to make. She asked only that the two dine with her again the next day.

Much happened before the next banquet. Early in the morning, in his own yard Haman had gallows constructed, on which to hang Mordecai. The king had a sleepless night and went over some of the court records, in the process of which he discovered that he had never rewarded Mordecai for saving his life. So he commanded Haman to bring great honor to his enemy Mordecai, by leading him through the streets of the city in a kind of ticker tape parade. Those close to Haman considered this an evil omen. At the second banquet Esther disclosed the wickedness of Haman, and he was hanged on his own gallows and his position given to Mordecai. Since Persian law prohibited reversal of an order previously given, the Jews were now permitted to defend themselves on the day appointed for their destruction. Thus the Jews were saved, and the day of their deliverance was thereafter celebrated as the Feast of Purim. Without this divine protection, all Jews would have died, because at that time the Persians ruled all areas where Jews were living.

What was going on in the eastern Mediterranean world at the time is this: In the ongoing struggle between the Greeks and Persians, the Greeks had won a significant victory over the Persians at the Battle of Marathon (490 B.C.) in the days of Darius I. Darius had not been successful in a later attack on the Greeks and left it to his son Xerxes (Ahasuerus) to defeat the Greeks. In Xerxes' third year (483 B.C., Esther 1:3) he organized a planning session for the invasion of Greece. And at the end of it he threw a banquet for the participants. During this banquet he deposed Queen Vashti and began the search for a new queen. Meanwhile Xerxes proceeded with the war against the Greeks and was soundly defeated in 480–79 B.C. And in the seventh year of his reign (Esther 2:16, 479 B.C.) he decided to bury his sorrows in his harem and concluded the choice of a new queen, namely Esther.

EZRA SEEKS SOCIAL AND SPIRITUAL RENEWAL

As already noted, the story of Ezra picks up again after the Esther narrative, in the seventh year of Artaxerxes (458 B.C.). Ezra 7 through 10 describes Ezra's return to Jerusalem under the favor of Artaxerxes and armed with his decree. He had permission to take along the Jews who wanted to go, to raise funds among the Jewish community in Persia, and to draw on the royal treasury for payment of supplies. His primary concern was social and spiritual improvement of the community in Judea. Some fifteen hundred men, plus their families, joined Ezra the priest in the return to Jerusalem. When Ezra arrived in Judea, the main problem he dealt with was the marriage of Jews with heathen neighbors, which in the end would utterly destroy the true faith. In fact, already there was evident slippage into the religious and social ways of pagan people of Palestine. The decision was then made that those who had taken pagan wives must be separated from them. The matter was not resolved in haste. It took three months to hear and decide problem cases.

NEHEMIAH REBUILDS THE WALL

Nehemiah completed the task of restoring the principality of Judea. Probably the area ruled by the governor in Jerusalem did not extend much more than about thirty miles north and south and an equal distance from east to west. Of course, this was just a province within the Persian Empire, and the Jews were not destined to have their political freedom again for another three hundred years.

Nehemiah was cupbearer to King Artaxerxes I (464–424 B.C.), and as such had the responsibility of tasting the king's wine to see that it was not poisoned. He was, therefore, a very trusted servant; often at the Persian court cupbearers became very powerful advisors. In Artaxerxes' twentieth year of rule (445 B.C.), Nehemiah's brother Hanani and some other Jews came from Jerusalem with a report of the dilapidated condition of the Jewish province. Terribly upset, Nehemiah prayed for about four months for the king's favor; and when the opportune time came, he laid his request before the king, with positive results. The king granted Nehemiah permission to rebuild the walls, furnished him with requisitions for supplies of building materials from the king's storehouses in Palestine, and sent along a military contingent to provide safe conduct.

Nehemiah knew he would face fierce opposition; so upon arrival in Jerusalem he worked secretly and rapidly. Three days after his arrival he made a moonlight inspection of the walls, then promptly called together the Jerusalem leaders and presented his plans. He then recruited workers and the work began. Opposition arose almost immediately under the leadership of Sanballat, governor of Samaria; Tobiah, possible governor of Ammon; and Geshem, an Arabian prince. Their tactics were first to mock and then to plan a frontal assault. When Nehemiah ignored the former and prepared to defend the work against the latter, his enemies changed their strategy. As the work progressed, they tried four times to lure him away from Jerusalem for a conference about the project. When, in effect, he said he was too busy, they then threatened to send the Persian king a report of Nehemiah's disloyalty. He brushed this off, too. Finally they employed a false prophet to bring him into reproach before his people. Nehemiah did not fall into this trap either, and the walls were completed in fifty-two days of intense effort.

Subsequently, Nehemiah called the people to assemble for the reading of the law. Over this religious function Ezra the priest presided; he was still active thirteen years after his return in 458–57 B.C. Nehemiah and many representatives of the people responded by making a covenant to keep the law faithfully, and sometime before the end of the year they formally dedicated the walls. Probably Nehemiah remained in Judah for only about a year and then returned to Persia, retaining the governorship in absentia.

A Final Purification of the Repatriates

Twelve years later, in Artaxerxes' thirty-second year (Nehemiah 13:6), Nehemiah returned to Judah to find that decline had rapidly set in. There was laxity toward the law, carelessness in keeping the Sabbath, and mixed marriages were again threatening the purity of the faith. Nehemiah took vigorous action on all three counts; but he did not demand divorce of Jews and non-Jews, only mandating that the practice of contracting mixed marriages would cease.

Two events shocked Nehemiah. Tobiah the Ammonite was actually living in a storage area of the temple, and a grandson of the high priest had married a daughter of his old enemy Sanballat. The former he expelled from the temple, and the latter, from Judah.

The restoration was relatively complete. The major return of the repatriates had occurred under the administration of Cyrus and the leadership of Zerubbabel. The temple had been rebuilt during the rule of Darius I and at the prodding of Haggai and Zechariah. The walls were restored and the city repopulated by permission of Artaxerxes I under the effective leadership of Nehemiah.

NOTE

1. Tradition concludes that Ezra and Nehemiah each wrote the book that bears his name. The author of Esther is completely unknown but the book almost certainly was also composed by about 400 B.C.

The Prophets of
the Old Testament

11

"Thus Says the Lord": An Overview of Prophets & Prophecy

TO many, an Old Testament prophet was a wild-eyed mystic who occupied himself with peering down the corridors of time to predict the future. To some, he was even a deranged person who fell into trances or had spells of wild mutterings that were then written down and preserved as the Word of God. Such approaches are a product of complete misunderstanding of what the prophet was or what he tried to do. One must not read the modern concept of "prophecy" into either the Old or the New Testament. The Old Testament word translated "prophet" seems to come from a root that means "to summon, announce, or call." Thus Gleason Archer concludes that the word *prophet* would "signify one who has been called or appointed to proclaim as a herald the message of God Himself."[1] Sometimes he was called a "man of God" (one devoted to God's cause) and sometimes a "seer" (one who could see things truly from God's point of view and one who might actually be able on occasion to look into the future).

Many of the Old Testament prophets were oral prophets, whose messages do not seem to have been written down because they dealt only with contemporary issues in the life of Israel (for instance, Nathan and Gad in David's day or Elijah and Elisha during the reigns of Ahab and subsequent Israelite kings). Some, however, had a message of continuing value to succeeding generations, and God led them to put their words in writing. But even the writing prophets were primarily concerned with the present. They were generally very practical people with both feet on the ground, concerned with the here and now. For instance, Isaiah, as court prophet, encouraged the good King Hezekiah during an Assyrian attack on Judah. Amos thundered against the luxurious living, moral corruption, and other sins of the Northern Kingdom. Haggai and Zechariah urged rebuilding of the temple in Jerusalem. Especially, they all had the responsibility of warning against idolatry and apostasy and calling the Hebrews to faithfulness to God's law and to dependence on His power to protect them against their enemies.

Normally the prophets made predictions about the future only in relation to the present. For instance, they warned that present idolatry would lead to divine punishment in the form of captivity by the Assyrians or the Babylonians. However, the prophets also made it clear that God would not utterly destroy the Hebrews; He would restore them to their land and allow them to enjoy a future utopian era under the rule of Messiah. The prophets talked not only about a Messiah who would rule, but also about One who would come as a suffering servant to provide for man's salvation from sin. Such predictions of future blessings were a guarantee of survival in the present and an assurance of a wiping away of the blot of sin that lay at the root of their current difficulties. Further, the prophets underscored the principle stated earlier in the Abrahamic covenant (Genesis 12:3) that God would judge the nations surrounding Israel on the basis of treatment of the Jews; thus, numerous predictions announced specific punishment of individual nations that had oppressed Israel.

ORDINARY PEOPLE WITH AN EXTRAORDINARY MESSAGE

In response to the view that a biblical prophet often appeared to be a wild-eyed mystic, one must conclude that, on the whole, they seem to have been a rather normal lot. Admittedly, Jeremiah used some rather unusual object lessons, but only under divine instruction and to arrest the attention of a people with apparently dulled sensitivities. Ezekiel's visions are hard to appreciate fully, but his primary purpose was to strengthen the faith of the exiles in Babylon by predictions of national restoration and national glory under the Davidic monarchy. A strictly ethical person will appear to be a little "strange" in the midst of a degenerate society. Someone caught up in the glory and excitement of divine revelation never will be understood by materialistically minded antisupernaturalists.

THE WRITING PROPHETS

Prophet	Approximate Date of Writing	Recipient of Message
Obadiah	840 B.C.	Edom
Joel	835	Judah
Jonah	760	Assyria (Nineveh)
Amos	755	Israel
Hosea	710	Israel
Micah	700	Judah
Isaiah	700	Judah
Nahum	650	Assyria (Nineveh)
Zephaniah	625	Judah

(Continued)

THE WRITING PROPHETS (Continued)

Prophet	Approximate Date of Writing	Recipient of Message
Habakkuk	607	Judah
Jeremiah	585	Judah
Ezekiel	570	Exiles in Babylon
Daniel	535	Babylon
Haggai	520	Judah
Zechariah	518? 480?	Judah
Malachi	435	Judah

The books of the prophets as they appear in the Old Testament are in approximate chronological order. Of the so-called Major Prophets, Isaiah dates to the Assyrian period (about 900–612 B.C.); and Jeremiah, Ezekiel, and Daniel date to the Babylonian period (612–539 B.C.). Of the so-called Minor Prophets, the first seven and the ninth belong to the Assyrian period: Hosea, Joel, Amos, Obadiah, Jonah, Micah, Nahum, and Zephaniah; Habakkuk belongs to the Babylonian period, and the last three belong to the Persian period (after 539 B.C.): Haggai, Zechariah, and Malachi. Discussion of the writing prophets is roughly in the order in which they were written.

NOTE

1. Gleason Archer, *A Survey of Old Testament Introduction*, rev. ed., p. 296.

12

Prophets of the Assyrian Period

Obadiah, Joel, Jonah, Amos, Hosea, Micah, Isaiah, Nahum, Zephaniah

OBADIAH

EVANGELICAL scholars generally tend to locate the prophecy of Obadiah during the reign of Jehoram of Judah (853–841 B.C.), at a time when there was an Edomite revolt against Judah and Philistine and Arabian plundering raids extended into Jerusalem itself (2 Kings 8:20; 2 Chronicles 21:16, 17). If this conclusion is correct, it is the earliest of the writing prophets. The message of this shortest book of the Old Testament (one chapter) is that because of her violence against Jacob and her pride, Edom shall be destroyed. She shall be dislodged from fortresses she thought impregnable and plundered and deserted. Judgment shall come upon Edom and other godless nations in the day of divine wrath. Israel is to be delivered and restored and will be an instrument in Edom's destruction. Verses 20 and 21 speak of reestablishment of the Hebrew kingdom and of the day when God will rule over the world from Mount Zion.

JOEL

It is commonly concluded that Joel wrote about 835 B.C. in the days of the young king Joash who was under the regency of the priests. (There is no reference to a ruling king of Judah.) At that time the enemies were Philistines, Egyptians, and Edomites (Joel 3:4, "coasts of Philistia," (Hebrew; 3:19), rather than Syrians, Assyrians, or Babylonians of a later time. The occasion of Joel's prophecy seems to have been a severe drought and plague of locusts in his day. Joel preached that the reason for this calamity was the sin of the people, and he urged national repentance to avoid further punishment. He also pointed to the invasion of locusts as symbolic of human incursion, either in the form of plundering expeditions or military activity No doubt this prophecy had partial fulfillment in the swarms of neighboring peoples who invaded in his own time or shortly thereafter, but some details have not yet been fulfilled and clearly point to the end times. Of special importance to understanding the book is the phrase "the day of the LORD"[1] (1:15; 2:1, 11, 31; 3:14), which seems to include the tribulation period, the second coming of Christ, and the Millennium and involves judgment on the wicked and salvation for the righteous.

Joel and other prophets predicted a time of trouble[2] or tribulation or judgment (seven years long) to come upon Israel and the nations at the end times. Just as the plague of locusts devours the land before it, so during the Tribulation an army from the north will bring great destruction; but God will intervene to save His people with forces of His own. This great time of tribulation will reach a climax with the personal return of Christ, who will judge the nations. At His return there will be great signs in the heavens and on earth, "The sun shall be turned into darkness, And the moon into blood" (Joel 2:30, 31, NKJV).

When God returns to save His people, He will pour out His Spirit in great power and blessing (Joel 2:28–32). What happened on the day of Pentecost (Acts 2:15–21) was just a foretaste or partial fulfillment or sample of the Joel promise. Complete fulfillment will come in the kingdom age. At last, unbelieving Israel will receive their Messiah and the law will be written on their hearts.

JONAH

The book of Jonah is one of the battlegrounds of modern destructive criticism. It is frequently considered to be an allegory rather than a factual account of events in the life of a real person. According to this theory, the book was written about 430 B.C. to counteract the exclusivism of Ezra and Nehemiah, and preaches the need for Jews to witness to the Gentiles rather than separating themselves from them. Presumably Jonah represents disobedient Israel; the sea represents the Gentiles; the great fish, Babylon; and the three days in the belly of the fish, the Babylonian captivity of the Jews. But according to 2 Kings 14:25–27, Jonah was not only a real person, but also an accredited prophet. His home was at Gath-hepher near Nazareth in Galilee. Moreover, Jesus Christ treated the experience of Jonah in the belly of the great fish as factual (Matthew 12:39–41). And the book of Jonah itself reads like a straightforward historical account. The 2 Kings passage connects him with the reign of Jeroboam II of Israel (793–753 B.C.).

Briefly, the story of Jonah is this. God commissioned him to go to preach salvation to Nineveh, but Jonah refused to do so and fled in the opposite direction toward Tarshish (possibly a Semitic mining colony in the vicinity of Gibraltar). While he was at sea, a storm blew up, and it was ultimately determined that God had caused the storm as a punishment for Jonah. He finally volunteered to have the crew throw him overboard to save the ship. When they tossed

Jonah into the water, a great fish swallowed him. While in the belly of the fish for three days, he prayed to God and renewed his dedication to Him. Then the fish disgorged the prophet onto dry land, and God renewed the command to go to Nineveh to preach repentance to its inhabitants. When Jonah obeyed the command, the Ninevites repented; and God spared them. This upset Jonah terribly, and he now declared his real reason for refusing to do God's bidding in the first place. It was not because of cowardice, but because Assyria was Israel's enemy. Jonah knew how gracious God was and that He would spare the Assyrians; this Jonah wished to prevent (4:12). Of course he was guilty of a false patriotism. The whole story was to teach the Jews that God was God of the Gentiles as well as the Jews and that He was interested in salvation of the Gentiles.

There are numerous interesting questions about the book of Jonah. One concerns the time when this revival may have broken out. Some suggest that it came during the reign of Adad-Nirari III (810–783 B.C.), when there was an approach to monotheism in the kingdom. Others put it in the days of Ashurdan III (771–754 B.C.) after the plague of 765, the eclipse of the sun in 763, and a second plague in 759. These staggering events could well have prepared the Assyrians to react favorably to Jonah's preaching of judgment upon their sin.

Amos

Amos, Hosea, Micah, and Isaiah were all roughly contemporaries during the last half of the eighth century B.C. Moreover, Amos was also partly contemporary with Jonah. Certainly this was a golden age of Hebrew prophecy. Amos himself was a shepherd from Tekoa, about five miles southeast of Bethlehem. Thus, he was a native of Judea, but he ministered in the Northern Kingdom (Amos 1:1). He began his ministry two years before the earthquake (1:1) and foretold that great catastrophe (6:11; 8:8; 9:5). It must have been a terrible calamity, because Zechariah referred to it even two hundred years later (Zechariah 14:5).

Although Amos was a prophet to Israel, he began his preaching with an announcement of judgment on surrounding nations: Damascus (Syria), Gaza (Philistia), Tyre (Phoenicia), Edom, Ammon, and Moab (1:3–2:3). Thus, he showed that since other nations were to be punished for their sin, the Jews could not hope to escape. Their condemnation would be greater because they enjoyed greater exposure to truth. Certainly God is no respecter of persons where sin is concerned. After a general statement showing both Judah and Israel guilty of neglecting God's word and therefore headed for destruction (2:4–16), Amos turned more particularly to Israel. He concluded that judgment on Israel was inevitable because of her depravity and dispelled the idea that Israel might be safe from destruction and captivity (4:2). The prophet denounced worship divorced from right conduct (5:21–24), violence and oppression, indolence, wanton luxury and gluttony, drunkenness, and false security (6:1–6). In 7:1–9:10, Amos saw five visions concerning Israel's future judgment:

1. Devouring grasshoppers or locusts (7:1–3),
2. Consuming fire (7:4–6),
3. Plumb line, symbolizing that Israel did not measure up to divine standards of integrity and was to be destroyed (7:7–9),
4. A basket of ripe fruit, portraying Israel ripe in her sins and the end near (8:1–14),
5. The Lord executing judgment (9:1–10).

But like most of the other prophets, Amos did not leave his listeners in despair. He predicted a coming restoration of Israel with the reestablishment of David's throne. Of course, he referred to something more than a mere restoration to the land, for at that time (538 B.C.) the throne and independent sovereignty were not to be restored. This political recovery is to be accompanied by magnificent fertility and permanent possession of the land (9:11–15). Certainly all this looks forward to the glorious millennial day at the end times when the Messiah will rule on the throne of David.

HOSEA

The prophecy of Hosea is a powerful attack on apostasy and corruption in Israel (the Northern Kingdom) and a call to return in penitence to their loving God. Hosea preached to his people for a very long time, perhaps longer than any of the other writing prophets. His ministry began sometime during the reign of Uzziah of Judah (791–740 B.C.) and continued into the reign of Hezekiah (716-687 B.C.); so probably he began to preach at least by about 760 B.C. and continued until 710 or later. Undoubtedly the book contains excerpts from messages delivered during his long career.

One of the greatest problems in the book concerns how one should view Gomer, wife of Hosea, described as a "wife of harlotry." To avoid the problem of a man of God marrying a harlot, which the Mosaic Law would condemn, some have tried to interpret Hosea's experience as a parable. But the narrative is straightforward, and there is no indication it should be interpreted that way. There is no reason it cannot be concluded that Gomer was an acceptable bride when Hosea married her and that she became a woman of loose morals subsequently. God knew what she would become; the prophet described her in retrospect. At any rate, the life experience of Hosea was intended to be symbolic of God's relation to Israel. The unfaithfulness of Hosea's wife was a picture of Israel's unfaithfulness to God, and his two sons and a daughter were given names symbolic of Hosea's chief prophecies: Jezreel, the dynasty of Jehu to be destroyed; Lo-ruhamah, "unpitied" a prophecy of Assyrian captivity; and Lo-ammi, "not my people," temporary rejection by God of His people. The central theme of Hosea's prophecy appears in 3:1–3, where the prophet brought back his unfaithful wife, disciplined her, and expressed his love for her, all of which God would do for Israel.

Hosea chapters 4 through 13 detail the prophetic indictment against Israel. She was addicted to idolatry, guilty of moral depravity, and polluted by idolatrous contamination and thus stood condemned. So God withdrew His favor from Israel, but He mourned over Ephraim and Judah and pursued them with undying love as Hosea pursued his faithless wife. The prophet concludes with a promise of ultimate complete restoration of Israel to paths of spiritual obedience and divine favor (14:1–9).

Micah

While Hosea was ministering to Israel and Isaiah to the court in Jerusalem, Micah preached to the common people of Judah, concentrating on personal religion and social morality. His active years must have been about 735–700 B.C.; and his book, composed about 700. As a social critic, Micah scorned the idle rich for their exploitation of poor defenseless people (2:1–13), the princes for devouring their subjects instead of rendering them justice (3:1–4), the false prophets for leading the people astray (3:5–8), and the people for their ingratitude and sin (6:1–7:6). For all their sins, the kingdom of Judah would be destroyed and Jerusalem "plowed as a field" (3:12). Previously Micah had already predicted the destruction of Samaria (1:2–7).

But God was not through with His covenant people. Micah gives one of the most exalted accounts of Israel's glorious future (chapter 4). Jerusalem will be the religious and political center of the earth. In it the Davidic kingdom will be restored, as will justice, peace, and security. The people will be regathered into the land. After this general statement about the kingdom age, the prophet backs up to talk about the first coming of the Messiah who would be born in Bethlehem (5:2), and events at His second corning when the Messiah will strike down the northern invader, purify His people, and bring judgment on the heathen (chapter 5).

There are three significant quotations of Micah in Scripture:

- by the elders of the land who, in appealing to Micah, saved the life of Jeremiah (Jeremiah 26:18, quoting Micah 3:12)
- by the chief priests and scribes in answer to Herod's question on where Messiah was to be born (Matthew 2:56, quoting Micah 5:2)
- by our Lord when sending out the twelve (Matthew 10:35, 36, quoting Micah 7:6).

One of the most quoted passages from Micah today is 6:8, which sets forth the three basic requirements for believers: "To do justice, to love kindness [mercy], And to walk humbly with your God" (NASB).

ISAIAH

Isaiah has always been considered the greatest of the Hebrew prophets. His is the longest of the prophetic books. He ministered to the Judean court when the nation was threatened with extermination at the hands of the Assyrians, and delivered God's message of preservation. He has the most of any of the prophets to say about the coming Messiah and how He would save people from their sins. Bible students often speak of the "gospel according to Isaiah." He has much to say also about the golden age of the future, when there will be peace and prosperity and a proper respect for moral and spiritual values.

Something has been said earlier in this book about the continuing relevance of the Old Testament; it provides answers to the big questions of life. Isaiah especially throws the spotlight on the questions of how to be right before God and what the future of the world is. He says that salvation comes through the provision of the Messiah in His substitutionary death and that faith in Him should issue in the determination of the believer to live right before God. Concerning the second question, he predicts that the future does hold a utopian experience for the world when, through God's intervention, humanity and nature will be at peace and the Messiah will rule in righteousness from His holy hill, Mount Zion.

Isaiah ministered primarily to Judah during the crucial last four decades of the eighth century B.C. under the kings Uzziah, Jotham, Ahaz, and Hezekiah (1:1). His great spiritual experience referred to in 6:1 occurred in the year King Uzziah died (740 B.C.). Often this is considered to be his prophetic commission, but he may actually have been in office before that time. At any rate, his ministry began at least by 740 and continued through the century. Tradition says the wicked king Manasseh martyred him sometime after 700, so his book probably dates around the turn of the century.[3] He evidently was the court prophet in the days of the good King Hezekiah and bolstered the troubled king in the face of the devastating attack by King Sennacherib of Assyria in 701 B.C. The Northern Kingdom had already fallen to Assyria in 723–22. According to Isaiah 7:3 and 8:3, the prophet was married and had children for signs: Maher-shalal-hash-baz, meaning "haste ye, haste ye to the prey" and signifying the captivity of Israel; and Shear-jashub, meaning "a remnant shall return" and signifying return from captivity.

The Coming of the Messiah and the Millennium

The book of Isaiah is especially rich in predictions concerning the Messiah, which clearly relate to the person and work of Jesus Christ. The prophet predicts:

1. His virgin birth (7:14; cf. Matthew 1:23): While some argue that the word translated "Virgin" here may mean "a young woman of marriageable age," the word is regularly used in the Old Testament to refer to a virgin.
2. His deity: Immanuel, meaning "God with us" (7:14; cf. Matthew 1:22, 23 and Isaiah 9:6).
3. His humanity: a branch from the root of Jesse (11:1).

4. His forerunner: John the Baptist (40:3, 4; cf. Matthew 3:1–3).
5. His ministry (61:1, 2a; cf. Luke 4:18; Isaiah 42:1, 6, 7).
6. His substitutionary sufferings and death on behalf of all humanity (52:13–53:12). Seven times we are told in Isaiah 53 that He has borne our sins. Some New Testament references will demonstrate clearly how Christ in His death fulfilled this preview of Him. "He was wounded for our transgressions" (53:5; cf. 1 Peter 3:18). "He was bruised for our iniquities" (53:5; cf. 1 Peter 2:21–23; 4:1). "And the Lord has laid on him the iniquity of us all" (53:6; cf. 2 Corinthians 5:21). "For the transgression of my people was he smitten" (53:8; cf. John 11:51, 52). "When you shall make his soul an offering for sin" (53:10; cf. Romans 8:32). "For he shall bear their iniquities" (53:11; cf. 1 Peter 2:24). "And He bare the sin of many" (53:12; cf. Hebrews 9:28).

Another major theme of the book is the future golden age or millennium that will come at the end times. Note, for instance, the following: Isaiah 2:1–5, Jerusalem to be the center of the earth religiously and politically and universal peace to be established as swords are beaten into plowshares; Isaiah 11, the Immanuel-King and His kingdom to be peaceful, to include Gentiles and to involve a regathering of Jews; Isaiah 35, the miraculous physical and climatic changes during the kingdom; Isaiah 59:20–66:24, the return of Messiah in glory and vengeance, establishing the kingdom, restoring and exalting the righteous remnant of Israel, but bringing judgment on apostate Israel and encompassing the Gentiles in His glorious kingdom.

Brief Outline

The book of Isaiah may be conveniently outlined in three parts: chapters 1–35, with the principal theme of judgment; chapters

36–39, with a historical interlude on the attack of Sennacherib; chapters 40–66, with the main theme of redemption. The first twelve chapters contain prophecies concerning Judah and Jerusalem, beginning with a scathing denunciation of Israel's religious formalism and sinfulness, and continuing with an intermingling of threats of judgment and captivity with promises of the glorious millennial kingdom. Nestled in this section is the magnificent vision of chapter 6. In a word, the message of this chapter is that with a vision of the holiness of God, we then realize by comparison our utter sinfulness. Once cleansed of sin and guilt, then in gratitude we will want to serve God. Chapters 13–23 detail prophecies against the nations: Babylon, Assyria, Philistia, Moab, Damascus, Ethiopia, Egypt, Arabia, Edom, Jerusalem, and Tyre. A study of history and archaeology reveals how these prophecies have been minutely fulfilled. Chapters 24–27 describe the Great Tribulation and establishment of the kingdom and are followed by prophetic warnings concerning Samaria and Judah in chapters 28–35.

After a historical interlude concerning the attack of King Sennacherib of Assyria on Judah (chapters 36–39) appears a section of comfort to the exiles in the promise of restoration (40–48). Even though God had warned that He would send the Israelites into captivity in Babylon for their sin, He did not intend to cut them off forever. He would one day raise up Cyrus to deliver them and would destroy Babylon and her idols in the process. Moreover, God would send the Messiah to judge Israel's oppressors, to redeem and restore Israel, and to provide worldwide salvation (49–57). In the remaining chapters of the book (58–66), the prophet extends comfort to the exiles in predictions of the future glory of Israel at the end times. Chapter 55 contains some of the most gracious invitations in the Old Testament: "Ho, every one that thirsts" (v. 1); "Seek the LORD while he may be found" (v. 6); "Let the wicked forsake his way . . . for he will abundantly pardon" (v. 7).

NAHUM

The main burden of Nahum's prophecy is execution of God's judgment on Nineveh, capital of Assyria, "the bloody city" (3:1). It is a message of comfort to the harassed Hebrews who stood in constant fear of utter destruction at the hand of the cruel Assyrians. But it is a message of warning to the effect that all God can do with an apostate nation is destroy it. Judah might rejoice in the destruction of idolatrous Assyria, but did apostate Judah have any real hope of escaping the same judgment? Obviously, Nahum wrote his prophecy before the fall of Nineveh in 612 B.C., and he wrote it after King Ashurbanipal of Assyria captured and sacked No (ancient Thebes, modern Luxor), the great capital of Egypt, in 663 B.C. (Nahum 3:8). Probably he wrote about 650 B.C.

The repentance in Jonah's day apparently had had only temporary effect. The Assyrians had quickly gone back to their old ways, making themselves particularly obnoxious to the Hebrews in the destruction of Samaria in 723–22 B.C. and in the near destruction of Jerusalem in 701 B.C. On the basis of the Abrahamic covenant alone, the Assyrians could expect judgment (Genesis 12:3), but Nahum notes special causes for Nineveh's destruction: violence, falsehood, plunder, ruthlessness, cruelty, and subjection of the nations (3:14). Moreover, he roots judgment ultimately in the holiness of God and the opposition of idolaters (Nahum 1:1–11); any nation guilty of the kind of things the Assyrians had said before the walls of Jerusalem in 701 B.C. is ultimately bound for trouble (see, for instance, Isaiah 36:18–20).

As noted above, Nahum is primarily concerned with the destruction of Nineveh; almost every verse from 1:12 through 3:19 relates to this catastrophe. Nineveh was to be besieged. The furious attack on the capital is described, as are the flight of her defenders and the sack of the city. Nineveh was to become a habitation of animals, and none would lament her distress. In large part, the prediction was fulfilled in 612 B.C. when the Babylonians,

Medes, and Scythians took Nineveh and destroyed it. Unlike other conquering capitals, it did not continue in a lingering twilight of decline after the center of power had shifted somewhere else. It simply passed out of existence.

ZEPHANIAH

Zephaniah focuses on the theme of the Day of the Lord and its accompanying judgment. In his pronouncement of doom, he addressed first Judah and Jerusalem (1:1–2:3) and then turned his attention to the surrounding nations: Philistia, Moab, Ammon, Ethiopia, and Assyria (2:4–15). The prophet carried on his ministry during the reign of good King Josiah of Judah (640–608 B.C., see Zephaniah 1:1) and apparently wrote his little book about 625. This may be concluded from the fact that in 621 B.C. a revival broke out in Jerusalem, during which many of the evils that Zephaniah scorned were either removed or at least greatly reduced. Presumably he had a part in bringing about the spiritual changes. The Hezekiah mentioned in Zephaniah 1:1 as the great-grandfather of the prophet was presumably the good King Hezekiah.

The Day of the Lord is described as imminent and no doubt refers, in the first instance, to a Babylonian attack under Nebuchadnezzar (1:14–18). But Nebuchadnezzar's invasion prefigures the Day of the Lord at the end times when there will be universal judgment and salvation of a remnant. The soon-coming judgment on Judah was to fall because of disobedience, opposition to correction, injustice of judges, godlessness of prophets and priests (3:1–4), and idolatry (1:4–6). These conditions came about especially because of the evil influence of the kings Manasseh and Amon. Zephaniah concludes his prophecy with the prediction of a remnant of Israel spiritually cleansed and restored to the land of Palestine at the end times, fully enjoying kingdom blessing (3:9–20).

Notes

1. Some commentators apply "the day of the LORD" to the Tribulation; others, to the Tribulation and the Second Coming; and yet others, to the Tribulation, the Second Coming, and the Millennium. If one accepts the latter view, the day refers to the whole process at the end times during which God intervenes in judgment and sets things right.

2. Jeremiah calls this "the time of Jacob's trouble" (Jeremiah 30:7). It is designed to purify Israel by means of adversity (see Zechariah 13:8–9; Daniel 12:1).

3. There is not room here to discuss the involved question of the unity of Isaiah. Those interested may consult works mentioned on pp. 206–7. Suffice it to say that no one has ever seen these supposed separate "books" of Isaiah. As far back as we can go—to the second Century B.C. Dead Sea Scrolls—Isaiah is always one unit.

13

Prophets of the Babylonian Period

Habakkuk, Ezekiel, Jeremiah, Daniel

A S the earlier prophets had foretold, Nineveh fell in 612 B.C. But the end of the Assyrian Empire did not mean relief for Judah. About three years later, Pharaoh Necho of Egypt carved out for himself a short-lived empire in Palestine and Syria. Meanwhile Babylon consolidated her power in the valley of the Tigris and Euphrates. When Nebuchadnezzar of Babylon defeated Necho in 605 B.C., he stood at the doorstep of the Judean kingdom and was in a position to wreak the havoc that the prophets predicted he would. The judgment of God was about to fall.

HABAKKUK

In those days when the power of Babylon was looming on the horizon, the prophet Habakkuk carried on a conversation with God about conditions in Judah and the imminent captivity. He has sometimes been called "the freethinker among the prophets" because he could not quite square his belief in a righteous God with conditions as he saw them. He had the temerity to ask God, *Why?* First he asked why God did not answer his prayers and why He apparently allowed the mounting evil of Judah to go unpunished (1:1–4). God answered that He was about to bring punishment on Judah for her sins by means of Chaldean invasion and then gave a graphic sketch of the Chaldeans (1:5–11).[1] Then Habakkuk had another problem: How could a holy and just God use a people more sinful than the Jews to bring judgment on them (1:12–2:1)? This time God replied that He was certainly aware of the wickedness of the Babylonians and would soon punish them also (2:2–20). Nestled in this section are two significant passages. The first states, "The just shall live by his faith" (2:4). Quoted by the apostle Paul in Romans 1:17 and Galatians 3:11 and by the writer to the Hebrews (10:38), it became the great theme of Martin Luther's preaching. Thus, in a very real sense Habakkuk became the grandfather of the Reformation, which emphasized the fact that one is made just or righteous before God on the basis of faith in the finished work of Christ on the cross, not on the basis of works. Habakkuk 2:18–20 effectively shows the folly of making a dumb idol one's god in preference to the sovereign God of the universe.

While Habakkuk has been called a freethinker, he has also been called the prophet of faith, not only because of the passage in 2:4 but also because of his attitude in chapter 3. Finding his difficulties solved and remembering God's care for Israel in the past, he breaks forth in a thrilling hymn of praise and confidence in God.

EZEKIEL

By the time of Ezekiel, the captivity anticipated by Habakkuk had begun. Daniel and others had been taken as hostages in 605 B.C., and Ezekiel was carried off in 597 with a second contingent of captives (numbering ten thousand, according to 2 Kings 24:14). In Babylonia, he was settled among a community of Hebrew captives south of the city of Babylon on the "river Chebar," evidently a major irrigation canal. A member of a priestly family, he apparently had a degree of freedom and economic independence, for he had a house of his own, where he gave religious instruction (possibly the early beginnings of the synagogue), and nothing is said about his financial needs (8:1; 14:1; 33:30–33). His ministry began with a call to the prophetic office in the fifth year of King Jehoiachin's captivity and of his own (593 B.C., Ezekiel 1:1–3) and continued at least to the twenty-seventh year of Jehoiachin's captivity (571, Ezekiel 29:17). Thus he was contemporary with Jeremiah's ministry to the Jews of Jerusalem.

Most of Ezekiel's prophecy is precisely dated and is generally in chronological order. Chapters 1–24, spanning the period 593–588 B.C., deal primarily with the imminent destruction of Jerusalem. Chapters 25–32 were revealed to the prophet during the years 587–585 B.C. (with the exception of 29:1), and concern prophecies against nations surrounding Israel. Chapters 33–48 were revelations to the prophet during 585–573 B.C. and tell of the future restoration of Israel.

The Uniqueness of Ezekiel

There are several insights and emphases or peculiarities of Ezekiel that deserve special attention. Over sixty times, the prophet used the expression, "They shall know that I am the LORD" in connection with reasons for judgment on Israel and prospects for her future salvation. At least twenty-five times, Ezekiel refers to the ministry of the Holy Spirit, especially in connection with prophetic inspiration (e.g., 2:2; 3:12, 14, 24). Fourteen times the prophet speaks of "the glory of the LORD." This is the visible light that shone between the cherubims in the holy of holies in the temple and symbolized the presence of God. Before the destruction of the temple, Ezekiel saw a vision of this glory leaving the temple (9:3). Above the ark, Ezekiel saw the likeness of God's throne that had wheels and was, therefore, a kind of royal chariot (10:1). The glory of the Lord removed to the threshold of the house (10:4), then to the east gate of the temple (10:18, 19), and then from the city eastward to the Mount of Olives (11:22, 23). At the end times it will return from the east to the city (43:2).

Only in this book appear details of a temple yet to be built in Jerusalem (chapters 40–42). Only in Ezekiel can one learn of Israel's idolatry while yet in Egypt (20:1–9). If one grants that 28:11–19 refer to Satan, as many Bible students conclude, only here do we have such information; this passage must be linked with Isaiah 14 for complementary data on the subject. Moreover, there is a wealth of symbolism, simile, or metaphor throughout the book. For instance, Nebuchadnezzar was a great eagle (17:3); Tyre, a stately ship that would be sunk (27:5ff.); and Egypt, a great sea monster that God would slay (32:1ff.).

The book of Ezekiel begins with an extended statement about the prophet's commission (chapters 1–3). As with Moses (Exodus 3:1–10), Isaiah (Isaiah 6:1–10), Daniel (Daniel 10:5–14), and John (Revelation 1:12–19), it begins with a revelation of the glory of God; but it includes also a special anointing with the Holy Spirit and an emphasis on the necessity for the word of God to permeate the whole being of the prophet. (Ezekiel ate the roll or scroll on which Scripture was written, 3:1–4).

The message of Ezekiel is, to a large degree, a message of doom. Chapters 4–7 concern the impending destruction of Jerusalem, describing its siege by the Babylonians in terms of several symbolic actions of the prophet (chapters 45) and including obliteration of the high places used for pagan worship (chapter 6). This destruction was to come because of the incorrigible sinfulness of Judah (chapters 8–24). Some of the sins especially singled out are idolatry (chapters 8–9), wickedness of political leaders (11:1–13), false prophetic activity (chapter 13), spiritual unproductiveness (chapter 15), violence and sexual promiscuity (chapter 22), and political and religious contamination resulting from alliances with surrounding nations (chapter 23). Having pronounced doom against Judah, Ezekiel next moves against the nations surrounding Israel (chapters 25–32). Attention focuses first on Ammon and then on Moab, Edom, Philistia, Tyre, Sidon, and Egypt. God was against these peoples for their idolatry and their ill treatment of Israel.

The Regathering of Israel

Ezekiel was not merely a prophet of doom. Occasional references to preservation and glorious restoration in a future day, sprinkled through the earlier chapters of the book, expand into a floodtide in the latter chapters. Events preceding the restoration of Israel appear in chapters 33–39; the account of the restoration is in chapters 40–48. God as the good Shepherd will regather the flock (34:11–16) and will set over them the true Shepherd, evidently referring to the Messiah ("my servant David," 34:24). In connection with this restoration there will be a judgment on Edom for her encroachment on southern Judah (chapter 35). The restoration will involve not only a regathering from among all nations, but also spiritual regeneration (chapter 36). The scope of this regathering is far greater than the restoration of the Persian period and is still future. Ezekiel's vision of the valley of dry bones (chapter 37) portrays divine power operative in restoring the national life of Israel. The exiles (bones) are regathered from the valley of dispersion and are given national life. All twelve tribes are involved, showing that Judah and Israel will again become one. After Israel is regathered in the land, a great northern confederacy, called Gog and Magog, will descend on Palestine. In this hour of trial, God will personally intervene and destroy the invaders (chapters 38–39).

Chapters 40–43 describe in detail construction of a new temple and a sacrificial system, and subsequent chapters tell of the division of the land into tribal territories. Many have tried to spiritualize the latter chapters of Ezekiel and apply them to the church age. Some view the prophecy as being fulfilled in the new earth. It should be pointed out that there are several chapters that assure the exiles that God has a definite plan for Palestine, Jerusalem, and the temple. If taken at all literally, they can have nothing to do with the church. Moreover, if they are fulfilled in the church, they provide no encouragement for Israel, which they are designed to do. In the new Jerusalem of Revelation 21, there is to be no temple at all; so this prediction cannot be realized in the new earth. It is best to regard this passage as applying to the Millennium, when Israel will inhabit the land and their Messiah will rule over them on Mount Zion. There is no special problem raised about a reinstitution of the sacrificial system because it may be viewed as having a memorial function as does the Lord's Supper in the Christian church. Certainly the sacrifices could not build merit for a people evidently regenerated by faith in the Messiah and His sacrificial work on their behalf.

JEREMIAH

Even though Ezekiel completed his ministry later than Jeremiah did, he is placed earlier in this book because for Ezekiel, the captivity had begun long before the destruction of Jerusalem. Jeremiah was the great prophet of the captivity and especially of the destruction of Jerusalem. He began his ministry in the thirteenth year of the good King Josiah, 627 B.C. (Jeremiah 1:2) and continued to preach in the capital until its destruction by the Babylonians in 586 B.C. Thereafter, the Babylonians permitted him to stay in Palestine during the days when Gedaliah was governor. After the assassination of Gedaliah, a group of Jews forced him to accompany them to Egypt; probably he died there. Presumably he completed his prophecy in Egypt about 585.

Jeremiah began his prophetic activities at a time when the Assyrian Empire was disintegrating and there was relative peace in Western Asia. Although the Babylonians under Nabopolassar managed to free themselves from Assyria in 626 B.C., they posed only a remote threat to the people of Judah. It was, therefore, difficult for

Jeremiah to persuade the people that God was about to destroy them for their sins at the hands of the Babylonians. This was especially true when false prophets continually preached peace and security. But Jeremiah remained true to his prophetic call. In spite of his youth (he was perhaps only about twenty when commissioned) and a natural tendency to reticence and gentleness, he proclaimed stern messages of irreversible gloom that brought intense opposition from all classes of the corrupt society of his day. As someone has said, it takes a tenderhearted individual to deliver with force and pathos a stern message of judgment. As long as the good king Josiah was alive (d. 609 B.C.), Jeremiah was protected, but then he suffered increasing opposition, beating, and imprisonment (see 11:18–23; 12:6, 18:18; 20:1–3; 26; 37:11–38:28). The book of Jeremiah is the most autobiographical of the prophets. In addition to statements about Jeremiah's call and priestly birth in chapter 1, personal references appear throughout the book, indicating his attitudes, outlook on life, relations with others, sufferings, and prohibition to marry (16:2).

Focus on Judah and Jerusalem

The bulk of Jeremiah (chapters 2–39) consists of prophecies against Judah and Jerusalem. The first half of the section is devoted to a series of six sermons or discourses delivered mostly during the days of Josiah (chapters 2–20). These may be summarized as follows:

1. Judah's apostasy (2:1–3:5)
2. The threatened invasion of Judah from the north and impending disaster (3:6–6:30)
3. The Babylonian exile and punishment of idolatry (7:1–10:25)
4. Judah's rejection for breaking God's covenant (11:1–13:27)
5. The inability of the prophet's prayers to prevent judgment (14:1–17:27)
6. The signs of the potter and the broken jar, predictions of coming exile (18:1–20:18)

The second half of the major portion of Jeremiah (21–39) consists of later prophecies against kings, prophets, and the people of
Judah. Jeremiah made very pointed predictions against reigning
kings of Judah, telling Zedekiah the Babylonians would defeat him
and burn Jerusalem (chapter 21) and likewise pronouncing judgment on Jehoiakim (22:13–19) and Jehoiachin (22:20–30), who
was deported to Babylon. (Jehoiachin is called Coniah in this passage and in 37:1.) The vision of two baskets of figs (chapter 24)
also concerned Zedekiah. The bad figs represented Jews remaining
in Jerusalem to support wicked Zedekiah, and the good figs were
the better people carried to Babylon with Jehoiachin (here called
Jeconiah; cf. Matthew 1:11) in 597 B.C. Next Jeremiah made a specific prediction that the captivity in Babylon would last seventy
years (chapter 25) and that the temple would be destroyed (chapter 26). For the latter he was threatened with death but was rescued by some of the elders. The Babylonian conquest is described
in another way in chapters 27–28, when the prophet symbolically
saddled himself with an ox yoke to indicate the Babylonian yoke
to come upon them. Subsequently, when Jeremiah tried to stir up
a spirit of revival, King Zedekiah burned the book of Jeremiah's
prophecy, but the prophet wrote it over again (chapter 36). Finally,
in fulfillment of prophecy, the anticipated siege of Jerusalem
occurred. Jeremiah counseled surrender and was imprisoned. The
city fell and was burned, but Jeremiah received kind treatment at
the hands of the Babylonians, being given the choice of staying in
the land or going to Babylon (37–39).

The Return of the Messiah

The book of Jeremiah is not an unrelieved prediction of doom,
however. In 23:3–6 appears a glorious prediction of regathering in
the end times and of the rule of Messiah. Chapters 30–33 provide
an extended prediction of the distant future. After a great tribulation (called "the time of Jacob's trouble"), during which Israel will

be purged, Christ will return and establish His kingdom. Restoration to blessing is to be based on the new covenant (Jeremiah 31:31–34), founded on the sacrifice of Christ. Israel will then enjoy kingdom peace and prosperity when "the Branch of Righteousness" will sit on the throne of David forever.

The two remaining shorter sections of Jeremiah concern a series of events after the fall of Jerusalem (40–45) and prophecies against foreign nations (46–51). Jeremiah elected to stay in Judah and support the governor Gedaliah, appointed by the Babylonians. Soon, however, an Ammonite plot against Gedaliah was successful. A group of frightened Jews then decided to flee to Egypt to escape possible Babylonian reprisals. Jeremiah urged them not to go, but they rejected the command of God and went anyway, forcing Jeremiah to go along with them. While there, he tried to persuade the Jewish groups in Egypt to renounce their worship of false gods, but without success. The last section of the book details prophecies against various heathen nations: Egypt, Philistia, Moab, Ammon, Edom, Damascus, Kedar and the kingdom of Hazor, Elam, and Babylon. Some of the reasons given for their judgment were pride, idolatry, and their treatment of Israel.

DANIEL

The book of Daniel is often called the key to biblical prophecy because it provides the means of unlocking numerous secrets of prophecy. Not only does it give necessary perspective on major prophetic themes (e.g., the Tribulation, the Antichrist, and the times of the Gentiles) but it also provides a means of interpreting numerous passages of Scripture (e.g., Matthew 24–25, 2 Thessalonians 2, and the book of Revelation). Put another way, the book provides a kind of framework on which to hang much of the prophetic plan of Scripture. While Daniel therefore has had a continuing significance for believers of all ages, it had a twofold message for contemporaries of the prophet: judgment on Gentile powers that plagued the Jews and hope of deliverance for the nation of Israel. Sometimes Bible students get so excited about the message of Scripture for their own times that they neglect the fact that the Bible was written to people thousands of years ago and had a special message for them in their particular needs. The book of Daniel falls logically into two parts: the first six chapters are generally historical in nature and relate to events in the life of the prophet; the last six chapters contain prophecies of future events.

Daniel was one of the hostages that Nebuchadnezzar carried off to Babylon in the third year of Jehoiakim of Judah (605 B.C.). A youth of perhaps fifteen or sixteen, he was apparently of royal blood (Daniel 1:1–6). Rising to power in Babylon, he held a position of leadership for most of the remaining days of the Neo-Babylonian Empire (612–539) and in the Persian period. According to Daniel 1:21, he continued to the first year of Cyrus (539 B.C.); and according to Daniel 10:1, he was still going strong in 537. These chronological references mean that he was contemporary with Ezekiel in Babylonia and Jeremiah in Jerusalem and the return of the Jews recorded in the early chapters of Ezra. The composition of the book that bears his name must be dated to about 535 B.C.

But the matter of authorship is not as simple as that. Ever since the third century A.D., when the Neoplatonist Porphyry asserted that the book was a forgery written in the Maccabean period (165 B.C.), opponents of the traditional view have been numerous. Primarily they have based their position on the denial of supernatural ability to predict prophecy along with alleged historical inaccuracies and textual problems in the book. Of course, it is impossible in the last analysis to prove the supernatural, but predictive prophecy has gained considerable support from the fulfillment of numerous prophecies in Isaiah, Jeremiah, Ezekiel, and other Old Testament books. Moreover, one by one, the supposed historical errors or difficulties in Daniel have melted away. For instance, as a result of archeological discoveries, Belshazzar is now known to have been acting as coregent with his father Nabonidus when Babylon fell, and he was apparently ruling monarch in the city when it capitulated to the Persians. This eliminates the old contention that secular history named Nabonidus king of Babylon at its fall, and Daniel named Belshazzar. Again, Daniel often has been dated late because of certain Greek words in the text. Newer scholarship no longer claims that some of these words are of Greek origin. Some that undoubtedly are Greek pose no problem because of information on the influence of Greeks in the Near East, even before Daniel's day. They served widely as mercenaries, even in the Persian armed forces. Moreover, the author of Daniel shows a knowledge of sixth century events that a second century writer could not have had. Of course, this whole subject is much too technical and detailed to discuss here.[2]

Daniel's Personal History

Absolute devotion to God stands out at the beginning of this prophecy. When put in a special training program that offered considerable opportunity for advancement, Daniel and his friends determined that they would not defile themselves with the king's food and wine. Perhaps this had been offered to idols; certainly it had not been prepared according to Levitical dietary laws. God prospered them in their decision to eat only vegetables (and possibly grain) and water (chapter 1). Throughout his long life at the pagan Babylonian court, Daniel maintained his saintly life. Ezekiel referred to him as a pattern or model of righteousness (Ezekiel 14:14–20; 28:3).

Presumably near the end of Daniel's special period of training, a crisis arose at court. Nebuchadnezzar had had a troublesome dream that he had forgotten. Wondering what it was all about, he had ordered the court wise men and diviners on pain of death to produce the dream and an interpretation. While they might offer an interpretation if they had known the dream, they could not reproduce the dream. At the crucial moment, Daniel, who also possibly would have been executed had they failed, stepped forward and asked for time to grant the king's wish. In answer to prayer, God revealed the dream and the interpretation. It concerned a great image that was meant to portray world history. The head of gold (Babylon) was to be succeeded by an upper body of silver (Medo-Persia) and in turn by parts of bronze (Macedonia) and iron (Rome). Toes of the feet represented panoramically a political development in the Roman Empire of a ten-king federation in a later day, which would be destroyed by Christ at the setting up of His kingdom. For his remarkable performance Daniel was rewarded with governorship over the province of Babylon (chapter 2).

Increasing Influence of Daniel

Possibly impressed by the dream that labeled him as the head of gold, Nebuchadnezzar erected a great image of gold ninety feet high and nine feet wide (chapter 3). Exactly what this was cannot be determined from the text. It may have been a kind of obelisk with a human figure on top. At any rate, it involved idolatry, and Daniel's three friends refused to worship the image. For this they were thrown into a fiery furnace, where they were joined by one who appeared to be the Son of God and may well have been a preincarnate appearance of Christ. Tremendously impressed by the fact that the Hebrews suffered no harm in the fire, Nebuchadnezzar ordered that all should respect the Hebrew God and that the three Hebrews should be promoted. Where Daniel was at the time is not stated, perhaps he was away on official business.

Later, Nebuchadnezzar had a vision or dream that Daniel interpreted as predicting a temporary insanity the king would suffer for seven years until he properly recognized the God of heaven (chapter 4). At this point the historical narrative breaks. Nebuchadnezzar's last days and the brief reigns of his successors are passed over. Chapter 5 picks up the history with the last king of the Neo-Babylonian Empire, Belshazzar. Apparently Daniel no longer had the same access to the court as he had had in the days of Nebuchadnezzar. At another moment of crisis, when handwriting appeared on the wall of the palace during a great feast, the queen recommended that Daniel be called to interpret it. Even though the interpretation spelled doom for the king, he rewarded Daniel and elevated him to a position roughly equivalent to prime minister. That night (October 12, 539 B.C.), the Persian armies seized Babylon without a struggle.

Remarkably, the new ruler made Daniel chief administrator. Presumably he felt comfortable with Daniel's leadership, in part because Daniel was the one who had pronounced judgment on Belshazzar and the Chaldeans. The identity of Darius, Daniel's immediate superior, cannot be determined with certainty. Critics often assert confusion with Darius the Great (521–486 B.C.) or the conqueror Cyrus by a supposed second century writer of the book of Daniel. It should be noted, however, that Daniel 5:31 calls him Darius the Mede (Cyrus and Darius the Great were Persians) and says he took (may also be translated "received," as if appointed to office) Babylon. Furthermore, this Darius the Mede was sixty-two at the time of conquest while Darius the Great was comparatively young when he became king. Moreover, if one takes Daniel 6:28 at face value, it would appear that Darius was a subordinate to Cyrus, and 9:1 says he "was made king over the realm of the Chaldeans," as if by a superior in the empire. Many would equate this Darius with Gubaru, governor of Babylon at the time.[3]

Whoever Darius was, he was pressured by jealous officials into a course of action that ultimately landed Daniel in the den of lions for his faith. It is significant that Darius had high respect for Daniel and his God and hoped that God would deliver Daniel. When Daniel came out of the lion's den, he was restored to his high position in the realm.[4] In passing, it is also significant that Daniel was the equivalent of prime minister in Babylon when the exiles returned to Judea (Ezra 1; cf. Daniel 1:21; 10:1) and that he was therefore in a position to facilitate their return.

Visions of the Future

As previously indicated, the last half of Daniel is a series of prophetic visions concerning the future. Chapter 7 presents a vision somewhat similar to chapter 2. In chapter 2, external features of the world kingdoms appear in connection with a human image. In chapter 7, four ravenous beasts portray the internal character of these Gentile kingdoms, and additional details are added. The lion is Babylon; the bear, Medo-Persia; the leopard with four wings and four heads, Alexander's empire and its subsequent four divisions; the fourth beast with iron teeth, Rome. The ten horns of the fourth beast represent a future and final stage of the Roman Empire in the latter days. The "little horn" is the Antichrist or beast of Revelation 13:4–10, who will be destroyed by Messiah at His second coming (Revelation 19:20; 20:10). Bringing an end to the power of Gentile nations, the Messiah will set up His kingdom.

Chapter 8 provides an enlargement on chapter 7. A ram with two horns (Medo-Persia) is destroyed by a he-goat (Alexander the Great). The one horn of the he-goat would be broken and become four small horns (Alexander's successors). Out of one of these horns (Seleucid kingdom or Syria) would rise a "Little horn" (Antiochus Epiphanes) who would abolish the temple worship in Jerusalem and bring on the Maccabean revolt of 167 B.C. Evidently, however, Antiochus was only to prefigure the Antichrist of the latter days (see Daniel 8:23ff.) whom Messiah will destroy when He comes at the end of the Tribulation (cf. Daniel 7:11; 8:25).

One of the most significant prophecies of all Scripture is the prophecy of Daniel's seventy weeks, or seventy sevens (9:20–27).[5] Most interpreters agree that these represent seventy weeks of years (70 × 7 or 490 years). This period is divided into three units: seven weeks (49 years), from issuance of the command to restore Jerusalem to completion of the work; sixty-two weeks (434 years), from completion of the work "unto Messiah the prince" (after which period Messiah would be cut off); and one week (7 years) of great trial. The prediction states it would take 49 years to complete rebuilding of Jerusalem and an additional 434 years would pass before the crucifixion of Messiah ("cut off"). After that, a lapse of time was to take place, during which Jerusalem would be destroyed (9:26). Then at some indefinite time in the future, a seventieth week would occur. At the beginning of the seventieth week, the Antichrist was to make a covenant with the Jews, and in the middle of the week would break the covenant, stop the sacrifice, and desecrate the temple (9:27; cf. 11:31; 12:11). Then he would persecute the Jews fiercely for "a time and times and half a time" (Daniel 7:25; 12:7) or three and one-half years, equal to the forty-two months of Revelation 13:5, the 1260 days of Revelation 11:3 and the rough equivalent of the 1290[6] days of Daniel 12:11. In his great discourse on the Mount of Olives, Christ referred to the abomination of desolation that Daniel said would introduce the Great Tribulation, and said He would return again at the end of that tribulation (Matthew 24:15, 29–31).

Daniel 10–12 constitutes a panoramic vision concerning Israel from Daniel's days to the second coming of Christ. After the greatness of Persian power passed (11:2), Alexander the Great would establish a Greek empire, which would be broken into four parts (11:3, 4). Then a conflict would take place between two of those parts, Egypt (the Ptolemies) and Syria (the Seleucids), over Palestine (11:5–20). Syria would win, and Antiochus Epiphanes of Syria next would come in for attention as a type of Antichrist (11:21–35). Then the prophecy clearly focuses on the Antichrist and the time of Jacob's trouble, or the Great Tribulation on Israel, followed by deliverance (11:36–12:1). After the Tribulation and at the second coming of Christ, there will be a resurrection of Israel (12:2, 3).

Notes

1. The Chaldeans were a Semitic people who invaded Babylonia c. 1000 B.C. and became the ruling element in the Neo-Babylonian Empire (612–539 B.C.).

2. Especially useful treatments of the issues of authorship and date may be found in Gleason Archer, *A Survey of Old Testament Introduction*, chapters 28, 29; Hobart Freeman, *An Introduction to the Old Testament Prophets* (Chicago: Moody, 1968), pp. 264–72; R. K. Harrison, *Introduction to the Old Testament* (Grand Rapids: Eerdmans, 1969), pp. 1105–1134; Merrill F. Unger, *Introductory Guide to the Old Testament*, pp. 396–99.

3. For discussion, see Freeman, pp. 267–68; and John C. Whitcomb, *Darius the Mede* (Grand Rapids: Eerdmans, 1959).

4. This episode occurred when Daniel was over eighty. The date of the event was 539 or 538 B.C., and Daniel had been carried to Babylon in 605, sixty-six years earlier. If Daniel was only fifteen at the time he went into captivity, he would have been eighty-one in 538. The stand he took in his youth (chapter 1) prepared him for the stand he was forced to take in old age.

5. For development see Robert D. Culver, *Daniel and the Latter Days* (Chicago: Moody, 1954), pp. 135–60.

6. Perhaps the additional thirty days here include a period of judgment of the nations and adjustment before beginning of the Millennium.

14

Prophets of the Persian Period

Haggai, Zechariah, Malachi

GOD had protected His people during the difficult days of Babylonian captivity. Moreover, with the Persian destruction of the Babylonian Empire, He had brought about restoration of the Jews to Judah under Cyrus the Great. The first contingent of exiles had laid the foundation of a new temple in about 536–35 B.C. but had left the structure uncompleted. Haggai and Zechariah joined their voices in encouragement to complete the project. Both began their Ministry in the second year of Darius the Great (520 B.C.), and the temple was completed in 515 B.C. The temple was of great significance as the focal point of the religious life of Israel and as the house of God. Failure to make progress in construction demonstrated the low priority the repatriates had assigned to the things of God.

HAGGAI

Haggai appeared on the scene rather suddenly in 520 B.C., preached four messages over a period of four months, and disappeared from history. Ezra recognized his contribution (Ezra 5:1; 6:14). Some conclude that Haggai was one of the few returning from exile who could remember the temple of Solomon (2:3). If so, he would have been at least eighty at the time of writing. Haggai's first message (1:1–11) was delivered on the first day of the sixth month (August-September). It was an encouragement to build the temple with an explanation that neglect of the central sanctuary was the reason for Israel's economic woes. The rulers seem to have fallen in line first; soon afterward, the people did also. Within twenty-four days, work had resumed.

About seven weeks after his first message, Haggai delivered a second (2:1–9). The builders had been discouraged over the comparative insignificance of the second temple; so Haggai encouraged them with the promise that this "latter house shall be greater than the former" and that God would "shake all nations." The reference point of the whole passage evidently is millennial. Zerubbabel was in the line of David and in the line of Christ (Luke 3:27). This chosen line would some day achieve real greatness in the person of its "greater Son" (Jesus Christ), and the line would stand while other dynasties and kingdoms would fall.

Two months after the second message, Haggai delivered two more messages on the same day (2:10–19; 2:20–23). The subject of the third discourse was essentially that though the repatriates offered sacrifice to God, failure to complete the temple constituted limited obedience. Thus sacrifices could not really cleanse if their obedience was incomplete. Rendering complete obedience in the form of temple construction would lift the burden of economic woes they were carrying. The fourth message was a prediction of God's triumph over the heathen nations at the end times.

ZECHARIAH

As already noted, Haggai and Zechariah worked together in their efforts to get the temple rebuilt in Jerusalem. While they both started their ministry in 520 B.C., Zechariah began his two months after Haggai in October-November (1:1). Although Haggai may have been an old man at the time, Zechariah was definitely young (Zechariah 2:4). How long he continued his prophetic activity is uncertain. The last dated reference in the book is 518 B.C. (7:1), but many conclude that the latter chapters of the book were written much later.[1] In this connection it is argued, for instance, that the reference to the Greeks in 9:13 may indicate composition some time after the Greeks had become significant in the Near East (after 490 B.C.).

Of priestly descent, Zechariah was the son of Berechiah, the son of Iddo (1:1 see also Ezra 5:1; 6:14; Nehemiah 12:16), and must be distinguished from over twenty other Zechariahs in the Old Testament.

While Haggai in his ministry emphasized the local historical situation, Zechariah to a large degree sought to encourage the despondent by predicting in glowing terms the glory of Israel in far-off ages. After an introductory call to repentance (1:1–6), the prophet records eight visions, all given in one night and designed for encouragement (1:7–6:15). Chapters 7 and 8 constitute an answer to questions raised by a delegation from Bethel. The rest of the book describes the future of Israel both in connection with the first coming of Christ and the establishment of the millennial kingdom at His second coming.

Greatness Begins With Repentance

In his introductory message (1:1–6), Zechariah extends a call to repentance, reminding the people of their fathers' sin and resultant captivity. As they lamented their departed greatness, they should not forget the reason for it.

The eight visions of 1:7–6:15 together speak of future deliverance for Israel and establishment of the kingdom. While it is not possible here either to go into details of interpretation or to defend the interpretations set forth, generalized statements will make possible an understanding of the prophet's message. The vision of the man among the myrtle trees (1:7–17) indicates that while Israel is downtrodden, God's concern for His people is great; He will yet restore them. The four horns and four craftsmen (1:18–21) represent empires that have oppressed the Jews and are to be destroyed. The man with the measuring line (2:1–13) portrays the fact that with her enemies fully overcome Jerusalem will enjoy glorious prosperity during the Millennium. Joshua, symbol of the priestly nation (3:1–10) pictures national pollution, cleansing, and restoration of the nation to priestly service. The golden lampstand and the two olive trees (4:1–14) presents the truth that Israel in the future will be God's lamp of witness under Messiah as priest-king. The flying roll or scroll (5:1–4) symbolizes the judgment of God against sinners. The removal of the ephah² to Babylon (5:5–11) is difficult to interpret, but certainly indicates removal of evil from Palestine. The four-chariot vision (6:1–8) presents divine judgment on the nations preparatory to Messiah's reign.

In 518 B.C. a delegation came to Zechariah from Bethel, with a question about observing certain fasts especially commemorating the destruction of Jerusalem (Zechariah 7–8). In reply, the prophet rebuked meaningless ritualism and predicted that fasts will some day be replaced by feasts when there is a full restoration of Jerusalem and when the city enjoys its millennial glory.

Prophecies of the future deliverance of Israel (chapters 9–14) begin with judgment on nations surrounding Israel, now largely fulfilled (9:1–8), continue with an announcement of the first coming of Christ (9:9), and develop with a description of the program of the King at His second coming (9:10–10:12). At that time He will punish the nation's oppressors and bring about national restoration and regathering to the land of Palestine. The prophecies of the latter part of the book are not in chronological order. Chapter 11 predicts the rejection of the good Shepherd (Christ at His first coming), punishment for it, and the acceptance of the bad shepherd (the Antichrist during the Tribulation). At the end of the Tribulation when there is a major attack on Judah and Jerusalem, God will protect the Jews and confound their enemies (12:1–9). Then He will bring about Israel's national conversion (12:10–13:9). The Messiah shall return bodily to earth and establish His kingdom.

One of the most significant aspects of the book of Zechariah is its teaching about the Messiah. He is the Branch (3:8; 6:12, 13), signifying that Christ would be of the seed of David; He would enter Jerusalem on a colt (9:9), would be betrayed for thirty pieces of silver (11:12, 13), would be pierced (12:10), would return to the Mount of Olives (14:3–8), and would reign over all the earth (14:9).

MALACHI

Malachi is the last of the Old Testament prophets. After him prophecy ceased for more than four hundred years, until the days of Christ's earthly life and the early church. Exactly when he ministered is uncertain. The two common suggestions are about 460 B.C. or about 435, when Nehemiah had returned to the Persian court. Probably the latter is to be preferred. It is argued that the sins Malachi denounced were those that Nehemiah scorned during his second term as governor: priestly laxity, neglect of tithes, and intermarriage with foreign women. A hundred years had passed since the return from Babylon and eighty years since completion of the temple. Evidently there was a general religious and moral decline that called for some rather direct preaching. Some indication of the nature and degree of Israel's spiritual lapse is provided by the eleven quotations that Malachi attributes to the people. Note the "you say" quotations in 1:2, 6, 7, 12, 13; 2:14, 17; 3:7, 8, 13, 14.

Malachi began his book with a declaration of God's love for Israel demonstrated in His choice of her, but Israel questioned that love (1:1–5). The prophet then condemned the priests for not giving God the honor due Him, for offering to Him what they would not offer the governor, for being lazy and mercenary and for leading many astray and causing them to lose respect for God and His word (1:6–2:9).

Next Malachi turned to deal with the sins of the laity. First he rebuked them for treachery against other men and for divorcing their wives and marrying heathen women (2:10–16). Then when they expressed unbelief in divine judgment, he uttered a prophecy of the coming of the Lord in judgment (2:17–3:6). This coming would be preceded by Messiah's messenger or forerunner (John the Baptist, Matthew 11:10). Messiah is here viewed particularly in connection with His second coming when He will purge and judge His people. Next the prophet condemned them for their sin of robbing God (i.e., withholding their tithes, 3:7–12). Last Malachi took to task those who argued that it was useless to serve God and that the wicked seemed to prosper. His answer was to commend the godly and predict their reward and to focus again on the second coming of Christ when He will punish the wicked (3:13–4:3). The book closes with a further exhortation to faithfulness and a prediction of Elijah's return before the day of the Lord (4:4–6).

Notes

1. Critics commonly argue that Zechariah 9–14 was not originally part of the book and that the prophet was not the author. For a conservative answer, see Gleason Archer, *A Survey of Old Testament Introduction*, pp. 411–415, and Hobart Freeman, *An Introduction to the Old Testament Prophets*, pp. 337–44.

2. An ephah is a measure a little larger than a bushel.

The Singers and Sages
of the Old Testament

The Art of Godly Living: Truth in Poetry

Job, Psalms, Proverbs, Ecclesiastes, Song of Solomon, Lamentations

THE NATURE OF HEBREW POETRY

PERHAPS the average Sunday school student who is taught that Job, Psalms, Proverbs, Ecclesiastes, the Song of Solomon, and Lamentations are poetry is quite confused and skeptical because these books do not seem to contain anything like the poetry with which he or she is acquainted. This is an understandable reaction; the King James Version quite effectively obscures the literary forms of the Bible, and many other versions do not do much better. Some of the more recent versions have sought to correct this difficulty by setting the poetic portions in poetic stanza form. Among such versions are Thomas Nelson's *New King James Version*, Moulton's *The Modern Reader's Bible*, the *New American Standard Version*, *The Complete Bible* by Smith and Goodspeed, the *New Revised Standard Version*, the *Revised English Bible*, the *New Jerusalem Bible*, the *New International Version*, and *A New Translation of the Holy Scriptures*, by the Jewish Publication Society of America.

But even a Bible that gives adequate attention to literary form cannot make Hebrew poetry appear to be like Western poetry. Hebrew poets did not employ either rhyme or meter until the seventh century A.D.[1] We must learn to appreciate biblical poetry on its own terms.

Characteristics of Old Testament Poetry

One of the basic principles of Old Testament poetry is parallelism of thought. Probably the most common type of parallelism is *synonymous*, in which the second line essentially repeats the thought of the first. Three verses from the Psalms illustrate this form well:

> He who sits in the heavens shall laugh;
>   The LORD shall hold them in derision (2:4, NKJV)
> They tested God again and again,
>   and provoked the Holy one of Israel (78:41, RSV)
> When He worked His signs in Egypt,
>   And His wonders in the field of Zoan (78:43, NKJV)

Antithetic parallelism, on the other hand, presents in the second line an idea which is opposite to that of the first line. Psalm 1:6 provides a good example:

> For Jehovah knows the way of the righteous;
>   But the way of the wicked shall perish. (NASB)

In *synthetic* parallelism, the second or succeeding lines add to or develop the thought of the first line of the verse. This is ably demonstrated in the first two verses of Psalm 1:

Blessed is the man who does not walk in the counsel of
    the wicked.
Nor stand in the path of sinners,
Nor sit in the seat of scoffers:
But his delight is in the law of the Lord,
    And in His law he meditates day and night. (NASB)

Emblematic parallelism is a type in which the second or succeeding lines give a figurative illustration of the first, as in the first verse
of Psalm 42:

As the deer pants for the water brooks,
    So my soul pants for Thee, O God. (NASB)

Several other types of parallelism could be enumerated, but they
are not very common. Perhaps it should be observed that Hebrew
poetry is not limited to couplets but may extend to triplets, qua-
trains, sextets, and octets. Moreover, parallelism is not restricted
to lines, but may extend to strophes or stanzas. This may be due in
part to the fact that it is characteristic of Hebrew music and speech
to chant or recite antiphonally; that is, the leader makes a statement or chants a portion of the text and he is answered by a group
he is leading. Psalm 136 was probably repeated in this way.
Sometimes two choirs are involved in the procedure.

A second principle of Hebrew poetry is rhythm, but it is not
strictly metrical in the sense of adhering to hard-and-fast rules governing balanced numbers of accented and unaccented syllables. Of
course it is impossible to display this quality of the original fully in
translation. It is possible, though, to observe the figurative nature
of biblical poetry in translation. Numerous rhetorical devices are
utilized to great effect. Simile, metaphor, hyperbole, and metonymy
are among the many figures of speech that appear.

A third characteristic of Hebrew poetry is the alphabetic
acrostic. An acrostic may be defined a set of letters—as the ini-

tial, middle, or final letters of lines or words—that when taken in order vertically or horizontally form a word or words. For instance

Forsaking
All
I
Trust
Him

may be read in order either vertically or horizontally, and each way makes sense. In alphabetic acrostic, each letter of the Hebrew alphabet (22 letters) is used to begin a verse, so that read vertically the alphabet is formed; read horizontally, the letter becomes part of the first word of the verse. This principle is beautifully illustrated in the book of Lamentations, where chapters 1, 2, and 4 are perfect single acrostics; in all three chapters there are twenty-two verses and each begins with a different letter of the Hebrew alphabet in alphabetical order. Chapter 3 has sixty-six verses, a multiple of twenty-two, and every fourth verse begins with a letter of the Hebrew alphabet. Chapter 5 continues the twenty-two-verse pattern, but the arrangement is not acrostic. Psalm 119 is another excellent illustration of this arrangement; there every ninth verse begins with the next letter of the Hebrew alphabet. The words or symbols at the head of each section in the English versions are letters or names of letters of the Hebrew alphabet, and each verse in the section under that name begins with the letter listed at the head of the section. Other Psalms are acrostic in nature but are not perfect acrostics.

TYPES OF POETRY

Though the principles of Old Testament poetry have been delineated, it remains to define the types of poetry. Epic is a kind of narrative poetry that deals with heroic action and is written in elevated style; drama is acted poetry; lyric is sung poetry and is reflective in nature. In the Bible there is no verse narrative (epic) as such, but it should be noted that Hebrew verse and prose systems overlap. When this is taken into consideration, it is evident that epic incidents are scattered through the historical books. Moreover, Scripture does contain mixed epic, for example, the story of Balaam (Numbers 22–24).

Probably the best example of Old Testament drama is furnished in the book of Job; there is found a considerable amount of dramatic dialogue arranged in cycles of development. At the beginning the reader is allowed to look behind the scenes and discover that all the distress which Job endures is caused by satanic temptation. Fleeting glimpses of the villain are caught in the early part of the drama. Then the plot thickens as messengers come with almost telegraphic speed to inform Job of the misfortunes that have befallen him. In short order his wife turns against him, and he is afflicted with physical suffering. The next scene pictures the erstwhile, wealthy patriarch sitting by the city dump. During the greater part of the drama he engages in a struggle with himself over the question of why he is thus made to suffer; all the while so-called friends offer a variety of suggestions. The tenseness of the situation rises as the reader wonders whether Job will be able to conquer himself. The climax comes as he reasserts his faith in God, and the drama concludes with a pronouncement of divine approval and benediction and restoration of Job's earthly goods.

Lyric is a classification that includes many types of poetry. There is the lyric idyl, which is a descriptive or narrative poem and is pastoral in nature. Those who believe that Solomon disguises himself as a shepherd in order to win the hand of the Shulamite maiden classify the Song of Solomon in this category. Another type of lyric is the ode, which is difficult to define specifically; but it may be distinguished from other kinds by greater elaboration and structural consciousness. It is also characterized by nobility of sentiment and dignity of style. Two very excellent examples of the ode are

found in Deborah's song of Judges 5 and in the song of Miriam and
Moses in Exodus 15. No doubt both of these were recited
antiphonally. A third type of lyric is the elegy, which is used primarily in professional mourning. Good examples of elegy are found
in Lamentations, Psalm 74, 80, 137, and 2 Samuel 1:19–27. Songs
in the lyric class abound in the Psalms, where they deal with such
themes as deliverance, providence, nature, judgment, trust, and consecration. Likewise, meditations and prayers appear frequently in
Hebrew poetry and are well represented in the Psalms.[2]

JOB

The book of Job is one of the most magnificent dramatic poems in
all literature. The elevated theme, the mystery of human suffering,
concerns tragedies that befell a wealthy, God-fearing inhabitant of
northern Arabia and the effort of his friends and himself to discover
the reason for his afflictions. That Job was a historical character
and not merely invented to teach a truth is supported by Ezekiel
14:14, 20 and James 5:11. The setting of the drama is clearly a
patriarchal society; so some conclude that it must have occurred
early in the second millennium B.C., not long after the days of
Abraham. Others argue that since Job lived on the edge of Arabia,
he may have had little or no contact with the more formal religious
and political institutions of Israel and that he may be dated much
later, perhaps even contemporary with David and Solomon. If so,
the book of Job would be roughly contemporary with Proverbs,
Ecclesiastes, and some of the Psalms, and would date during the
golden age of Hebrew wisdom literature.

Since the book shows an ignorance of the Hebrews or of Hebrew
history in general and of the Mosaic Law in particular, it would seem
that it was written in a non-Hebrew context and before Israel had
settled in Canaan. The land of Uz probably was located in northern
Arabia. Job himself may have composed the book, or Elihu may have
written it in close collaboration with Job. In any event, some careful

observer of the dialogues must have recorded them.[3] The book itself may be the earliest book in the Old Testament.

In form, the book of Job consists of a prologue, three cycles of speeches by Job's friends with the patriarch's replies, a series of four speeches by a fourth observer, two speeches by God, and an epilogue. As the curtain rises on the drama, Job appears as prosperous and upright in conduct and character. Then with telegraphic rapidity, a series of calamities falls on his children and possessions, and destroys them, and finally even Job's health fails. At length his wife calls on him to curse God and die.

The Three Cycles of Speeches

But Job as a true believer in God refuses to do that. When his three friends, Eliphaz, Bildad, and Zophar come to mourn with him over his losses, he does, however, curse the day he was born. The first cycle of speeches occupies chapters 3–14. In essence, what his "comforters" say in this section, as in their later statements, is that suffering is the result of personal sin. They end each speech with an appeal to Job to repent of his sin so that his prosperity will return. Eliphaz backs up his arguments by lessons received in a dream or vision; Bildad, by old proverbs, and Zophar, by appeal to reason and experience. In all this discussion, Job protests his innocence of any great wrongdoing (though admitting he is a sinner) and raises the fundamental question of the book, "Why does God constantly bring suffering on me? Why doesn't He pardon my sins?" (6:11–21). Job as an Old Testament believer longed for a "daysman" or umpire or mediator who "might lay his hand upon us both" and bring a reconciliation between God and himself (9:32–33). The New Testament believer rejoices in Jesus Christ as the one mediator between God and humankind (1 Timothy 2:5). Through His finished work on the cross, He made the perfect sacrifice for sin and thus dealt with the fundamental issue separating God and humanity.

In the second cycle of speeches (chapters 15–21), the discussion grows more heated. The "comforters" deal with the terrible sufferings and end of the wicked and harshly reproach Job. Upset and puzzled by all he is going through, Job does not lose his faith. In fact, in 19:25–27, he utters one of the most sublime statements of faith in the entire Old Testament: "For I know that my redeemer liveth, and that he shall stand at the latter day upon the earth: And though after my skin worms destroy this body, yet in my flesh shall I see God: Whom I shall see for myself, and mine eyes shall behold." Though Job generally holds the same views as his friends (and that is why he is so puzzled about his own suffering), in chapter 21 he sets forth the argument that the wicked often spend their lives in prosperity.

The third cycle of speeches (chapters 22–31) repeats many of the same arguments of the first two cycles. Job's friends continue to assert his sinfulness, and Job pleads his innocence and integrity. As the discussion seems to wind down, with no new ground being covered, another speaker comes on the scene. Elihu in his four speeches (chapters 32–37) does cover new ground, stating that God teaches people through affliction, that God is a just God, that while the wicked may seem to prosper temporarily, God does want men and women to be righteous, and that God has a purpose in afflicting the godly: to show His disciplinary grace and love. He concludes with the observation that God's ways are above human understanding.

Elihu prepares the way for God to speak. In chapters 38–41, God demonstrates His own great power and contrasts it with human frailty. Job is forced to stop finding fault with God. Note especially God's word in 40:8 (NKJV), "Would you condemn me that you may be justified?" Finally, Job catches a true vision of God (42:1–6). Perhaps his experience was a little like that of Isaiah in Isaiah 6. When a person sees God as He really is, all self-righteousness and pleas of goodness go out the window. Job now confesses his sin before God; and God vindicates the patriarch, rebukes his "friends," and restores his health and prosperity, even giving him a new family.

The Eternal Question of Suffering

In conclusion, we should perhaps stop to ask why Job suffered.[4] At least a partial answer can be given: to judge sin, to reveal Job's character, to provide an object lesson for others, to strip away all self-righteousness, and to bring Job to complete trust in God. But behind the scenes of Job's trials, and of all modern believers, there is something far more sinister than these suggestions intimate. Commentators generally ignore the full significance of the appearances of Satan in 1:6–2:10. He will do what he can to destroy the work of God and the witness and effectiveness of believers in the world. He is the god of this world (2 Corinthians 4:4; cf. John 12:31; 16:11), the prince of the power of the air (Ephesians 2:2), and especially the accuser of believers. In this age, he apparently also has access to God in this capacity. In fact, he will not be prohibited from presenting his accusations until the end times (Revelation 12:10). Believers today have wonderful consolation, however, for whenever a charge against them is brought before the Father, Christ is there at the Father's right hand to make intercession. Christ does not merely plead leniency, but presents the fact that all our sins were taken care of by His death and resurrection (Romans 8:33–34).

PSALMS

The book of Psalms is a collection of 150 spiritual songs or poems, many of which were set to music for tabernacle or temple worship. It has been called "an inspired prayer book and hymnal" and is often viewed as the devotional book of the believer. Calvin said it was "an Anatomy of all the Parts of the Soul" because of its wide range of emotions. Certainly it expresses the spiritual experience of an individual and provides something of a manual on how better to pray and to praise. From very ancient times the psalms were divided into five books (Psalms 1–41; 42–72; 73–89; 90–106; 107–150) that are thought to correspond to the five books of the Law of Moses. While many of the psalms in the King James Version are widely recognized as among the greatest poems ever written, and many of these are greatly beloved by multitudes of Christians, the translations appearing in the *New American Standard Bible*, the *New International Version*, and the *New King James Version* have some magnificent passages and are rapidly gaining favor.

The only real indications of *authorship* of individual psalms are provided in the titles (dating to very early times), but not all scholars are very sure about that evidence. If accepted, it appears that David wrote seventy-three psalms; Asaph, twelve; descendants of Korah, ten; Solomon, one or two; Moses, one; Heman, one; Etham, one. In some cases at least, references within the psalms support authorship claims of the titles; moreover; some of the psalms without titles seem to be Davidic in character. In addition to authorship, psalm titles often have musical notations which apparently intend for individual psalms to be sung to the accompaniment of stringed instruments or wind instruments or a specific instrument (e.g., lute) or to a specific tune.

A Book of Praise

Since limitation of space makes it impossible to comment on 150 separate chapters of the Psalms, it seems that the best way to describe the book is to note some of the major topics or themes evident in it. Preeminent is the theme of praise. In fact, the Hebrew title of the book is "Songs of Praise." More than twenty psalms have praise as their keynote, and in many others there are outbursts of thanksgiving. Note especially 47, 66, 67, 96, 98, 100, 103, 107, 113, 117, 118, 134–36, 138, 145–50. With rich vocabulary and wonderful variety the poets extol the goodness and glory of God.

If the Psalms are to be thought of as the devotional book of the believer, then they must express the soul's thirst for God. This theme appears especially in 42, 43, and 63. (Note particularly 42:1.) Of course, one will especially come to find God and learn more about Him in His Word. The two great psalms of the Word are 19 and 119. The latter is the most extensive statement on the Word of God in Scripture. God may also be seen in nature. Psalms 19, 29, and 104 especially center on this theme. When one has found God, he or she will revel in loving fellowship with God the Shepherd and Protector (23, 91), will find great blessing in being in the house of God (84, 122), and will find God to be a great refuge and stronghold (46, 61, 62).

As one spends time in the Word and enjoys the presence of God or grieves over broken fellowship with God, he or she will become greatly impressed with personal sin and break down in deep contrition for sin committed. Great penitential psalms include 6, 25, 32, 38–40, 51, 102, 130, 143. Of this group, Psalm 51 is the greatest.

As believers learn to walk with God and serve Him more fully, they will suffer persecution. Numerous psalms (normally classified as imprecatory psalms) refer either to personal enemies or enemies of God's people and call down curses on them. There is no basic difficulty in reconciling these pronouncements of wrath with Christian thought. The only way an Old Testament saint had of knowing tangibly the truth of the Word of God, His holiness, and His sovereign power was through judgment falling on the wicked and deliverance granted to followers of God. If enemies of the truth and enemies of Israel constantly triumphed, there was some doubt of the validity of serving God. In this category, note Psalms 7, 35, 52, 55, 56, 58, 59, 68, 69, 79, 83, 109, 137, 140.

Some of the psalms were used in corporate worship. A special group of these are 120–134, called ascent psalms. These were apparently recited or sung by pilgrims on the way to Jerusalem for the annual feasts.

Foretelling of the Messiah

A last major group of psalms speak of the future and predict aspects of either the first or second coming of Christ. These are called Messianic psalms. Some are referred to specifically in the New Testament and can, therefore, be certainly identified as Messianic. Others apparently have Messianic intent. Outstanding examples of Messianic psalms include Psalm 2, which pictures Christ rejected and coming again to judge the wicked and establish His Kingdom (see Matthew 3:17; Acts 13:33; Hebrews 1:5; 5:5; 7:28; 2 Peter 1:17); Psalm 8, which portrays Christ coming in humiliation, a little lower than the angels, to taste death for every human being (see Hebrews 2:6–9; Matthew 21:15, 16); Psalm 16:10, which predicts Christ's resurrection (see Acts 2:25–28); Psalm 22:1, which Jesus quoted as He hung on the cross (Matthew 27:46); Psalm 45, which speaks of Christ's future glorious rule (see Hebrews 1:8, 9); Psalm 69:4, 9, which makes reference to aspects of Christ's earthly life (see John 15:25; John 2:17); Psalm 110:1, which refers to the future rule of Christ (see Matthew 22:44; Mark 12:36; Luke 20:42, 43; Acts 2:34; Hebrews 1:13); and Psalm 118:22, 23, which predicts both the rejection and ultimate triumph of Christ (see Matthew 21:42). Other psalms generally believed to be Messianic are 40, 41, 45, 68, 72, 102, 110, 132.

PROVERBS

The book of Proverbs is a library of wisdom that provides moral and ethical principles to guide believers in the present life and to bring them reward in the life to come. The Hebrew word of which *proverb* is a translation signifies a maxim or saying or parable that is a statement of principle. More than a collection of human wisdom, Proverbs contains divine wisdom intended to rule our daily lives and teach us how practical godliness is. Of course, these instructions governing conduct were not designed to provide a means by which individuals might do good works that would accumulate merit and lead to salvation. The standard, in both Old and New Testaments is that salvation comes by faith in God and His gracious provision for our salvation.

Apparently Solomon wrote most of the collection of Proverbs: 1:1–9:18, according to 1:1; 10:1–22:16, according to 10:1; 25:1–29:27, according to 25:1, though the latter were selected from Solomon's collection in the royal library by King Hezekiah's committee. According to 1 Kings 4:32, Solomon wrote/spoke 3000 proverbs and 1005 songs. The sayings of the wise (22:17–24:34) are thought to be proverbs selected by Solomon himself from a collection that existed in his day. Who Agar and Lemuel (composers of chapters 30–31) were is not otherwise known.

The first section of Proverbs (1:1–9:18) may be described as a book of wisdom. In it a father delivers instruction to his son that becomes a general book of admonition for youth. At the outset it is important to recognize that the fear of the Lord is the beginning of knowledge or wisdom (1:7; 9:10). The wise person, then, is the one who walks in God-honoring paths and receives blessings for such wise conduct. The wisdom and instruction inculcated in this section spells out warnings against violence, gives practical advice on relations with one's neighbor, admonishes to faithfulness in marriage and warns against adultery, describes the folly of the sluggard and stirs to industriousness, condemns the evil of the troublemaker, and commends acts that promote harmony in society.

The second section of Proverbs (10:1–22:16) is a collection of about 375 short proverbs (each verse contains a complete proverb) almost exclusively arranged in antithetic couplets. The tone, of this section is happier than the previous one; in it virtue is uniformly rewarded. Because there are so many individual proverbs here, it is hard to classify them. Moreover, description is complicated by the fact that after a proverb is given, it is frequently repeated elsewhere with variations. Generally speaking, these proverbs contrast righteousness and wickedness or goodness and evil. The wrong use of the tongue comes in for its share of criticism.

The sayings of the wise (22:17–24:34) are like the first section addressed to "my son." Again the subject changes frequently and the topics are practical in nature. Admonitions cover such subjects as being a guest, parental discipline, envy, wisdom, and laziness. Proverbs of Solomon chosen by Hezekiah's committee (25–29) deal with wise conduct before a king, in speech, in dealing with enemies; and they condemn the fool, the lazy, the liar, the contentious, and other unappealing kinds of individuals. Highlight of the last two chapters, and probably the best-known passage in Proverbs, is the poem in honor of the virtuous woman in 31:1–31. By the standards indicated there a godly woman may evaluate her life.

ECCLESIASTES

In many ways the book of Ecclesiastes appears to be out of keeping with the rest of the Old Testament. On the surface it seems to glorify human values; it seems worldly in outlook rather than spiritual; it seems to have little place for God. One of the key phrases is "under the sun" (which occurs twenty-nine times); therefore some have called Ecclesiastes "the book of the natural man," for it describes life on earth apart from a divine perspective. But such life is declared to be "vanity" (the word appears thiry-seven times). So the real purpose of the book seems to be to demonstrate the uselessness of living a life of mere human enjoyment; the fulfilled life is one that gives proper recognition to God and that is lived in His service. If one grants that Solomon is the author,[5] this book is probably not merely a theoretical discussion but an autobiography of the great king as he drifted away from God and tried various methods of securing happiness.

The king found that great wisdom, good as it is, could not bring true happiness (1:12–18), nor could pleasure and wealth (2:1–11; 5:8–6:12), nor the enjoyment that comes with work well done

(2:17–3:15), nor popularity which is fleeting (4:13–16), nor large family nor long life (6:1–6). The king was further frustrated as he recognized that wickedness and oppression were prevalent on earth (3:16–4:6); that there seemed to be no advantage in being righteous (7:13–21); that life is full of uncertainties about which nothing absolute can be known and that death is a puzzle (8:1–9:18).

The speaker does not give up completely on the life of the natural man. Occasionally he points out the value of wisdom and gives suggestions on how to live a "better life" on earth. But preeminently he seeks to rise to a higher level. For instance, in 2:24–26; 5:18–20; 8:15; and 9:7–9 God is acknowledged as the giver of all the good things that may be enjoyed in life. Finally, asserting the futility of a life apart from God, the speaker comes down to the grand conclusion: reverence God, keep His precepts, and live in the light of eternity. And this must be regarded as the theme and purpose of the entire book (cf. 3:14; 5:7; 7:18; 8:12, 13). When human beings live in that manner, the whole of life begins to fit into a meaningful pattern and takes on a new significance. A proper relationship is established between Christ and culture and one will avoid pagan solutions to the quest for happiness.[6]

Song of Solomon

The natural rendering of the first verse of the Song of Solomon is that it belonged to Solomon rather than being *about* or *concerning* Solomon. Therefore, the claim is to Solomonic authorship. Numerous internal evidences are marshaled by scholars to support the claim of the first verse. The book is a lyric poem in dialogue form describing King Solomon's love for a Shulamite lass (a girl of Shunem), whom he had met somewhere in the hill country of Samaria. The king had come in disguise to her family's vineyard, where she was made to work very hard. There he had won her heart and promised to return to her. This he ultimately did and made her his bride.

How this book should be interpreted has stirred considerable discussion. Some view it literally and claim that it teaches the dignity of human love. Others interpret it allegorically—Jews saying it represents God's love for Israel; Christians, that it represents Christ's love for the church—and do not view it as in any sense historical. Yet others interpret it typically, accepting the historical nature of the events but finding in them a typical relationship of God's love for His people and anticipating the mutual love of Christ and His church.

While it is difficult to analyze this book, the following will give some idea of the contents. The lovers sing their mutual affection in 1:1–2:7. Next the Shulamite speaks of her lover and recounts her first dream of him (2:8–3:5). As the drama heightens, Solomon comes in all his glory from Jerusalem to take his bride back to the palace and once more praises her beauty (3:6–5:1). Some apply this coming to Messiah's return in glory for Israel; others, to Christ's coming for His church. Next the bride has a dream of being separated from her bridegroom; this only heightens her realization of her love for him (5:2–6:3). The book closes with the bride and bridegroom expressing their ardent love for each other (6:4–8:14).

LAMENTATIONS

Lamentations is a book of mourning over the destruction of Jerusalem. While the book includes no claim to authorship, tradition is early and consistent that Jeremiah wrote it shortly after the destruction of the city (perhaps 585 B.C.). Thus, he has come to be known as "the weeping prophet." The poetic form of the book has already been indicated.

The lament begins with Jerusalem represented as a widow bereft of her children, sitting and weeping with none to comfort. She recognizes that God is just in punishing her for her sin, but appeals to the Lord for vindication against her enemies (chapter 1).

Chapter 2 provides a description of the siege and ruin of Jerusalem and the scorn and taunts of passers-by, with emphasis on God as the inflicter of these punishments. In chapter 3 the prophet identifies himself with his people in their affliction, but he also pours out his heart to God in faith and hope. (Verses 22 and 23 inspired the hymn "Great Is Thy Faithfulness"). The latter part of the chapter contains first an appeal to the Jews to repentance, then an appeal to God to punish Israel's oppressors. The fourth lamentation depicts the horrors of the siege, alluding to famine, cannibalism, and carnage, and justifies God's actions in bringing judgment. The book closes with a long, earnest appeal to God as the repentant nation casts itself on His mercy (chapter 5).

Notes

1. F. Delitzsch, *Commentary on the Psalms* (Grand Rapids: Eerdmans, 1949), p. 28.

2. This discussion on Hebrew poetry is largely reproduced from *Effective Bible Study* by Howard F. Vos (Grand Rapids: Zondervan, 1956), pp. 90–94.

3. For a helpful summary of the questions of authorship and date and place of writing, see Gleason L. Archer, Jr., *The Book of Job* (Grand Rapids: Baker Book House, 1982), pp. 12–16.

4. It should be noted that the book of Job is neither a systematic nor a complete answer to the question of why the righteous suffer, nor does this brief discussion of the book make any attempt to be complete on this issue.

5. Ecclesiastes 1:1; 1:12 imply that Solomon is the author, and Jewish and Christian tradition standardly supported that view until the rise of higher criticism in recent centuries. For a very detailed discussion of the problem of date and authorship, see Gleason Archer, *A Survey of Old Testament Introduction*, chapter 35.

6. A refreshing and satisfying discussion of the message of Ecclesiastes appears in Walter C. Kaiser, Jr., *Ecclesiastes: Total Life* (Chicago: Moody, 1979).

FOR FURTHER OLD TESTAMENT STUDY

ONE could go on almost indefinitely listing books on the Old Testament. It would seem, however, that a list in a book of this sort should be brief and that it should consist of publications that are in print or at least readily accessible, fairly recent, nontechnical, and theologically conservative. It should also include materials on Bible study methods.

Three books will prove to be especially helpful in providing information on such matters as authorship, occasion for writing, date of composition, and integrity of the Old Testament text: Gleason Archer's *A Survey of Old Testament Introduction*, rev. ed. (Chicago: Moody, 1973); Roland K. Harrison's *Introduction to the Old Testament* (Grand Rapids: Eerdmans, 1969); and Merrill F. Unger's *Introductory Guide to the Old Testament* (Grand Rapids; Zondervan, 1951).

Such issues as inspiration and accuracy of the text of the Old Testament are discussed in a helpful way in Rene Pache's *The Inspiration and Authority of Scripture* (Chicago: Moody, 1969); Clark Pinnock's *Biblical Revelation* (Chicago: Moody, 1971); R. Laird Harris' *Inspiration and Canonicity of the Bible* (Grand Rapids: Zondervan, 1957); and Norman Geisler and William Nix's *General Introduction to the Bible*, rev. ed. (Chicago: Moody, 1986).

Five excellent survey books deserve careful attention. The best full-length conservative survey of the Old Testament is *The Old Testament Speaks* by Samuel J. Schultz, 3rd ed. (New York: Harper & Row, 1980). A more thematic or topical treatment is found in Eugene H. Merrill's *Kingdom of Priests* [a history of Old Testament Israel] (Grand Rapids: Baker Book House, 1996). Another good discussion of Old Testament history is *A Survey of Israel's History* by Leon Wood, rev. by David O'Brien (Grand Rapids: Zondervan, 1986).

Note also John J. Davis and John C. Whitcomb, *A History of Israel* (Grand Rapids: Baker Book House, 1980) and Walter C. Kaiser, Jr., *A History of Israel* (Nashville: Broadman & Holman,

1998). Hobart Freeman has rendered a great service to students of Old Testament prophecy with his *An Introduction to the Old Testament Prophets* (Chicago: Moody, 1968). A newer one-volume source of information on the Old Testament is Peter C. Craigie's *The Old Testament: Its Background, Growth, and Content* (Nashville: Abingdon, 1987).

Three of the better one-volume Bible commentaries of note are the *New Bible Commentary*, edited by D. Guthrie and others, 3rd ed. (Grand Rapids: Eerdmans, 1970); *The Wycliffe Bible Commentary*, edited by Everett F. Harrison and Charles F. Pfieffer (Chicago: Moody, 1962); and *The Bible Knowledge Commentary: Old Testament*, edited by John F. Walvoord and Roy B. Zuck (Wheaton, IL: Victor Books, 1985).

Several publishers are producing inexpensive paperbound commentaries on individual books of the Bible. Note, for instance, Baker Book House's *Shield* series, Moody Press's *Everyman's Bible Commentary* series, and Zondervan Publishing House's *Bible Study Commentary* series, now out of print.

Of course, Bible students should learn to study the Bible for themselves and not depend exclusively on commentaries produced by others. Materials of help in this regard are *Effective Bible Study* by Howard F. Vos (Grand Rapids: Zondervan, 1956); *Independent Bible Study* by Irving Jensen, rev. ed. (Chicago: Moody, 1991); Bible Self-Study Guides begun by Grace Saxe and revised and continued by Irving Jensen (Chicago: Moody) and the Teach Yourself the Bible series by Keith L. Brooks and others (Chicago: Moody). Both the Saxe-Jensen and Brooks series are paperbound and consist of separate titles on individual books of the Old Testament. In addition, Irving Jensen has produced a *Survey of the Old Testament* (Chicago: Moody, 1978), which applies Bible study methods to the entire Old Testament.

A book that discusses the literary structure of the Old Testament is Leland Ryken's *How to Read the Bible as Literature* (Grand Rapids: Zondervan, 1985).

PART

IV

Between the
Testaments

When There Was No Word from the Lord: The Four Hundred Silent Years

THE Old Testament closes with the Persians in control of Palestine and all other lands where Jews lived. The New Testament opens with the Romans in charge in Palestine and the rest of the Mediterranean rim. A Sassanid Persian Empire ruled eastern regions where some descendants of exiled Jews remained. The period between the Old and New Testaments is often called "the four hundred silent years"—aptly named so far as biblical revelation is concerned, for no inspired writer took up his pen between the days of Malachi (c. 435 B.C.) and the founding of the Christian church. But to the historian these were anything but silent centuries, and the New Testament student needs to know what went on then in order to understand better the unfolding of the New Testament drama.

PRESERVATION IN CAPTIVITY

That the Jews survived at all as a separate people during the Babylonian captivity is nothing short of a miracle. An enslaved people torn from their homeland, they could well have concluded that their God had deserted them. Tempted by the allurements of the brilliant civilization of Babylon, they might easily have succumbed to a process of assimilation. Militating against such assimilation, however, was, first, the fact that for the most part the Jews settled in cohesive groups. Second, many priests and Levites had been carried off in the deportations from Canaan. They knew the Law and a great many of them could read and write. No doubt they rallied their people with a prophetic message of hope; probably they also reminded them that they had gone into captivity as a punishment for idolatry and that they should not now succumb to a worship of the pagan gods enshrined in their imposing temples. Moreover, apparently most of the Jews who had been carried off in captivity came from the upper classes, and they were more conversant with the religious institutions of Israel and the claims of God than the masses in the rural areas.

An important new institution that evidently originated in Babylon during the captivity was the synagogue (derived from the Greek meaning "to bring or come together"). Initially referring to a gathering for any purpose, but especially for worship, it also came to include the building in which such meetings were held. The origin of the synagogue seems especially to have been connected with the event mentioned in Ezekiel 14:1: "Now some of the elders of Israel came to me and sat before me" (NKJV, cf. Ezekiel 20:1), presumably for instruction and inspiration. As it developed, the synagogue served a threefold function: worship, education, and some governmental role in the community. Thus it provided a cohesive and self-perpetuating element for the covenant people. Judaism itself became less tied to physical institutions and rituals and more spiritual and abstract.

PERSIAN AUSPICES

As is clear from the discussion of Ezra, Nehemiah, and Esther earlier in this book, the restoration of the Jews to Palestine after the Babylonian captivity occurred under Persian auspices. Cyrus the Great authorized the return of the first contingent of Jews during the first year of his rule over Babylon (539–38 B.C.). Other groups returned later, but evidently only a fraction of those living in exile ever went back to Palestine. Those exiles, who had been the more resourceful and better educated upper classes, by dint of hard work and prospering under divine blessing, soon enjoyed living standards in Mesopotamia superior to what they had known in Palestine. After a couple of generations of material success in Mesopotamia, they were not willing to undergo the hardships of relocating in their homeland. But of course many did go back, and they finished the temple in the days of Darius I (515 B.C.) and the walls of Jerusalem during the reign of Artaxerxes I (444 B.C.).

By the time of Artaxerxes' death in 424 B.C., the governorship of Nehemiah and the prophetic ministry of Malachi had almost certainly ceased and Old Testament history had come to an end. Judah was a small unit in the fifth satrapy or province of the Persian Empire, able to develop its unique characteristics in relative security. In general, the Persians seem to have taken a greater interest in the welfare of their subjects than other rulers of the ancient Near East, and the Jews appear to have enjoyed a considerable amount of religious freedom under their administration during the following century.

Though the Jews gradually enhanced their position in Judah, they never were able to dominate all of Palestine. In the central part of the country Samaritans held forth. These people were a mixture of Jews and Gentile colonists the Assyrians had brought in after conquering the Northern Kingdom (723–22 B.C.; cf. 2 Kings 17:24–29). Not only were they racially mixed but they also combined elements of paganism with Hebrew beliefs and practices.

During the captivity they were able to assert a fair amount of economic and political dominance in Judah. Naturally they resented a return of the Jews from Babylonia, and the antipathy between Jews and Samaritans that developed during the restoration of Judah (see especially Nehemiah) continued on into the New Testament period (see John 4). The Samaritans built their own temple on Mount Gerizim, about thirty-one miles north of Jerusalem.

Space does not permit discussion of all the colonies of Hebrews scattered from Egypt to Persia during the intertestamental period, and it is not important to this survey to try to do so. But one group is of some interest. Located on the island of Elephantine in the Nile River at Aswan, these Jews had built a temple that local Egyptians razed to the ground, and the Jews then sought help from the Persian governor of Judea and the Samaritans (in a letter dated 407 B.C.) in rebuilding it. Not only did those Jews have their own temple, but they also seem to have worshiped deities other than Yahweh. It is possible, however, that they merely worshiped aspects of the nature of God in the titles they employed for deity. It is not clear when this colony was established in Egypt, but one theory is that Ashurbanipal brought them from the Northern Kingdom after Assyrian destruction of Samaria and left them as a garrison after his conquest of Egypt in 667 B.C.[1] A study of this colony is interesting from the standpoint of a possible mixture of pagan elements in worship where the separatist spirit of an Ezra or Nehemiah was not present.

ALEXANDER THE GREAT

Alexander's Conquests

Ever since Darius I of Persia crossed the Hellespont and invaded Greece in 512 B.C., Greeks and Persians had been at war, or at least looking over their shoulders to see what the other side was up to. Finally Philip II of Macedon planned a Panhellenic war against the

Persians in an effort to remove them from the Greek sphere of operations once and for all. When Philip fell to an assassin's dagger in 336, he was unable to realize his life dream and his mantle fell on his young son Alexander. After establishing himself as head of state Alexander launched the long-anticipated attack on Persia in 334 B.C. The size of his army has been estimated at 48,000 with about 16,000 other personnel and about 6,000 cavalry horses.[2] But Alexander had more than military concerns. Schooled at the feet of Aristotle, he was impressed with the superior culture of Athens and sought to internationalize that culture. Becoming something of an apostle of Hellenism, he took along with his army historians, scientists, and geographers.

Alexander conquered the Persian Empire with lightning speed. Crossing the Hellespont in 334, he soon won a battle at the nearby Granicus River, which opened up all of Asia Minor to him. The following year he defeated the Persians at Issus, at the eastern end of Asia Minor. During 332, after stubborn resistance at Tyre and Gaza, he secured the eastern end of the Mediterranean and went on in 331 to take Egypt and then to win a single victory over Darius III at Gaugamela in northern Mesopotamia. Before that, Darius had offered to give Alexander the western half of the empire, but the conqueror turned him down. It is not at all clear what Alexander had in mind when he attacked Persia, beyond a desire to remove the Persians from access to the Greek world; but he soon discovered that he could take the entire Persian Empire if he persevered. During the year after Gaugamela Alexander pursued Darius eastward, finally coming upon his corpse after attendants had assassinated him.

How Alexander was able to take this largest of all empires of western Asia in ancient times is no great mystery. He was a commander of superior generalship, with slightly superior weapons and body armor. The morale of his forces was high. The Persian Empire itself was in a moribund condition, but even in good times the Persians faced serious problems in maintaining their control. They were perhaps only one-sixtieth of the population of their empire, which consisted of a large variety of peoples. What had brought them to power in the first place was the fact that the independent spirit of Near Eastern peoples had been broken by generations of imperialism, and the Persians needed only to defeat ruling minorities whose armies consisted largely of mercenaries. Now it was the turn of the Macedonians, with their fierce nationalistic spirit, to unseat a Persian ruling minority.

As Alexander the Great came through Palestine in 332, Jerusalem surrendered to him without a struggle, and the outlying towns apparently also received him with kindness. Josephus tells a dramatic account of how the high priest, Jaddua, went out in procession with the priests and many of the populace to welcome Alexander. The conqueror then reportedly offered sacrifice in the temple and promised to permit the Jews in Judah and the eastern provinces to practice their religion without interference.[3] Though this account is frequently considered to be unhistorical, at the least it reflects the generally good relations between Alexander and the Jews.

Alexander's Legacy

Many view Alexander as just a great conqueror. He was that, and if his only achievement was destroying the Persian Empire in four or five years, he would be remembered as "the great" for that reason alone. But Alexander's legacy to world civilization was much more significant than that. He universalized the Hellenic culture of Athens and the tongue of that culture, contributing to the rise of Koine Greek, the common Greek of subsequent centuries. When the Romans later fell under the spell of this Hellenistic culture, the entire Mediterranean world had a single culture and a single language. Thus, during the first Christian century, Paul and others who sought to reach the Mediterranean basin with the gospel of Christ did not have to learn new languages or pass through stages of culture shock. They knew instinctively how to evangelize that world. Alexander's openness and tolerance toward native cultures also contributed to Greek cultural absorption of Oriental culture. Thus an internationalism and cosmopolitanism developed in the Hellenistic world that was perhaps even greater than during the Roman period.

Alexander's foundation of Greek cities at strategic points was also destined to change his world. His cities served as centers for political administration, military control (because they were garrison centers), and cultural diffusion, for they were places from which a gospel ("good news") of Hellenism could spread to the surrounding, supposedly "unenlightened" countryside. The use of city foundations to hold down a whole region and create a common culture for that region was taken up by Alexander's successors in the East and by Rome in later centuries. Using this contribution of Alexander, the apostle Paul developed an urban strategy for the spread of the gospel of salvation. His eighteen-month stay at Corinth and his two-to-three-year stint at Ephesus are cases in point. Actually Alexander's successors founded more cities than he did; he lived long enough to establish only about a dozen of them. Queen of his foundations was Alexandria in Egypt, which dominated the eastern Mediterranean world politically, culturally, and economically for some 650 years. Alexander was also significant for his favorable treatment of the Jews, a practice followed by his successors in Egypt and Syria.

SUCCESSORS OF ALEXANDER:
PTOLEMIES AND SELEUCIDS

Ptolemies

After Alexander died in Babylon in 323 B.C., members of his inner circle struggled to take over his empire. Soon it became clear that no one of them could succeed in doing so. Details of the contest are not important for this account. Suffice it to say that, of the group, Seleucus, who controlled Syria and points East, and Ptolemy, who dominated Egypt, both fought hard for control of the buffer region of Palestine. From 323 to 301 B.C. this strategic land bridge passed back and forth between them, but finally Ptolemy gained control in 301 B.C. and his descendants held it for a century.

Though the history of the period is not well documented, apparently the Ptolemies were generally well-disposed toward the Jews and allowed them considerable religious and cultural freedom. A large community of Jews gathered in Alexandria and those people gradually forgot their Hebrew. Since Greek had now become their mother tongue, they proceeded to translate the Old Testament into Greek. This version, called the Septuagint, gradually came into being between 250 and 150 B.C. and was destined to serve as the Bible of the early church. More than the Greek language rubbed off on the Jews, however. Some of them also bought into the Hellenistic thought patterns and turned their backs on aspects of their supernatural faith. Of course the cultural impact of Hellenism made inroads among the Jews of Palestine as well as those of Egypt.

Seleucids

When Ptolemy IV of Egypt died in 203 B.C., the land was torn with rebellion and unrest. The accession of Ptolemy V to the throne as a young boy did not help matters any. Antiochus III of Syria took advantage of the situation and scored important victories against Egyptian forces at Gaza in 200 and Banias in 198 B.C. With the latter, Palestine came under the control of the Syrians or Seleucids. When Antiochus subsequently came to Jerusalem, the inhabitants reportedly gave him a cordial welcome, apparently hoping to exploit this new relationship to their advantage.

Developments in the West were destined to complicate and even destroy this new relationship, however. The Romans had worsted Carthage in the Second Punic War; and after the final battle at Zama (202 B.C.), Hannibal, the famous Carthaginian general, had fled to the court of Antiochus. There he sought to stir up trouble for Rome and persuaded Antiochus to invade Greece. Roman forces repelled Antiochus' advance, threw him back into Asia Minor, and defeated him decisively at the battle of Magnesia in 190 B.C. This defeat cost him much territory in Asia Minor, the surrender of his navy, and a huge indemnity. As part of the guarantee of payment, Antiochus' younger son, the future Antiochus IV, was taken to Rome as a hostage. During his twelve years there he gained great respect for Roman power and Roman (i.e., Hellenistic) ways. Collection of funds to pay off the indemnity to Rome rested heavily on the Jews, along with other peoples of the Seleucid kingdom. And, as sovereigns, the Seleucid kings now reserved the right to appoint the high priests of the Jews and through them to maintain Seleucid sovereignty over their people. Both actions were destined to create serious friction between the Jews and the Syrian monarchy.

This friction need not have brought on a Jewish revolt, however, if the Jews had remained united. As a matter of fact they did not, and the divisions not only provided an opportunity for the Seleucids to exploit the differences but also seemed to require that they take action to maintain order. When the Seleucids occupied Palestine, they initially upheld Jewish customs and exempted the temple in Jerusalem from taxes. Onias III, an orthodox Jew, served as high priest. By the time Antiochus IV (175–163 B.C.) came to the Seleucid throne, however, many Jews had become so Hellenized that they wanted change in the religious system. At that point apparently some accused Onias of Ptolemaic leanings, and his brother Joshua paid a huge bribe for appointment as high priest and the right to build a gymnasium in Jerusalem (2 Maccabees 4:8–10).[4] Taking the Greek name Jason, Joshua proceeded to build the gymnasium, to introduce athletic competition in the nude, and to encourage other actions totally repugnant to orthodox Jews. The orthodox organized under the name *Hasidim* (pious), a movement from which the Pharisees eventually arose.

After three years in office (175–172 B.C.) Jason was deposed by a close associate, Menelaus, who outbid him in the bribery game (2 Maccabees 4:23–26), and Jason fled to Transjordan. Menelaus proved to be an even more thoroughgoing Hellenist than Jason, and more unscrupulous as well. He helped himself to temple assets to pay off his debt to Antiochus. Jason waited impatiently in Transjordan for a chance to regain his lost position. Finally, in 168 B.C., when Antiochus was busy with a military campaign in Egypt, Jason raised a force and attacked Jerusalem. The disorders that followed evidently were clashes primarily between those loyal to Jason and Menelaus and between the pro-Egyptian and pro-Syrian factions, but Antiochus chose to regard them as open rebellion against his rule. He sent a force to Jerusalem that broke down the walls, destroyed many houses, slaughtered countless inhabitants, and built a fortified citadel for a Syrian garrison.

Then, in 167 B.C., realizing that Jewish opposition against him rose ultimately from their religion, Antiochus decided to destroy Judaism. He made such religious observances as circumcision and Sabbath keeping and the possession of a copy of the Law punishable by death. The temple was dedicated to the Olympian Zeus, and it was desecrated with a sacrifice of swine on the altar. Worship of heathen gods became compulsory.

THE MACCABEAN REVOLT

Response to these severe measures was predictable. Some capitulated; some offered passive resistance; and some decided to fight for their faith. The spark that touched off open revolt was struck at the mountain village of Modin, west of Jerusalem. There a priest named Mattathias lived with his five sons. When a royal officer came to town to enforce the decree requiring the Jews to perform pagan sacrifice, Mattathias killed a Jew who was about to offer sacrifice, as well as the officer. Then he fled to the hills with his sons, there to conduct guerrilla warfare. The insurgents raided towns and villages, killing Syrian officers and Hellenized Jews who supported them. A few months after the beginning of the struggle Mattathias died, but before he did he saw to it that the mantle of leadership fell on his third son Judas, "the Maccabee" (interpreted to mean "the hammer").

Under Judas

Judas received increasing numbers of recruits from the towns and villages. Both because the Syrians underestimated the valor of Judas and the power of the Maccabees and because they had to deal with a revolt in Parthia to the east, they sent fairly small and inferior armies against the Jews. When Judas defeated them, the Syrians sent stronger forces. A particularly important victory at Emmaus permitted Judas to march on Jerusalem. As he entered the city, Menelaus and his supporters fled and Judas took everything but the fortified citadel. He was able to cleanse the temple, where for three years sacrifices had been offered to the Olympian Zeus, on the twenty-fifth of Chislev (December), 165 B.C. The day has been celebrated ever since as the Feast of Hanukkah or Rededication or Lights.[5]

All did not go well for the Jews, however. Lysias, commander of the Syrian forces, now descended on Judah, defeated Judas near Jerusalem, and then besieged the capital. But in the Maccabees' blackest hour a sudden reversal occurred. With news of an enemy force marching on the Syrian capital of Antioch, Lysias now offered peace, repeal of the laws proscribing Judaism, removal of Menelaus from the high priesthood, and amnesty for Judas and his followers. The Hasidim accepted the terms because their goal of religious liberty had been achieved. Judas, not satisfied with anything less than full political liberty as well, left the city with a small force. Soon the new high priest, Alcimus, seized and executed a number of Hasidim, and Judas renewed the war. With greatly reduced forces, he was defeated and killed on the battlefield in 161 B.C. To put the Maccabean conflict in proper perspective, it is necessary to recognize that the Jews were not united. The Maccabees drew much of their support from the rural peasants and faced the animosity of the well-to-do Hellenizing priests of Jerusalem. The latter won over many of the followers of Judas so he faced the Syrians in a much weakened position and suffered defeat at their hands.

Under Jonathan

Judas' younger brother Jonathan now became leader of the band of Maccabeans, who maintained themselves virtually as freebooters in the Wilderness of Tekoa, as David had, and in Transjordan. Jonathan constantly augmented his forces. Ultimately, the Syrian general, Bacchides, found it impossible to destroy Jonathan and made peace with him in 158 B.C. Thus, during the following five years Jonathan was able to consolidate his power. Meanwhile, the Seleucids, through their dynastic quarrels, proceeded to commit national suicide and gave Jonathan a chance to win by diplomacy what Judas had not been able to accomplish by force of arms.

In the struggle between the pretender Balas Alexander and Demetrius I (after 153 B.C.), Jonathan received generous offers from both sides. The latter withdrew almost all Syrian garrisons from Judea, and the former appointed him military and civil governor of Judea. Jonathan threw in his lot with Balas, who killed Demetrius I in 150 B.C. When Balas was assassinated five years later, Jonathan was strong enough to stand up to the Syrian Demetrius II. His brother Simon became military governor of coastal Palestine from Tyre to the Egyptian border. Although a general of Balas' killed Jonathan in 143 B.C., the Maccabean cause was too well established to be snuffed out. Simon rushed to Jerusalem and took over leadership of the nationalist movement and gained independence of the Jews from Syria the following year.

THE HASMONEANS

With Simon, the Hasmonean line took over rule of the Jews and held sway until the Roman conquest in 63 B.C. The name *Hasmonean* is thought to be derived from an ancestor of the Maccabeans named Asmoneus. In 141 B.C. the Jews conferred on Simon and his descendants permanent authority as ruling high priests (1 Maccabees 14:25–49), and the Roman Senate recognized him as a friendly independent ruler (1 Maccabees 14:16–19, 24; 15:15–24). In international affairs, for the next eighty years the Romans valued the Hasmonean dynasty as a counterbalance to the Seleucid state. Domestically, the Hasmoneans depended on the aristocratic Sadducean party with its power base in the Temple. Partially Hellenized, this sect usually contested with the Pharisees— with their power base especially in the synagogue—for control of the public at large. The Hasmoneans gradually increased their military strength, expanded their borders in all directions, and transformed their body politic from a religious community into a secular state on Greek lines.

Simon

Simon (142–135 B.C.), as noted, won for himself and his posterity permanent authority as ruling high priests and the recognition of Rome. Moreover, he secured Joppa as a Jewish harbor and conquered Gazara (Gezer), Beth-zur, and the Acra or citadel in Jerusalem where Seleucids had continued to hold out. When in 138 B.C. Simon rejected the demands of Antiochus VII for return of these conquests to Syria, Antiochus attacked the Jewish state. Simon's sons repulsed the Syrian, and he did not renew the attack during Simon's lifetime. As with other sons of Mattathias, however, Simon also met a violent death. The governor of Jericho assassinated him and two of his sons in 135 B.C. But John Hyrcanus, a third son, was in Gezer at the time and escaped to become the next high priest (1 Maccabees 16:18).

John Hyrcanus

John Hyrcanus (135–104 B.C.) began his reign fighting for his life and his kingdom but ended it with the Jewish state at the height of its power. Antiochus VII of Syria attacked Hyrcanus at the beginning of his reign, devastated Judea, forced the surrender of Jerusalem and the payment of a huge indemnity, and then compelled Hyrcanus and a Jewish army to accompany the Syrian in a renewed war against the Parthians on his eastern front. But there Antiochus met more than his match and committed suicide to avoid capture (129 B.C.). The lifting of the strong hand of Antiochus from Syrian affairs was very beneficial to Hyrcanus; for the next several decades Syria was convulsed by dynastic struggles.

Hyrcanus was avowedly expansionistic. First he reestablished control of the coastal cities of Palestine and promoted the development of Jewish commerce. Then he conquered east of the Jordan and followed that with the capture of Shechem and the destruction of the Samaritan temple on Mount Gerizim. Next he subjugated the Idumeans (Edomites) in the south and forced them to accept Judaism and be circumcised.

Internally the Jewish state changed significantly too. It transformed itself from a religious community into a secular state. Though the Hellenistic party as a separate group disappeared with Syrian interference in Jewish affairs, the Sadducees perpetuated its views, as the Pharisees perpetuated the views of the Hasidim. Those two parties, so prominent in the New Testament, first surfaced during Hyrcanus' reign. Hyrcanus publicly aligned himself with the Sadducees, but he was safely Jewish (reflective of his Hasidic background), having brought both the Samaritans and the Edomites to heel. Thus he did not unduly upset the more conservative elements of the realm. But his sons received an education in Greek culture and tended to repudiate the Pharisees.

Aristobulus

Aristobulus (104–103 B.C.), the eldest of those sons, emerged as victor in the dynastic struggle that erupted after the death of Hyrcanus. Then he proceeded to imprison his brothers and his mother to guarantee his position as chief of state. It is said that his mother starved to death in prison, and he unjustly executed his brother Antigonus on the supposed involvement in a plot against him. Aside from these family tragedies, he apparently ruled well. He continued the expansionist policies of his father and extended Jewish rule into Galilee. He also continued the Hasmonean tendency to transform the religious community into a secular state, adopting the title *Philhellene* ("love of things Greek") and taking the title of king.

Alexander Jannaeus

When Aristobulus died from drink and disease, his widow, Salome Alexandra, released his brothers from prison and married the eldest, Alexander Jannaeus (103–76 B.C.). Jannaeus continued the expansionistic policies, of his predecessors, and by the time he died he had extended the borders of the Jewish state to include almost all the territory that Solomon had ruled. Jannaeus was almost constantly at war, however, and more than once suffered almost total disaster. Defeated by Ptolemy Lathyrus, he was saved by the forces of Cleopatra III, who headed another faction in the Egyptian government (100 B.C.). Suffering complete destruction of his army at the hands of Obadas, the Nabatean king (94 B.C.), he faced a violent rebellion when he returned to Jerusalem without his army. This rebellion had also been occasioned by Jannaeus' violation of temple ritual at the Feast of Tabernacles. At that time the crowd had assaulted him for his impiety and he had called in troops to restore order, with a resultant death of a large number (Josephus said 6,000) of defenseless people. The rebels called on Demetrius III of Syria to champion their cause. It is sometimes stated categorically that the Pharisees, usually pacifistic, were responsible for the rebellion and the Syrian alliance, but it is not certain that the Pharisees had instigated the violence. At any rate, a rebellion did take place and the Syrian king did decisively defeat Jannaeus, forcing him to flee to the Judean hills. At that point, apparently many Jews began to fear Syrian annexation of Palestine, and 6,000 Jews transferred their loyalty to Jannaeus, enabling him to regain the throne. After he had reestablished his control, Jannaeus hunted down his enemies and crucified about eight hundred of them.[6] Subsequently Jannaeus suffered defeat at the hands of the Nabatean king Aretas, but again managed to restore his personal and national power.

Salome Alexandra

When Jannaeus died, his widow Salome Alexandra (76–67 B.C.) succeeded him on the throne, as she had when Aristobulus, her first husband, died. Because she was a woman, she could not exercise the high priesthood. Her eldest son, Hyrcanus II, filled that position. Her more able second son, Aristobulus II, received command of the army. The Pharisees, who had enjoyed little influence under earlier Hasmonean rulers, now played an important role in the government and for the first time were admitted to the Sanhedrin. This change in their fortunes seems due in part to the fact that Alexandra's brother was the famous Pharisee, Simon ben Shetach. In general, Alexandra's reign was peaceful and prosperous. The only military action of her reign, against Damascus, was unsuccessful. She was saved from potentially disastrous invasion by the king of Armenia by bribing him and especially by Roman attack on his domain. When she died at the age of seventy-three, the days of Jewish independence were nearing an end. Though Jannaeus had established control over an extended territory, his hold upon it was somewhat tenuous (as implied above), and Roman power loomed on the horizon.

As a matter of fact, it was sparring between Alexandra's two sons that gave the Romans a chance to add Palestine to their empire. Hyrcanus II, the elder son and legitimate successor, was weak and incompetent. Aristobulus II, the younger son, was more aggressive and had control of his father's veteran troops. Three months after the death of Alexandra, Aristobulus managed to defeat the forces of Hyrcanus at Jericho, and the latter gave up all rights to the high priesthood and the crown and retired to private life.

All might have gone well for Aristobulus, had it not been for the ambition of Antipater, military governor of Idumea and father of Herod the Great. Antipater saw that he could manipulate the weak Hyrcanus but had no future under a strong leader like Aristobulus. So he arranged with Aretas, king of the Nabateans (with their capital at Petra), to put Hyrcanus on the throne in exchange for some towns on the Nabatean frontier. Meanwhile the Roman general Pompey had become involved in conquests in the East, in Pontus and Armenia. In 66 B.C. one of his lieutenants visited Judea, where he heard appeals from representatives of both brothers and made some tentative decisions, pending the later actions of Pompey. When Pompey came to Damascus in 63 B.C., he heard appeals from Hyrcanus and Aristobulus and the Jewish people, who wanted abolition of the monarchy and return to priestly government. He promised a decision after a campaign against the Nabateans.

When Pompey's general, Gabinius, returned, he found that Aristobulus had locked the gates of Jerusalem against him. Gabinius then issued an arrest warrant for Aristobulus. Presently the followers of Hyrcanus opened the city gates, and Pompey launched a siege of Aristobulus' forces holding out on the Temple hill. When the battle was over Palestine passed under Roman rule. All non-Jewish areas (the Mediterranean coastlands, Transjordan, and Samaria) were detached from the Jewish state, and what was left was placed under the rule of Hyrcanus II as high priest. Thus the kingship was abolished, as the representatives of the Jews had asked, and Hyrcanus (with Antipater at his elbow) controlled the Jewish state, at the pleasure of the Romans. Aristobulus was taken to Rome, where he marched in Pompey's triumph, along with many Jews who were sold into slavery in the capital. In later years, as they won their freedom, they became the nucleus of the Jewish community there.[7]

Roman Rule in Palestine

After Palestine passed under Roman rule in 63 B.C., it became embroiled in Roman politics. So over the following decades there were factions loyal to Hyrcanus, Aristobulus, Pompey, Julius Caesar, Mark Antony, Augustus, Herod the Great, and others. It is very difficult even for the best informed scholar to follow accurately the history of the period, and the task becomes confusing and virtually impossible for the general student. Some details come clear, however. First, Hyrcanus II continued as high priest and ruler of the Jews during the confused period from 63 to 40 B.C. During almost all those years, Antipater was the real power in the state and faithfully carried out Roman policies. Second, the Aristobulus faction did not easily give up trying to regain power. Aristobulus' son Alexander stirred up rebellions in 57, 56, and 55 B.C. and both Aristobulus and Alexander were assassinated by Pompey or his supporters when they tried to help Julius Caesar in 49 B.C. Third, after Pompey's defeat at the hands of Julius Caesar in 48 B.C., Hyrcanus and Antipater became loyal supporters of Caesar. In appreciation, Caesar confirmed their political position in Judah, added some of the Mediterranean coastland in Palestine to the Jewish province, and showed numerous favors to Jews of the Dispersion, many of which continued under subsequent rulers. Fourth, after the assassination of Julius Caesar (44 B.C.), Hyrcanus and now Herod gave their loyalty to Mark Antony, who appointed Herod and his brother Phasael tetrarchs of Judea (41 B.C.), with the approval of Hyrcanus.

Fifth, at that point the Parthians on Rome's eastern frontier took advantage of her political and military weakness and invaded Syria and Palestine. They made Antigonus, son of Aristobulus II, king and high priest of the Jews (40–37 B.C.). The Jews hailed the Parthians as deliverers from the Romans, and all classes supported the rule of Aristobulus. When Hyrcanus and Phasael went to negotiate with the Parthian king, he threw them in prison, where Phasael committed suicide; Hyrcanus was carried off to Babylonia. Herod put his family in the fortress of Masada for protection and went to Rome to get help from Antony. He was appointed king of the Jews in 40 B.C. Of course the Romans counterattacked. Herod managed to rescue his family and with Roman help eventually to take much of Palestine. After the fall of Jerusalem (37 B.C.), Antony ordered the execution of Antigonus.

Herod the Great

Now Herod could become king in fact and ruled until his death in 4 B.C.[8] He remained loyal to Antony until Octavian (Augustus) defeated him (31 B.C.). Then Herod offered his total loyalty to Augustus as he had given it to Antony, and the Roman emperor accepted.[9] Augustus gave Herod additional territories along the Mediterranean coast and Jericho, all of which had belonged to Cleopatra, and later wild regions east of the Jordan. Herod held the position of an allied king, with local autonomy but subject to Rome in foreign affairs. Rome used him like other allied kings to pacify a recalcitrant frontier province and prepare it for a stage when Rome could directly appoint governors. Those direct appointees ruled Judea in the days of Jesus and Paul, when such governors as Pilate and Felix and Festus held the reins of government. His pacification of territory east of the Jordan also made possible organization of the Roman province of Arabia.

Herod also served the Romans as an agent for the spread of Hellenism, which he greatly admired. Rome sought to bring unity to the empire through the inculcation of a single Greco-Roman culture and through establishment of the emperor cult. Herod's outstanding city constructions in Palestine were Samaria and Caesarea. Samaria he renamed Sebaste in honor of Augustus (Greek, *Sebastos*) and built there a temple to Augustus, an agora with a Roman basilica, a Greek-style colonnaded main street, and more. About twenty-five miles south of the modern city of Haifa, he constructed the great city of Caesarea (22–9 B.C.), about half the size of Manhattan Island, again named in honor of Augustus Caesar. This was a thoroughly Greco-Roman city flung down on the coast of Palestine. Its temple to Augustus, hippodrome, theater, magnificent artificial harbor and port facilities, and other accouterments qualified it to be a first-class Roman capital of Palestine. In Jerusalem he built a theater and amphitheater.

A complete list of Herod's building activities would tire even the most patient reader. Examples include his reconstruction of Antipatris, northeast of modern Tel Aviv; the fortresses of Machaerus in Transjordan, of Masada along the Dead Sea, and the Herodeion, south of Bethlehem; and the palace complex at Jericho and his great palace in the western part of Jerusalem. His zeal for Hellenism also led him to get involved in numerous building projects all over the eastern Mediterranean—in Rhodes, Greece, Lebanon, and Syria. The glory of Antioch when Paul launched his three missionary journeys from there was due in part to the beneficence of Herod.

But of course pride of place in all his building activities goes to the temple in Jerusalem. Reconstruction began in 20 B.C. and continued for forty-six years, to the days of Jesus' ministry on earth (John 2:20), but was not actually completed until about A.D. 64— just a few years before it was destroyed in A.D. 70. This was especially a propaganda effort to win support of the Jewish populace, but also reflected Herod's love of grandeur. The work proceeded in such a way as not to hinder the temple ritual, and priests and Levites did much of the work. A magnificent structure, it was arranged in terraces, with the temple itself at the highest point. The outer and lower court was the court of the Gentiles, then came the court of the women and the court of the Israelites, and finally, the temple precincts.

While the Romans considered Herod to be an able vassal king, the Jews never accepted or respected this Idumean "half-Jew," and considered him a tyrant, a bloodthirsty oppressor who extorted all he could from the people. He was vengeful, jealous, and suspicious of intrigue or conspiracy. These defects in his personality led to his execution of one of his wives (Mariamne) and three of his sons. This jealous insecurity also led him to kill the infants of Bethlehem at the time of the birth of Christ in an effort to destroy the "king of the Jews" so He would not usurp the throne.

The Later Herods

The final revision of Herod's will divided his kingdom among three of his sons: Archelaus was to be king of Judea, Antipas the tetrarch of Galilee and Perea, and Philip the tetrarch of Trachonitis, Batanea, and Gaulanitis (the area northeast of the Sea of Galilee). After some consideration, Augustus approved the division, but made Archelaus ethnarch instead of king. Archelaus proved to be totally unacceptable to the Jews, so Augustus exiled him to Gaul and Judea became a Roman province (A.D. 6–41). Antipas (4 B.C.– A.D. 39) was a clever and vain person; Jesus called him a fox (Luke 13:32). He launched numerous construction projects, including Tiberias on the Sea of Galilee, named for Tiberius Caesar. He is especially noted in Scripture for his execution of John the Baptist. He was finally exiled for a supposed plot against Caligula. Philip (4 B.C.-A.D. 34) apparently ruled justly and well. He built as his capital Caesarea Philippi (Matthew 16:13; Mark 8:27). Herod Agrippa 1, grandson of Mariamne, the Hasmonean wife of Herod the

Great, received from Caligula the tetrarchy of Philip in A.D. 37, with the title of king. Subsequently he received the holdings of the other two sons of Herod and from A.D. 41 to 44 ruled all the territories Herod had controlled. He seems to have been well received by the Pharisees but persecuted Christians (Acts 12). When he died in 44, the emperor Claudius converted the Jewish kingdom into a Roman province, ruled by procurators. Under the procurators relations between the Jews and Romans gradually deteriorated until the outbreak of open hostilities in A.D. 66, which resulted in the destruction of Jerusalem and the temple (A.D. 70).

JEWISH SECTS

A concluding word about sects or factions in Jewish society during New Testament times will help to throw light on the New Testament text.

Pharisees

One of the most prominent groups was the Pharisees, presumably successors of the Hasidim (the Pious), who originated when Antiochus Epiphanes proscribed Judaism (168 B.C.). Zealous for the observance of the Law, the Hasidim fought in the forces of Judas Maccabeus. The Pharisees first appear by name in historical literature in the days of Jonathan (161–143 B.C.).[10] *Pharisee* comes from a word meaning "separated" and may indicate that separation was from the common people, but it more likely signifies separation from the influences of Hellenism.

The Pharisees were sticklers for observance of the law and paid great attention to ceremonial purity, fasting, and Sabbath observance. Concerned with both the written and oral law, they subscribed to the canonicity of the entire Old Testament writings and continued to refine and add to the interpretation of the Scripture.

By the time of Christ they seemed interested in little more than details of law observance, and they developed an inordinate pride in law keeping. Jesus scorned them for their lack of a true love for God and told them that if their desire was to be known for their public show of piety, "they *have* their reward" (Matthew 6:2, 5, 16). In the Greek papyri the construction used here is an economic or legal term, signifying "receipt in full." In other words, for all their efforts they have their reward in full in the esteem in which the public regards them, and they can expect no further reward in the hereafter. The Pharisees were progressive in their constant reinterpretation of the Law and in their seeking proselytes to Judaism and baptizing them, but they were conservative in theology, holding strictly to a supernatural faith. They also kept alive the Messianic hope. Their sphere of influence centered primarily in the synagogue.

Sadducees

While the Pharisees were progressive in relation to the Law, the Sadducees were conservative. They recognized only the Pentateuch as binding on Jews and interpreted it more literally than did the Pharisees. They did not accept the oral law. In theology they were antisupernaturalists, not believing in the resurrection or spirits or angels (Mark 12:18; Luke 20:27). The Sadducees belonged to the wealthy priestly aristocracy and were primarily concerned with temple administration and ritual. They made their peace with the Roman rulers and tended to be influenced by Hellenism. Holding themselves aloof from the masses, they became increasingly unpopular. Because of their theological and social position, the Sadducees were usually at odds as well with the Pharisees. Occasionally the two groups could get together on their opposition to Jesus, however. Because the Sadducees were so closely identified with the affairs of the temple, they passed out of existence soon after its destruction in A.D. 70.

Herodians

The Herodians are a third group or party appearing in the Gospels (Matthew 22:16; Mark 3:6; 12:13) and in Josephus (*Antiquities*, XIV.15.10). Evidently not an organized political party, they were merely adherents or partisans of Herod and his family. In the Gospel references they seem to be influential men who supported Herod Antipas and evidently were loyal to the Roman rule that provided the underpinning for the dynasty.

Zealots

Another group active during the New Testament period were the Zealots. They were an extremist party who followed Judah (Judas) the Galilean, who opposed the Roman census when Judah became a Roman province in A.D. 6. He denied the right of Rome to collect taxes from the Jews and considered it a sin to acknowledge loyalty to Caesar. One of Jesus' disciples, Simon the Zealot, evidently had once been a member of the group. They gained in popularity during the first Christian century and had great influence during the Jewish revolt in A.D. 66 and following.

Essenes

A group that does not appear in the New Testament but which occupied an important place in its background was the Essenes. An ascetic group, they not only sought separation from defilement (as the Pharisees did), but separation from institutional Judaism as well. These people tended to live in monastic communities, to practice community of goods, to engage in the study and copying of Scripture and other religious books, and to live lives of simplicity. Their communities were self-supporting. It is usually assumed that the Qumran community was Essene, but such a view should not be dogmatically held.

That Jesus and His followers had anything in common with the Essenes is highly doubtful. There is no evidence that Christianity was a division of Essenism or that Jesus was initiated into its teachings, as some have claimed. Jesus opposed the legalism and asceticism of the community, did not repudiate the temple services, did not oppose marriage, and had an active ministry to the common people who "heard Him gladly." The faith of Jesus was a vibrant faith for all of society. It was not exclusivistic, nor did it in any way advocate good works or an ascetic lifestyle as a means of gaining God's favor. It met people in the hurts and joys of life. And Jesus apparently had fun with people in their moments of happiness.

Notes

1. Charles F. Pfeiffer, *Between the Testaments* (Grand Rapids: Baker Book House, 1959), p. 57.

2. Donald W. Engels, *Alexander the Great and the Logistics of the Macedonian Army* (Berkeley: University of California Press, 1978), p. 18.

3. Josephus, *Antiquities*, XI.8.4–6.

4. New translations of the intertestamental books of the Maccabees may be found in *The Revised English Bible with the Apocrypha* (Oxford: Oxford University Press, 1989) and in the *New Revised Standard Version* (New York: Oxford University Press, 1989).

5. 1 Maccabees 4:52–59; John 10:22; Josephus, *Antiquities*, XII.7.7.

6. Josephus, *Antiquities of the Jews*, VIII.13.5–14.2.

7. Manumission was easy in Rome and in the empire, and in time freed slaves of a variety of nationalities came to outnumber the native population in Rome and some other places.

8. It is known that the calendar is somewhat in error. Christ was born up to a couple of years before Herod died, perhaps in 6 B.C.

9. A biography of Herod appears in Josephus, *Antiquities*, Books XV-XVII and *Wars* 1:18–33. For other listings see the Bibliography.

10. Josephus, *Antiquities*, XIII.5.9.

FOR FURTHER INTERTESTAMENTAL STUDY

Avi-Yonah, Michael, ed. *The World History of the Jewish People: The Herodian Period*. New Brunswick, New Jersey: Rutgers University Press, 1975.

Bowman, Alan K. *Egypt after the Pharaohs*. Berkeley: University of California Press, 1986.

Cohen, Shaye, J.D. *From the Maccabees to the Mishnah*. Philadelphia: Westminster Press, 1987.

Eban, Abba. *My People: The Story of the Jews*. New York: Behrman House, 1968.

Fairweather, William. *The Background of the Gospels*. 4th ed. Edinburgh: T & T Clark, 1926.

"First and Second Maccabees," *The Revised English Bible with the Apocrypha*. Oxford: Oxford University Press, 1989.

Grant, Michael. *From Alexander to Cleopatra*. New York: Charles Scribner's Sons, 1982.

Jones, A.H.M. *The Herods of Judaea*. Oxford: Clarendon Press, 1938.

Perowne, Stewart. *The Later Herods*. New York: Abingdon Press, 1958.

———. *The Life and Times of Herod the Great*. New York: Abingdon Press, 1956.

Pfeiffer, Charles F. *Between the Testaments*. Grand Rapids: Baker Book House, 1959.

Pfeiffer, Robert H. *History of New Testament Times*. New York: Harper& Brothers, 1949.

Sanders, E.P. *Judaism, Practice and Belief, 63* BCE-66 CE. London: SCM Press, 1992.

Stambaugh, John E. and Balch, David L. *The New Testament in Its Social Environment*. Philadelphia: Westminster Press, 1986.

PART

V

The Life of Jesus

In "the Fullness of the Time": The Resumption of Revelation

FOR over four hundred years God had remained silent. To be sure He may have communicated with individuals who sought Him. And He must have had much to say to angels and to Old Testament saints who were with Him in heaven. But he had delivered no recorded public utterance through a prophet or any other public religious figure. To the world at large and even to faithful, practicing Jews the heavens must have seemed as brass.

Then, finally, in the last days of Herod the Great, God began to speak again. First He came privately and quietly to Zacharias to tell of the birth of John the Baptist and his strategic ministry of preparing for the coming of the Messiah (Luke 1:5–23). Then He revealed Himself to the Virgin Mary (Luke 1:26–38) and to Jesus' legal father Joseph (Matthew 1:20–24) to announce the forthcoming birth of Christ. Subsequently a small group of friends of Zacharias and Elizabeth heard a word from God at the birth of John (Luke

1:57–80), and a larger public experienced the communication of God at the birth of Christ (Luke 2:8–20, 25–38—shepherds, Simeon, Anna, and the magi from the east, Matthew 2:1–12). Then in a crescendo of communication, John the Baptist spoke in thunderous tones to proclaim the coming of the Messiah and repentance and forgiveness of sin (Mark 1:2–11; Luke 3:1–20). Finally, Jesus Himself began His ministry as the full revelation of the Father. Though God in earlier millennia had spoken through the prophets and others in a variety of ways, in the Son came the fullness of revelation: "He is the radiance of His glory and the exact representation of His [the Father's] nature" (Hebrews 1:3, NASB).

The New Testament is an account of God's renewal of revelation to the world and especially of His full revelation in His Son. It tells of the coming of the Son to earth, of His teachings, of His death on the cross to pay for the penalty of human sin, of His resurrection and ascension to heaven, of the founding of His church and the spread of His message throughout the world by means of the preaching of the apostles, and of His predicted personal return to earth to judge and to rule.

WHAT IS THE NEW TESTAMENT?

New Testament is the name given to the second part of the Bible and is a collection of twenty-seven documents written by the disciples of Christ or their contemporaries. Apparently all the authors were Jews, with the exception of Luke.

Testament is the translation of the Greek word *diathēkē* that might better be rendered *covenant*. It denotes an arrangement made by God for human spiritual guidance and benefit. This arrangement is unalterable; men and women may accept it or reject it but cannot change it. Covenant is a common Old Testament word, and several covenants are described in the Old Testament, the most prominent being the Mosaic. While Israel chafed and failed under the Mosaic Covenant, God promised them a "new covenant" (Jeremiah 31:31).

The term *new covenant* appears several times in the New Testament. Jesus first used it when He instituted the ordinance we call the Lord's Supper; by it He sought to call attention to the new basis of communion with God He intended to establish by His death (Luke 22:20; 1 Corinthians 11:25). The apostle Paul also spoke of this new covenant and taught that the old covenant was done away by the work of Christ on the cross (2 Corinthians 3:6, 14). The writer to the Hebrews called attention to God's promise to make a new covenant (Hebrews 8:8). He declared that the new covenant fulfilled and superseded the old covenant because it made provision of a sacrifice adequate to remove all sin through the blood of Christ, who was the Mediator of the new covenant (Hebrews 9:11–15). The detailed description of this new method of God's dealing with humanity is the subject of the twenty-seven books of the New Testament. Perhaps it should be noted that Latin church writers rendered the Greek *diathēkē* by *testamentum*, and from them the use passed into English; so old and new covenants became Old and New Testaments.

How Can a Reader Make Sense out of the New Testament?

On the whole, the New Testament follows a very logical and easily understood arrangement. It begins with the four gospels, which describe the birth, life, death, and resurrection of Christ. These four books provide glimpses into His teaching, give evidences of His deity and humanity, detail His training of His disciples, and generally make it possible for the reader to gain insights into the very nature of God—for Christ came to reveal the Father.

The book of Acts continues the historical narrative where the gospels end. It tells of Christ's return to heaven and His commission to His followers to continue His work. Then it proceeds to describe the founding of the church and its spread through Palestine and Syria. At this point, the apostle Paul assumes special leadership in the church expansion movement, founding congregations in Cyprus, Asia Minor, and Greece. The book of Acts closes with Paul in prison and his ministry largely completed.

Next come the epistles that arise out of the ministry of Paul and are simply letters addressed to churches he founded or to young ministers he tried to encourage and disciple. These letters provide an enduring body of instruction concerning many facets of doctrine, church order, and Christian conduct. Following the Pauline epistles appears a group commonly called the general epistles. James, Peter, or John wrote most of these to individuals or churches to deal with problems that had arisen among early congregations.

The last book, the Revelation, is a prophetic work that details events of the end times. In it the apostle John describes tribulation, a utopian state, judgment of Satan, a final resurrection and judgment, and the establishment of a new heaven and a new earth with the triumphant Lamb as ruler over all. The New Testament begins with a helpless babe in a Bethlehem manger and ends with Christ as the acknowledged King of kings and Lord of lords.

What Does Inspiration of the New Testament Mean?

The inspiration of Scripture (of the Old Testament in particular) is discussed early in this book (see pages 8–12). Regarding specifically the inspiration of the New Testament, it stands or falls with that of the Old Testament, for claims of the New Testament build on the assumption that the Old Testament is truly God's book. Old Testament writers insisted in literally thousands of passages that they were uttering the words of God. The Old Testament was accepted as God's word by Jewry, by Christ, and by the early church. Its prophecies came to fulfillment as attested by history and the New Testament. Historical and archaeological studies have confirmed its historical accuracy at innumerable points.

The New Testament goes on then to build on that concept or foundation of inspiration. The connection is clear from such a passage as 2 Peter 3:2: "That you may be mindful of the words which were spoken before by the holy prophets, *and of the commandment of us*, the apostles of the Lord and Savior" (NKJV). Peter is obviously putting his own writings and those of the other apostles on the same level as the Old Testament and claiming their authority. He extends the same recognition to Paul's writings: "Our beloved brother Paul, according to the wisdom given to him, has written to you, as also *in all his epistles*, speaking in them of these things, in which are some things hard to understand, which untaught and unstable people twist to their own destruction, as they do also the rest of the Scriptures" (2 Peter 3:15, 16, NKJV). Jude claimed that "the words which were spoken before by the apostles of our Lord Jesus Christ" were absolutely reliable (v. 17, NKJV).

The apostle Paul on several occasions asserted that his words were divinely inspired and authoritative. For instance, he told the Corinthians, "the things that I write unto you are the commandments of the Lord" (1 Corinthians 14:37). He wrote the Galatians that he had received his gospel by revelation from Christ (Galatians 1:11, 12). He charged Timothy to "hold the pattern of sound words" which the younger preacher had heard from the apostle as if divinely uttered (2 Timothy 1:13, author's trans.). The apostle John warned against adding to or subtracting from the words of the book of Revelation under pain of being blotted out of the book of life (Revelation 22; 18, 19).

Their hearers accepted the claims of the New Testament writers to their inspiration. Historical portions of the New Testament are completely reliable as Sir William Ramsay and numerous other archaeologists and historians have shown. And especially the truth of the New Testament message has been verified as that truth has made men and women free (John 8:32); the changed lives of believers are the best testimony of all to the divine origin and power of the New Testament.

Before leaving this subject, it is necessary to distinguish inspiration from two other terms. Inspiration has to do with accurate reception and recording of God's truth. Revelation involves communication of God's message, and illumination concerns the Holy Spirit's ministry of giving understanding of truth already revealed (John 14:26).

Are the Text and History of the New Testament Reliable?

Some have argued that it does not matter if the New Testament was inspired in the original writings. Those writings no longer exist and copyists made thousands of mistakes as they reproduced the books of Scripture during the fifteen hundred years before the advent of printing. Scores of textual critics, many of them unsympathetic to evangelical Christianity, have laboriously compared the approximately 2900 biblical manuscripts, the numerous fragments of biblical papyri, and quotations of Scripture in the church fathers. Their conclusions have been that: (1) though many variant readings occur in the New Testament manuscripts, most of them appear in manuscripts considered to be of inferior value in determining a true text and are therefore not important; (2) variant readings do not destroy or pervert one article of faith; (3) not more than one word in a thousand is even subject to serious question; (4) the New Testament has come down to us substantially as it was originally written. (For fuller discussion, see Howard F. Vos, *An Introduction to Bible Archaeology*, rev. ed. [Chicago: Moody, 1983], pp. 45–51.)

It is one thing to verify the New Testament text; it is another to confirm its historical accuracy. Sir William Ramsay (1851–1939) especially led the way in exploring areas where New Testament events had occurred. Starting out with a highly skeptical view of Luke's accuracy in his book of Acts, he became convinced of the absolute authenticity of this account by Luke. (See W. Ward Gasque, *Sir William Ramsay: Archaeologist and New Testament Scholar*

[Grand Rapids: Baker Book House, 1966].) Numerous others have followed in Ramsay's train (and some preceded him), minutely investigating biblical sites in Palestine, Syria, Asia Minor, Cyprus, Greece, and Italy—always with the same results. Investigations have tended to support the New Testament narrative; to date at least they have not proved it wrong. There are still numerous points at which the student encounters problems with historical or geographical items in the New Testament, but successful investigations already conducted give us faith to believe that remaining difficulties may yet be solved.

How Was the New Testament Compiled?

Some people seem to have the impression that a group of church leaders met on a hot summer afternoon many centuries ago to decide what books should be included in the New Testament. Since they were in a hurry to get their job over with, they agreed to all sorts of compromises and came out with the twenty-seven books we now accept. Being imperfect men, they could easily have made mistakes.

No idea is farther from the truth. The process actually was long and involved. Behind the concept of a body of New Testament Scripture stood an already acknowledged collection of Old Testament Scripture. Gradually a new compilation of apostolic literature came into existence. Some of Paul's epistles were probably the earliest written portions of the New Testament. Their recipients apparently accepted these immediately as inspired and authoritative. Paul himself in one of his earliest epistles had told the Thessalonians to see that "this letter be read to all the brethren" (1 Thessalonians 5:27). To the Colossians he gave instructions to have the letter written to them read also in the church of the Laodiceans, and he charged the Colossians to get a copy of the letter written to the Laodiceans (Colossians 4:16). As time went on, churches other than those to which the epistles were originally written sought copies of Paul's letters for their edification and accepted them too as God's word and binding on them. In this fashion Paul's writings came to be collected and to circulate as a group during the second century.

Meanwhile, the apostles or persons closely associated with them were writing the gospels, and they were finding acceptance in the early church. We read in early church literature that the "Memoirs of the Apostles" (the gospels) came to be read in church services alongside portions of the Old Testament as being God's Holy Word. The acceptance of Luke carried with it that of Acts. First John and 1 Peter enjoyed apostolic origin and therefore apostolic authority.

Some books did not travel a smooth road to acceptance, however. Revelation, although written by John, had some difficult language; there was a question about the authorship of Hebrews but certainly not about the inspired nature of its contents; and questions arose over the authorship of 2 John, 3 John, 2 Peter, James, and Jude.

But forces were at work that demanded a decision on what should be regarded as Scripture. About A.D. 140 the heretic Marcion set forth his own collection of sacred writings. His assertion had to be met head on. Heretics began to promulgate a variety of teachings; church leaders sought to condemn them as being untrue or "unbiblical." It was necessary, therefore, for all to agree on what belonged in the Bible in order to make such charges of heresy. Also, a few, such as the Montanists, were traveling about claiming to have a gift of continuing revelation. Again orthodox church leaders made pronouncements, this time that revelation had ceased and that God had given believers all the Scripture He intended for them to have. Moreover, gospels, acts, and epistles attempting to fill in gaps in the narratives of the life of Christ and the apostles and to round out the theological message of the church appeared in profusion. Then as the great Diocletian persecution raged at the beginning of the fourth century and individuals could be martyred for possession of Scripture, they certainly wanted to be sure of what really belonged in the New Testament. These and other factors required a decision on what books should be accepted.

Gradually uncertainties about the disputed books were overcome and they became universally accepted. Questions asked by churchmen over the centuries as they sought to settle on the contents of the New Testament were:

1. Was the book inspired?
2. Was it of apostolic authorship or by someone of the apostolic circle?
3. Was it universally recognized?

If a book passed all these tests, it became a candidate for official adoption at a church council. A local council meeting at Carthage in North Africa in 397 declared for the present twenty-seven books, with the proviso that no other books were to be used in the churches as authoritative Scripture. When the Sixth Council of Carthage (419) reaffirmed the earlier decision on the canon, it directed that the statement be sent to the Bishop of Rome and other bishops. From that time on there was little further debate on the subject in the West. The example of the West and the influence of several great theologians in the East finally settled the matter there also. Since the fifth century there has been no serious controversy over the contents of the New Testament canon. The process of canonization was a long one and the decision did not come easily in some cases. But when it did come, there was great unanimity and certainty that what believers had in their hands was truly the Word of God.

HOW DOES THE NEW TESTAMENT RELATE TO THE OLD TESTAMENT?

The Old and New Testaments are simply component parts of one divine revelation. The Old Testament describes man and woman in the first paradise on the old earth; the New Testament concludes with a vision of redeemed humanity in the new heaven and new earth. The Old Testament sees human beings as fallen from a sinless condition and separated from God; the New Testament views them as restored to favor through the sacrifice of Christ. The Old Testament predicts a coming Redeemer who will rescue humanity from the pit of condemnation; the New Testament reveals the Christ who makes salvation possible. In most of the Old Testament the spotlight focuses on a sacrificial system in which the blood of animals provides a temporary handling of the sin problem; in the New, Christ appears as the One who came to put an end to all sacrifice—to be Himself the supreme sacrifice. In the Old Testament numerous predictions foretell a coming Messiah who will save His people; in the New, scores of passages detail how those prophecies were minutely fulfilled in the person of Jesus Christ, the son of Abraham and the son of David.

In the Old Testament most of the time the Hebrews are at center stage and God works with them to make them truly a people of God. There are occasional hints, however, that God planned to reach out to a wider constituency. In fact, near the beginning of Hebrew history, God told Abraham that in or through him all the people of the earth would be blessed (Genesis 12:3). In the New Testament, Jesus Christ, as a descendant of Abraham, makes available a salvation for all peoples. Jews such as Philip who preached to the Ethiopian eunuch, Barnabas who evangelized in Cyprus, and Paul who became the great apostle to the Gentiles, made it clear that the good news—salvation through Christ—was for all people. Thus, through Jesus Christ and the Jewish evangelists that descended from Abraham, all peoples of the earth have indeed eventually been blessed. The more we look at the two testaments, the more we recognize how integrally they are linked. As St. Augustine said more than fifteen hundred years ago, "The New is in the Old contained; the Old is in the New explained."

18

"Render . . . to Caesar": The World of Jesus and the Early Church

I N the midst of the Christmas story stands the assertion "that a decree went out from Caesar Augustus that all the world should be taxed" (Luke 2:1, NKJV). Of course reference here is to the Roman world, the world of the people with whom Jews and Christians (in the earliest days of the church) would be dealing.

That world was essentially the Mediterranean world, for the sea was the highway on which merchants, officials, and soldiers moved about to hold that world together. The land areas immediately adjacent to the Mediterranean were the only ones the Romans controlled: North Africa, Palestine, Syria, Asia Minor, Southern Europe (Greece, Yugoslavia, Italy, France, Spain), and the islands of the sea. During Paul's mature years the Emperor Claudius was destined to conquer Britain, and just after the apostle John passed off this earthly scene, the Romans subdued Dacia (Romania) and the Tigris-Euphrates Valley (modern Iraq). But for all practical purposes, the Empire was bounded by the deserts of North Africa and the Near East, the Black Sea, the Danube, and the Rhine. Of course the Romans depended on more than the Mediterranean sea lanes to keep their world together. They built a marvelous highway system, which, by the time the apostle John died, consisted of some 250,000 miles of improved roads—a distance that would encircle the globe at the equator ten times.

Romans were quite well aware that their world was not the entire world. They had failed to subdue the Germanic tribes east of the Rhine, the Parthians along the Syrian frontier, and the Picts and Scots in the north of Britain. The barbarians of the Danubian region posed a continuing threat to the security of the Empire, and the Emperor Hadrian (A.D. 117–138) would build extensive defenses there as well as a seventy-three-mile wall across Britain. Moreover, Romans would be even more impressed with the existence of other worlds as contacts with India and the Han Dynasty in China gradually increased during the first century A.D. and as the silk route opened up with the Far East.

Because the Mediterranean world was a Roman world, its fortunes were closely linked to Roman developments. Unfortunately, during most of the century 133–31 B.C. revolution plagued the Romans. The personal ambitions of such leaders as Marius, Sulla, Pompey, Julius Caesar, Mark Antony, and Octavian periodically convulsed Italy and the Empire in military struggles. Finally in 31 B.C., Octavian (Augustus Caesar) became master of the Empire and introduced the Pax Romana, two centuries of virtually unbroken peace and effective Roman dominance of the Mediterranean world. The prosperity that disappeared during the years of revolution gradually returned.

AUGUSTUS' REORDERING OF HIS WORLD

A grateful populace all over the Mediterranean world hailed Augustus as "Savior" and many sought to worship him. Thus developed the cult of the emperor and the goddess Roma. As this cult progressed, those who refused to participate came under increasing pressure and finally persecution. Jews and Christians alike were victims of this persecution. When Domitian turned his wrath against the Jews at the end of the first century, the church also became involved because it was not yet viewed as separate from Judaism. Among the Christians to suffer at that time was the apostle John, who was exiled to the Isle of Patmos where he received the Revelation. This seems to have been the first widespread persecution, though Nero had launched a local persecution against the Christians of Rome after the devastating fire of A.D. 64.

After Augustus became master of the Empire, he sought to bring order out of chaos. Instead of becoming a military tyrant he reestablished the civilian nature of the state. He shared administration with the Senate both in Rome and in the Empire. The Empire was organized into senatorial and imperial provinces and client kingdoms. The first were provinces most thoroughly Romanized (such as Sicily) and therefore needing only a few local police to keep order. Imperial provinces, on the other hand, required Roman legions under direct orders of the emperor to keep the peace.

Client kings in places like Galatia and Judea ruled fairly autonomously under the blessing of Rome. In such areas native rulers served a useful function of pacifying the countryside and preparing for ultimate direct Roman control. In Judea, after the transitional rule of Herod the Great and his son Archelaus, Rome instituted the rule of procurators—direct appointees of the crown. Best known of these was Pontius Pilate, who sentenced Jesus Christ to death during the reign of Augustus' successor, Tiberius.

In his effort to tidy up the Empire, Augustus also called for the first empire-wide census-designed not only to number the populace but to collect a poll tax. This census required people to return to their ancestral homes for registration (at least in the eastern Mediterranean); Joseph and Mary had to go back to Bethlehem where Jesus was born. What the population figures were for any given area of the Mediterranean world cannot be certainly known.

Italy probably had about fourteen million people in Augustus'
day and some twenty million by A.D. 70. The population of the
Empire as a whole possibly reached eighty million during the first
Christian century.

ROMAN VALUES AND RESISTANCE

As prosperity increased throughout the Roman world and as
Roman citizenship and its benefits were extended, increasing numbers of people adopted Roman ways. Romanization brought pacification and gradually there developed an Italian nation of the
Empire. Even the lot of slaves was not as bad as it could have been.
Manumission was common and relatively easy, and freed slaves
often achieved citizenship.

Under the circumstances, many provincials tended to value
security and prosperity and personal preferment above freedom.
Rebellions in the provinces became extremely infrequent. While
it is true that there was a year of rebellion and military unrest in
A.D. 68–69 when Nero was unseated, the uprisings were not of
provincials seeking freedom but ambitious soldiers on the lookout
for benefits and military commanders vying for the emperor's chair.
Of course one exception to this was the province of Judea. There
the problem was not merely one of continuing nationalism but of
exclusivistic, monotheistic religion that refused to be submerged in
a sea of polytheism. Revolution broke out in 66 and culminated
in the destruction of Jerusalem and the temple in A.D. 70.

Actually, however, the same thing was happening among other
peoples of the Empire as among the Jews. Many of the high priestly
group and their associates were influenced by the antisupernatu-
ralist approach of pagan society. These Sadducees came to deny the
resurrection and became the theological "liberals" of New
Testament times. Presumably this element of Jewish society sought
social and economic preferment at the hands of the Romans as did
their counterparts in other provinces.

But the Pharisees preached strict adherence to the law and to supernaturalistic aspects of Judaism, along with the Messianic hope. These leaders held forth in the synagogues of the land. Generally they supported Jewish nationalism, but they did not go so far as the Zealots in advocating military action to obtain political independence.

Synagogues served as training and worship centers for faithful Jews, not only in Palestine but all over the Empire. Jewish communities had settled in Syria, Asia Minor, Greece, Italy, Egypt, and elsewhere. In every city where they were sufficiently numerous they built a synagogue. These synagogues became beacon lights of monotheism in a poly theistic Greco-Roman society, and the Old Testament translated into Greek (the Septuagint) was a Bible that could be read everywhere in the Greco-Roman world. Thus many Gentiles became God fearers or proselytes to Judaism (Acts 2:10; 13:43), spiritually prepared for the coming of the Christian gospel. It was the strategy of the apostle Paul in his missionary efforts always to go first to the synagogues because there he could expect to find hearts prepared to receive the gospel of Christ.

The Roman world of the New Testament era was fundamentally different from the Mediterranean world of the twenty-first century. There was a cultural unity: Greco-Roman culture dominated the entire region, and the language in which people had to function to carry on economic, political, and cultural affairs was Greek. Anyone who sought to spread the gospel did not have to learn a new language first or to suffer culture shock. Then there was a political unity. Passports and visas were unknown. Roman power subdued piracy on the sea and brigandage on land. Roman prosperity and the bureaucracy maintained the infrastructure, especially the magnificent road system. If one were so fortunate as to possess Roman citizenship, he had special rights and protection that would facilitate his evangelization efforts (e.g., the apostle Paul). The Jews, as noted, through their synagogues (some 150 scattered over the empire) provided a witness for monotheism and an expectation of a coming Messiah. Moreover, they had completed translation of their Bible into Greek (the Septuagint) in Alexandria, Egypt before the end of the second century B.C. Culturally, politically, and religiously the Mediterranean world was prepared for the coming of Christ and the church during the first Christian century. It may be argued that there was no other time in world history when conditions were just right for God to do a new thing on earth. The "fullness of the time was come" (Galatians 4:4).

19

The Promised Messiah Comes: The Gospels

Matthew, Mark, Luke, John

THE New Testament is put together in a logical fashion. First appears the record of the life and work of Christ on earth in the gospels. Next the book of Acts describes the early history of the church that Christ left behind to continue His work. Especially it tells of the founding of churches through the ministry of the apostle Paul and his associates. Then appear letters that Paul and others wrote to churches and church leaders to instruct them in the truth. Finally in the Revelation comes a description of the return to earth of Christ who will judge all peoples, right wrongs, and institute the new heavens and the new earth.

The books in the New Testament do not necessarily appear in the order in which they were written. Paul penned some of his letters before the gospels were composed, and John wrote his gospel after almost all the rest of the New Testament had come into existence. When the collection was completed, by A.D. 100, it provided an adequate account of the life of Christ on earth, of His provision of salvation, of the founding of the church—the institution to which He committed the task of world evangelization—and of the doctrine, practice, and mission that constituted the marching orders for the church. Thus, modern believers have in a manageable and understandable body of literature all they need to know about the life and work of Christ, their privileges and responsibilities in the world, and the divine resources available to empower them to fulfill those obligations.

SYNOPTIC PROBLEM AND AUTHORSHIP OF THE GOSPELS

The first three gospels—Matthew, Mark, and Luke—are frequently called the synoptic gospels (a term which means "seeing together") because they see nearly eye to eye concerning many events of the life of Christ. Briefly stated, the synoptic problem is, "How can we account for the extremely close similarity of such a large proportion of these three gospels?" To illustrate, over ninety percent of Mark's material appears in both Matthew and Luke, comprising about half of each of those gospels. Of the remaining fifty percent of the contents of Matthew and Luke, about half is found in both of them; the remainder appears only in one gospel. On the other hand, less than ten percent of John is found in all three of the synoptics.

A Question of Sources

Modern scholars have expended great effort to account for this literary phenomenon. Of the solutions they have offered, the most commonly accepted is the two (or four) document theory. This teaches that Mark (either a primitive Mark or the Mark we have) was written first, and the other gospels borrowed narrative information from it. Discourse material was, however, taken from a supposed Q document. Subject matter peculiar to Matthew or Luke came, respectively from M or L sources.

By way of answer, it should be pointed out that there is no objective evidence for the existence of Q, L, or M. Moreover, it is unnecessary to degrade Matthew to the position of a plagiarist, because he was an apostle and accompanied Christ during the occurrence of nearly everything that appears in his gospel. If John were brought into account, the same may be said of him. Since tradition has it that Mark (who was not an apostle) wrote under the influence of Peter, we might expect that he would find it necessary to borrow part of his material from Matthew or someone else, rather than acting as a source for Matthew and Luke. Luke alone had to do research in order to write his gospel. He apparently had access to various brief accounts of the work of Christ on earth (Luke 1:2) as well as to an apostolic tradition concerning Christ's ministry (1:1). And of course he was very close to the apostolic circle. But research never implies copying most of one's material from a single source, as would be the case if Luke copied from Mark.

Also, we should note that only when the Bible began to lose its prestige as a divine product did the synoptic problem seriously plague Bible students (evolutionary and higher critical thought of the nineteenth century contributed to this decline in prestige). Among reverent believers down through the ages, it has always been held that God the Holy Spirit desired in the four gospels to emphasize various phases of the person of Christ, the totality of which would form a reasonably complete picture of His person. In presenting these four aspects of the person of Christ, there would naturally be a certain amount of repetition and divergence.

Remarkable Similarity

But having said all this, we still have not accounted for the similarity, even verbal in spots, between the first three gospels. This similarity may be explained in at least three ways. First, there may have been short written accounts of aspects of the works and teachings of Jesus on which all three could have drawn. That there were such written records seems certain (Luke 1:1). But if the writers of the canonical gospels drew upon them, we should probably expect a more exact verbal correspondence at certain points than we find in the synoptics. Second, Matthew, Mark, and Luke may have known each other in Jerusalem and/or in Antioch of Syria and have discussed Christ's earthly ministry on various occasions. This possibility deserves further investigation. Close similarity in phraseology indicates strong evidence of interdependence.

Third, apparently there was an oral tradition about the life and teachings of Jesus Christ that circulated in the early church. If Jesus' followers were to present Him properly, they had to tell a consistent story about His career. With the constant telling, that story would fall into a rather set pattern. That there was such a common core of accepted truth is indicated in such passages as Luke 1:1, 2 ("things . . . believed among us . . . delivered . . . unto us") and 1 Corinthians 5:2, 3 ("keep in memory what I preached unto you . . . I delivered unto you . . . that which I also received"). If the apostolic tradition were oral, there would be some flexibility in order of phrases and words and in emphases as does in fact occur in the synoptic gospels. So then, Matthew, Mark, and Luke may have drawn on the body of apostolic oral teaching as it suited their purposes and even have changed phraseology or emphases as they were led to do under the guidance of the Holy Spirit. Their personal research and difference of perspective and purpose would explain the materials peculiar to each; the many differences in the gospels indicate their independence. The similarities stem from common subject matter, common sources of information, and common divine inspiration. In any case, we must reverently believe that what appears in each of the synoptic gospels is exactly what the Holy Spirit wanted there.

Tradition is strong that Matthew, Mark, Luke, and John each wrote the gospel that bears his name. In the case of Matthew and John, considerable internal evidence supports tradition. Internal evidence for Luke's authorship becomes equally great when linked to information from Acts, Luke's other canonical production. Internal evidence for Markan authorship is weaker, but there is no valid reason for denying that he or any of the other gospel writers penned the books attributed to them.

OCCASION AND DATE

In the opinion of the writer, the dating of the gospels depends on at least four considerations: the order of the gospels in the lists of the early church, the historical situation giving rise to the gospels, internal evidence, and the dating of Acts.

In the lists of the gospels remaining to us from the early days of the church, Matthew and John appear first, never Mark or Luke. Since it is well known that John wrote last, the primacy of his gospel must have been due to the great spiritual significance of his message. Some think that Matthew was listed first because he wrote first, and this is a possibility. As Matthew was inconspicuous among the disciples, we must find some good reason for putting his gospel first on several of the lists. Perhaps date of composition is as good as any.

Historically there was a need first for a gospel for the Jews; Matthew is clearly that gospel. Next, the need arose for a gospel for the Greek-speaking world; Luke qualifies. As the message of redemption traveled west, the third gospel was needed—written particularly for the Roman mind. Mark fits. Then, as early church tradition has it, John attempted to produce a universal gospel, one that would be a spiritual interpretation of the synoptic narrative.

Internal evidence indicates that Matthew, Mark, and Luke were all written before the fall of Jerusalem in A.D. 70, and John long after that time. Moreover, it seems that Matthew and Luke were written before the book of Acts. At least Luke was, because the introduction to Acts says so. If the historical occasion for the writing of the gospels and indications from the early lists of the gospels be taken into account, we should conclude that Matthew was also written before Acts.

Acts 28:30 implies that Acts was written just before the end of Paul's first Roman imprisonment. Two of the most commonly accepted chronologies of the life of Paul place this prison term in 58-60 or 59–61. So Acts was probably written in 60 or 61. Many think that Luke did the research for his gospel during Paul's Caesarean imprisonment (assigned by some to the years 56–58 and others to 57–59). If this is true, Luke must have written around 58–61. At least he composed his gospel not long before the Acts. Assuming that Matthew was written before Luke, we could assign the general period 50–60 to its composition. Possibly it was written in Antioch. Various considerations seem to require that Mark wrote after the death of Peter at the hands of Nero. If the gospel were written before the fall of Jerusalem, we could date it about 66–69. Tradition gives Rome as the place of publication. John is commonly thought to have composed his gospel in Ephesus between 85 and 95.

Carsten Thiede and Matthew D'Ancona in their *Eyewitness to Jesus* (New York: Doubleday, 1996) argue that papyrus fragments of Matthew's gospel located at Magdalen College (Oxford) date to about A.D. 60. Acceptance of such a date would make the writer an eyewitness to Jesus and would make the gospel the earliest of the four gospels.

MATTHEW: FOCUS ON THE MESSIAH

In writing a gospel designed particularly for Jews, Matthew emphasizes the Messiahship of Christ. This he demonstrates by reference to Christ's lineage, His deeds, His teachings, and the constant fulfillment of prophecy in His life. Moreover, he stresses the reign of the Messiah, the term *kingdom of heaven* appearing thirty-three times. Reference to the Old Testament is more frequent here than in any of the other gospels; in all there are about fifty-three quotations from the Old Testament and seventy-six allusions to it. These are drawn from twenty-five Old Testament books.

At the beginning of the Hebrew nation, God told Abraham, ". . . in you shall all families of the earth be blessed" (Genesis 12:3). He assured David that his kingdom and throne would be established *forever* (2 Samuel 7). Such tremendous covenant promises could be fulfilled only by an infinite person, i.e., Christ. It is logical, then, in presenting a gospel of the Messiah that Matthew would begin by demonstrating that Christ was in the line of Abraham and David. One should not pass too hurriedly over this rather uninteresting list of unfamiliar names, however. Startling is the realization that the line of Jechonias (Jeconiah or Jehoiachin, Matthew 1:11) was cursed (Jeremiah 22:30; 36:30); and therefore Christ could not possibly have been born in his lineage, though he was descended from David. For this reason, among others, many Bible students conclude that recorded here is the legal line of Christ, the genealogy of Joseph. If so, it constitutes one of the most powerful arguments for the virgin birth. With the line of Joseph cursed, it was necessary for Christ to be born of Mary, also descended from David. In this connection, it should be pointed out that the "of whom" in Matthew 1:16 is feminine singular in the Greek.

The rest of chapter 1 comments on the virgin birth in fulfillment of prophecy. It is of utmost importance to remind ourselves that if Christ had been born in the cursed line of Joseph instead of virgin born, God's prophetic plan for the ages would have gone awry! All families of the earth could never have been blessed in Him, as promised to Abraham; nor could He reign perpetually on the throne of David. On the other hand, Mary, according to Luke's genealogy (Luke 3:31), descended from David through Nathan—a line not cursed.

But Matthew is not a gospel for Jews alone; Gentiles are also in view there. The Magi came from a far country to share in the worship of the newborn Babe of Bethlehem (2:1–12). Two non-Jewish women appear in His genealogy (1:5). Matthew is the one Gospel that mentions the church (16:18; 18:17), and it is clear from the Great Commission that more than Jews are to be included in that church (28:19). Moreover, Jesus states specifically that the kingdom will be taken from Israel and given to a people producing the fruits of it (21:43) and that the nations will enter into the inheritance of Israel (8:11, 12).

In chapter 2, the Messiah was recognized and worshiped by Eastern royalty; and in 3:1–4:11, He was prepared for His public ministry in a threefold way: by the ministry of John the Baptist, by the baptism, and by the temptation. John's work was merely to introduce the ministry of our Lord. Being filled with the Spirit from birth, John had the perception to recognize his role in life and the humility to give rightful to place to his Lord (see Isaiah 40 for prophecy of John's ministry). Much ink has been consumed in discussing the import of Christ's baptism. Whatever was involved, it seems safe to say that the event marked the inauguration of our Lord's public ministry. At the baptism, the other members of the Trinity expressed their pleasure in the divine mission of salvation He was now undertaking. Divine approval did not, however, render Christ immune to satanic opposition. Not only was it Satan's desire to thwart the redemptive plan of God, but it was in the plan of God that Christ should undergo such temptation. (Note that the Holy Spirit led Him into the wilderness to be tempted, Matthew 4:1.) Perhaps by this, in part, Christ was tempted in all points as we are and therefore is a perfect High Priest (Hebrews 4:15). What must be intended by the Hebrews reference is that He experienced temptation in the variety of categories in which we experience it. As we face temptation we may meet it head on as He did in His humanity, by recourse to the Word of God.

The Ministry in Galilee

In general, the vast section of Matthew from 4:12 to 18:35 describes the Galilean ministry. In 4:12 He enters Galilee; in 19:1 He leaves Galilee for Judea. Between these two references tremendous events transpire. In the latter part of chapter 4, Jesus calls His disciples; four are mentioned at this point. Then He proceeds to instruct them by means of the great Sermon on the Mount (chapters 5–7). This passage often has been called the proclamation of the King; here is set forth the nature of the kingdom. The beatitudes, describing the character of the members of the kingdom, begin the discourse. Then Jesus discusses and interprets the law, showing that the Old Testament law is not a matter of externals only but of the heart. Faith and entrance into the kingdom constitute the concluding topics of the sermon. The Sermon on the Mount has suffered greatly at the hands of many well-meaning folk who have tried to make it a means of salvation. Say they, "If we will live according to the Sermon on the Mount we will have done all that God expects of us. Therefore we can be assured of salvation." But such teaching constitutes a gospel of works and is at variance with the grace teachings of Christ and Paul (John 3; Ephesians 2:8, 9; Titus 3:5, 6). What unregenerate person could hope to live up to the beatitudes, for instance? The only one capable is the believer enabled by the Holy Spirit.

Power Through Miracles

The miraculous works of Christ dominate chapters 8–12. His Messiahship is attested by a demonstration of power. Chapter 13 deals with the great kingdom parables, which describe the course of the age. Briefly, the significance of these earthly stories with a heavenly meaning may be noted as follows. The sower parable describes the varying results that may be expected when the seed of the gospel is sown (13:1–23). The mixture of wheat and tares in the field demonstrates the fact that during this age Christendom will consist of a mixture of true believers and those making an empty profession (13:24–30). The mustard seed parable teaches the insignificant beginning of the kingdom and its unusual and unexpected growth (13:31, 32), while leaven or yeast in the meal points up the fact that as leaven produces a ferment or dynamic or resistless process, so the sowing of the Word will produce a new kingdom by a quiet and irresistible working from within (13:33–35). The hidden treasure and the pearl probably refer to the value of believers for whom Christ made the supreme sacrifice (13:44–46). Some relate the former to Israel and the latter to the church. The dragnet parable clearly describes the judgment to occur at the end of the age (13:47–50).

Four developments are outstanding in the remaining chapters of the Galilean section: miracles, the great confession, passion announcements, and the Transfiguration. Among the great miracles are feeding the five thousand, Jesus' walking on the water, and feeding the four thousand. In the great confession (16:13–20), Peter, possibly speaking for all the disciples, recognized Jesus as the Christ, the Messiah. Having elicited this confession, Jesus proceeded to foretell His death and resurrection. But between His two passion announcements (16:21; 17:22, 23), the Transfiguration occurred. Perhaps the purpose of this event was to provide strength for both the disciples and Christ during difficult days ahead. God often prefaces the valleys with mountaintop experiences. Note that as they came down from the mountain, Jesus again concerned Himself with His forthcoming suffering (17:9, 12).

The Rising Opposition

After the Galilean ministry, Jesus made the journey to Jerusalem; chapters 19 and 20 describe events along the way. The rest of the gospel narrative is staged in and around Jerusalem. Chapters 21–23 outline Israel's rejection of the Messiah. In spite of the fact that they initially hailed Him as king as He entered Jerusalem, the opposition grew rapidly until it was solidly arrayed against Him. Herodians, Sadducees, Pharisees, and scribes clashed with Him. That this opposition was not restricted to the leaders of the people is obvious from Matthew 23:37, 38: "O Jerusalem, Jerusalem, who kills the prophets and stones those who are sent to her! How often

I wanted to gather your children together, the way a hen gathers her chicks under her wings, and you were unwilling. Behold your house is left to you desolate!" (NASB).

Messiah's predictions of the end times consume chapters 24 and 25. This passage, known as the Olivet discourse, tells of the Great Tribulation, the second coming of Christ at the end of it, and the judgment of the nations that will take place when He returns. The sequence of events is clearly seen by skipping over the illustrative parables located after 24:31 and resuming reading at 25:31. That the judgment mentioned in 25:31–46 occurs before the Millennium is evident from the fact that the sheep are rewarded by entering the kingdom. The basis of the judgment is treatment of "my brethren," apparently the Jews of the Tribulation period. It should not be felt, however, that salvation referred to here is by works. In the first place, that would be inconsistent with the clear teaching of Scripture. In the second place, it might be suggested that only Christians would risk their lives in befriending Jews during the Tribulation. So helping Jews becomes an evidence of salvation and not a means toward gaining it.

Recognition of Jesus as the Son of God

The Messiah's passion, resurrection, and the Great Commission occupy the last three chapters of the book. Christ's intense suffering is thrown into bold relief by the betrayal of Judas, the slumber of the disciples in the garden, the mocking of His accusers, and the denial of Peter. But even in His death the Messianic element is present. In mockery Roman soldiers hailed Him as king of the Jews; the superscription above the cross read: THIS IS JESUS THE KING OF THE JEWS. The centurion who saw Him die testified, "Truly this was the Son of God." As evidence that His redemptive work was accomplished, the veil of the temple was torn down the middle—access into the presence of God now being available to every believer through Christ our high priest. Further evidencing

His deity, Christ rose from the dead. For the time being, His work was finished on earth; His followers would have to carry on the task He had begun. So before He left, He commissioned them for this tremendous responsibility: "Go therefore, and make disciples of all nations, baptizing them in the name of the Father and the Son and the Holy Spirit, teaching them to observe all that I commanded you" (Matthew 28:19, 20, NASB). But it was a command with a promise, "lo, I am with you always" (Matthew 28:20, NASB).

An abbreviated outline of Matthew, focusing on the Messiah, is as follows:

1. Messiah's Coming and Preparation, 1:1–4:11
2. Messiah's Ministry in Galilee, 4:12–18:35
3. Messiah's Ministry in Jerusalem, 19:1–28:20

MARK

From the beginning of the second century, early church leaders were unanimous in speaking of Mark as the author of the second gospel, under the influence of or as the interpreter of Peter. Thus the book gained apostolic authority or sanction. They disagreed, however, as to whether Mark wrote during Peter's lifetime or in Rome after his death. Perhaps the truth is that he began to write while Peter was still alive and issued the gospel after his death. One would not expect a tradition of Mark's authorship to develop if it were not true; he was after all a minor figure. It is significant that no worthy alternate proposal as to authorship has been made. The few modern critics who have sought to dismiss support for Mark's authorship have not been widely followed.

Internal evidence for Markan authorship or composition in Rome is minimal. As to Roman origin, it is often noted that Mark 15:21 names Simon of Cyrene, father of Alexander and Rufus, as bearer of the cross of Christ and that Rufus and his mother were living in Rome at the time the epistle to the Romans was written

(Romans 16:13). If one accepts identification of the Rufus of Mark 15:21 and Romans 16:13, as many do, Mark's inclusion of this detail would have had significance for the Roman church. Moreover, Latinisms in Mark are often pointed out. Transliterations of Latin words into Greek are more frequent than in other gospels. Certainly the contents of the gospel reflect an eyewitness to the events; if he were not Peter, he had to be one of the other apostles. Commentators frequently suggest that the young man who fled when Jesus was arrested was Mark (Mark 14:51, 52), but one cannot be sure of such an identification.

As to Mark's biography, it is known that he had a home in Jerusalem. It is also suggested that the upper room of that home was used for the Last Supper and also for the gathering at Pentecost. John Mark, a cousin of Barnabas (Colossians 4:10), joined Barnabas and Saul on the first missionary journey and ministered with them in Cyprus (Acts 13:5), but left the party in Perga and returned to Jerusalem (Acts 13:13). At the time of his second journey Paul refused to take John Mark along again (apparently feeling he was too undependable). Barnabas took Mark off on another mission to Cyprus and Paul took Silas and went to Asia Minor and Greece. Mark showed up in Rome during Paul's imprisonment there and sent greetings to the Colossians and Philemon (Colossians 4:10; Philemon 24). In 1 Peter 5:13 Peter refers to Mark as "my son"; perhaps he was Peter's understudy as Timothy was Paul's. At any rate, Paul spoke well of Mark in 2 Timothy 4:11 and desired his company during his last days on earth. Whatever Mark's failures earlier in life, he had subsequently proved himself.

Jesus as Servant

While Matthew emphasizes the kingly aspect of Jesus' Messiahship, Mark presents Him as the Servant of Jehovah. These two concepts are not the least incompatible; Isaiah's prophetic description of the Messiah includes both. In line with Isaiah's teaching concerning the ministry of the Servant of Jehovah, Mark divides into two rather equal parts; the first having to do with His *works* performed in Galilee and the second with His *passion* in Jerusalem. The key verse, Mark 10:45, admirably sums up these two portions: "For even the Son of man came not to be ministered unto, but to minister, and to give his life a ransom for many." A simplified outline based on content and key verse follows:

1. Preparation of the Servant, 1:1–13
2. Proclamation of the Servant, 1:14–8:30
3. Passion of the Servant, 8:31–16:20

Not only does Mark's gospel provide an emphasis on the work of the Messiah—an element minimized in Matthew—but it is particularly designed as a gospel for Roman readers. This fact is asserted by several church fathers and supported by internal evidence. Mark has fewer references to the Old Testament than the other gospels; Aramaic words are interpreted for those who would not know the language (e.g., 5:41; 15:34); Jewish customs are explained; and a number of Latin words appear only here in the gospels. Moreover, action and power, both greatly admired by the Romans, are stressed in the book. The narrative is swift moving; the word *immediately* appears forty-one times. Miraculous demonstrations of power are present everywhere; in all, eighteen miracles are recorded.

Now let us return briefly to a consideration of the outline of Mark presented above. The preparation is quickly described. The preparation for Christ is seen in the ministry of John the Baptist. The preparation of Christ is marked by the baptism and temptation.

Concentrated Ministry

With the exception of short excursions to such regions as Tyre and Sidon and Decapolis, the entire section on the proclamation takes place in Galilee. As we move through these chapters, events develop with lightning-like speed. Jesus calls His first disciples and launches His ministry in 1:14–45; in 2:1–3:6 opposition to Him begins as He heals the palsied and on the Sabbath picks grain and heals the man with the withered hand. In 3:7–35 He commissions the twelve and declares the new relationship of discipleship: "For whosoever shall do the will of God, the same is my brother, and my sister, and mother" (3:35). In chapter 4, He instructs the multitudes by means of parables, which have as their central theme the beginning and growth of the kingdom. The chapter is similar to Matthew 13 (see comments on that chapter under Matthew). Both Mark 4 and Matthew 13 explain the sower parable. An added note here is the purpose of parabolic teaching (Mark 4:11, 12). Apparently, these verses teach that parables were used to prevent His enemies from grasping the truth and to avoid sweeping multitudes with only superficial belief into the kingdom. Surely He was not generally trying to hide His message; He came to seek and save that which was lost. Moreover, He generally spoke plainly so all could understand, and He constantly pled with men and women to receive the truth. By way of contrast, 4:35–5:43 introduces a great display of power—something all should understand. He stilled the sea; delivered the Gadarene demoniac; healed a woman with an incurable issue of blood; and restored a child to life. Here Jesus' power over nature, satanic forces, disease, and death is demonstrated.

Calling of Workers

When we enter chapter 6, a new phase of our Lord's work appears: He associates His disciples with Him in His ministry. Previously they have been largely observers; now they become co-workers. In 6:7, He sends them out to preach, even giving them power over demons. The account of John the Baptist's murder is introduced to demonstrate the perils of discipleship. The disciples serve at the feeding of the five thousand and the four thousand.

Something else is clear in this last part of the section on the proclamation: increasing conflict and opposition. At Nazareth Christ met unbelief (6:6); from Herod came increasing political pressure (6:14ff.); His disciples did not clearly understand Him (6:52); the Pharisees opposed Him (7:1ff.; 8:10ff.).

Throughout chapters 1–8 Jesus remained the perfect servant, a true pattern for the believer. His was a tender, loving, compassionate ministry (6:34; 8:2). His was an active service, a self-denying service (3:20; 6:31), a misunderstood service (3:21), and a costly service—a God-fearing service that would eventuate in death.

Focus on the Passion Week

Perhaps it is rather arbitrary to begin the passion section of the gospel with 8:31; most would begin it later in the book. And yet, the first passion announcement occurs in 8:31. From then on, the passion theme heightens. In 9:9 His death is mentioned. In 9:31 He made the second passion announcement; and in 10:32–34 He delivered the third. The Transfiguration is recorded (9:1–13); and as mentioned in the discussion of Matthew, a probable reason for the Transfiguration was the preparation of both Jesus and the disciples for dire days ahead. After the journey to Jerusalem in chapter 10, for the purpose of offering His life a ransom, the Servant begins the main period of the passion.

It is interesting that this section, beginning with 11:1, constitutes about three-eighths of the gospel and that most of it takes place within one week. The earlier five-eighths occupy approximately three years. After all, the sinless life of Christ alone could not save us (though He had to be sinless to be our Redeemer); so it is only fitting that great emphasis be placed on His death and resurrection.

In general, this portion divides into three sections: ministry in Jerusalem (11–13); submission to death (14–15); and resurrection and ascension (16). In chapter 11, Jesus makes His official appearance as king and cleanses the temple; in chapter 12, He wins a victory over the leaders of the Jews; in chapter 13, He presents a revelation of the future, one which includes the Tribulation and Second Coming. Highlights of chapters 14 and 15 in order are the plotting of the chief priests and scribes, Mark's anointing of Jesus, Judas' betrayal plot, the Lord's Supper, the agony in the garden, the arrest of Jesus, Jesus before the high priest and Sanhedrin, Peter's denial, Jesus before Pilate, and the crucifixion and burial. The book closes with the suffering Servant's triumph over death and His ascension to the Father—His servanthood having been accomplished.

The question of the ending of Mark is one of the thorniest in all of New Testament scholarship. The best manuscripts stop in chapter 16 at verse 8. The great scholar Eusebius of Caesarea, writing in the fourth century, said that nearly all copies of the gospel ended with verse 8. Jerome, translator of the Vulgate, said almost the same thing shortly after A.D. 400. Moreover, many argue that verses 9–20 are not in the same style as the rest of the book. So the tendency of modern textual scholars is to omit these verses. One should not be too hasty in throwing out Mark 16:9–20, however. Justin Martyr, Irenaeus, and Tatian witnessed to its inclusion in the second century, and the earliest translations—the Latin, Syriac, and Coptic—all include it. Hopefully new manuscripts bearing on the question will yet come to light.

LUKE

The authorship of Luke is bound up with that of Acts. The writer addresses both to Theophilus. As is noted in the discussion of Acts, the "we sections" of that book help to establish Luke as the author of those passages. An analysis of the Greek shows that the style and vocabulary of the rest of Acts are the same as in the "we sections." Moreover, a study of the vocabulary and style of Acts demonstrates their close agreement with the narrative of the gospel. The emphasis on the ministry of the Holy Spirit is likewise a characteristic of both books (see, for example, Luke 1:35; 3:22; 4:1; 4:18; 10:21; and Acts 10:38). The support in church tradition for Lukan authorship is early and widespread and few question it today.

Luke is thought to have been an Antiochian Gentile, converted there a few years after Pentecost. He joined Paul in Troas on his second missionary journey (Acts 16:10) and then accompanied him to Greece. He remained at Philippi as pastor while Paul went on to Thessalonica and eventually to Athens and Corinth. On Paul's third journey, Luke joined him again and accompanied him to Jerusalem. What Luke was doing during Paul's Caesarean imprisonment is not known, but some think he was engaged in the research for his gospel. Subsequently he accompanied Paul to Rome and was present when the apostle wrote Colossians (4:14) and Philemon (24). During Paul's second Roman imprisonment, Luke was the only one who stood with him (2 Timothy 4:11).

Evidently Luke was not satisfied with the accounts of the life of Christ that existed in his day (1:1). No doubt some were inaccurate and others fragmentary. If Matthew's account had been composed by that time, it was written to a large degree for Jewish consumption and did not meet the need for a gospel for Gentiles (Greeks). Mark and John must have written their gospels later. Evidently also Luke was not an eyewitness of the events he chronicled, so he had to engage in research. This he did meticulously: ". . . I myself have carefully investigated everything from the beginning . . ." (Luke 1:3, NIV). Especially did he interview the "eyewitnesses" (v. 2) available to him during his stay in Palestine.

The Gospel for the Gentiles

That Luke wrote his gospel for Gentiles, and more particularly for Greek Gentiles of the eastern Mediterranean area, was a conviction of early church leaders. Internal evidence corroborates their position. For instance, Luke gives explanations of Jewish customs and localities (e.g., "Capernaum, a city of Galilee," 4:31; "the feast of unleavened bread, which is called the Passover," 22:1; "Arimathaea, a city of the Jews," 23:51). Everywhere the air of universality pervades. Luke's genealogy makes Christ a son of Adam rather than merely a son of Abraham; Christ's birth was good news "to all the people" (2:10); He was "a light to lighten the Gentiles" (2:32); Luke alone quotes Isaiah 40:5, "all flesh shall see the salvation of God" (3:6); Luke alone speaks of the "times of the Gentiles" (21:24); Luke's record of the Great Commission notes "that repentance and remission of sins should be preached in his name among all nations" (24:47). Moreover, the Greek style is more literary than that of the other gospels; and the author substitutes a number of Greek names for Hebrew names (e.g., "skull" for "Golgotha," 23:33; cf. Matthew 27:33).

In providing a gospel for the Greeks, Luke emphasized Christ's humanity. Greek thought was man centered; it put much stress on the individual. It had high esteem for the genius, the hero, the ideal man. Christ was all that the Greek could wish for—and more; for the Greek never knew a perfect man, one who was above the moral and spiritual imperfections of his gods. Here is *the man* par excellence.

In the first four verses of the gospel, two things stand out. First, the book is addressed to Theophilus, who was also the recipient of Acts. It is often suggested that Luke may have written under literary patronage. Second, as noted, Luke was not an eyewitness of the narrative he records and he had to do research to produce his gospel.

Because they are utilized in such detail in Christmas programs on television, radio, and in churches, the early chapters of Luke are among the Scripture portions most familiar to Christians and non-Christians alike. The prophecy of the birth of John the Baptist, the annunciation to Mary, the song of Mary, the birth of John and Jesus, the adoration of the shepherds and Simeon and Anna, the account of Jesus' visit to the temple at the age of twelve, and the ministry of John have become almost trite to many. That is unfortunate, for here is drama of the most intense sort. More than that, here are events that are of utmost significance for the spiritual welfare of humanity: "Unto you is born this day . . . a Savior which is Christ the Lord" (2:11). Possibly Luke heard from Mary's own lips the events surrounding the birth of Christ.

At the end of chapter 3 is a genealogy of Jesus. Comparing it carefully with that of Matthew, the student may become puzzled, for from David to Jesus there is great divergence of names. When all the facts are taken into consideration, it seems that here we have Mary's genealogy. She descended from David by a line different from Joseph's, a line that was not cursed. Therefore, Christ could one-day rule on the throne of David (see discussion under Matthew). The first three chapters have to do with the preparation *for* the Son of Man. In 3:21, 22 and 4:1–13 we have the preparation *of* the Son of Man by baptism and temptation.

Jesus' Ministry in Galilee and Judea

The Galilean ministry of Christ occupies 4:14–9:50. After His temptation in the Judean wilderness, Jesus returned to Galilee, where He immediately became famous. His message was not well received at His hometown of Nazareth, however. In fact, He found it necessary to escape from the town because His synagogue hearers plotted against His life. It was in the synagogue at Nazareth that Jesus announced the purpose of His ministry, "to preach the gospel to the poor" (4:18).[1] Then Jesus went to Capernaum to establish His headquarters. Events described in this section do not differ greatly from those mentioned in connection with the Galilean ministry in Matthew or Mark. Familiar to the reader are such occurrences as the call of the disciples, the healing of Peter's mother-in-law, the paralytic carried by four men, the man with the withered hand, the feeding of five thousand, stilling the storm, uttering the sower parable, and curing the Gadarene demoniac. Two miracles appearing in this section and not elsewhere in the gospels are the miraculous draught of fish (5:1–11) and the raising of the widow's son (7:11–17).

The situation is quite different with the next section, however, with the Judean ministry, 9:51–18:30. Most of the material is peculiar to Luke. There appear nine parables which are mentioned in none of the other gospels: the good Samaritan, the rich fool, the fig tree, the seats at the marriage feast, the great supper, the lost coin, the prodigal son, the unjust steward, and the Pharisee and publican. Also, three miracles are peculiar to this section: healing a deformed woman (13:10–17), a man with dropsy (14:1–6), and ten lepers (17:11–19). From the above listing of parables, it is evident that much discourse material appears in this section. Jesus discusses prayer, denounces religious formalism and hypocrisy, exhorts to repentance, warns against untrue discipleship, and utters parables concerning salvation and the use of wealth.

The Parables

While it is impossible to comment at length on all the features of this portion of Luke, it may be well to stop for a moment on the parables of chapter 15 (the lost sheep, the lost coin, and the lost son), as the interpretation of them has suffered greatly in the bands of well-meaning Bible students. In the first place, note the occasion for uttering these parables. The Pharisees and scribes were complaining because Jesus ministered to the publicans and sinners. Jesus had repeatedly made it clear that He had come to save humanity; the scribes and Pharisees did not want to admit that they needed saving. After all, they kept the law; were they not all right? So Jesus directed these three parables at them. The ninety-nine sheep, the nine coins, and the elder brother all represent the Pharisees, who did not want the salvation of God. The lost sheep, the lost coin, and the prodigal son represent the publicans and sinners—those who by everyone's standard needed spiritual regeneration. The point illustrated here is that Jesus would not concentrate on those who did not want to be or did not think they needed to be saved; instead He would spend His time with those who needed and wanted Him. The fact that in each parable some were considered religiously safe does not mean that they were. They merely considered themselves safe (note in this regard Luke 16:14, 15). Christ can find only those who realize they are lost.

The unjust steward (16:1–13) is another parable that requires brief comment. Students of the Word are often puzzled by it, thinking that Christ commends dishonesty on the part of His followers. But such is not the case. The steward was not commended for his dishonesty but for his wisdom and foresight. The point is, he recognized that a day of accounting of his stewardship was coming; he wanted to be ready for it. The disciples were told to take a lesson and be diligent in their lives as believers because a day of accounting would be ahead for them, too.

Luke's Unique Emphasis

In Luke's account of the passion of our Lord (18:31–23:56), there is not great divergence from the general pattern followed by Matthew and Mark. The order includes the entry into Jerusalem, debate with the leaders, a discussion of the future, the last Passover, the betrayal, the trial before the high priest and before Pilate, the crucifixion and burial.

Luke's discussion of the resurrection differs markedly from that of the other synoptics, however. Here he develops a certainty of the resurrection of Christ. The two on the road to Emmaus experience Christ's living presence and come to understand, under His tutelage, the significance of Old Testament Scripture in terms of Himself. He appeared to the eleven and ate with them, thus confirming His resurrection and humanity. Peter saw the empty graveclothes in the tomb; had his body been stolen, these wrappings would certainly have been taken also. Moreover, Christ reminded His disciples that His sufferings and resurrection were in fulfillment of prophecy and that they were foundational to a universal message. And last, He promised His followers power from on high for their future ministry on behalf of the risen One. Having made this promise, and having given them a command to wait in Jerusalem for bestowal of this power, He ascended to heaven.

JOHN

According to Clement of Alexandria (about A.D. 200), the apostle John was urged by friends and moved by the Holy Spirit to write a spiritual gospel. In so doing he tried to supplement the other gospels that put more stress on the humanity of Christ (Eusebius *Ecclesiastical History* 6.14). Origen, Tertullian, and a number of other early church fathers support the testimony of Clement.

Corroborating external evidence for John, the son of Zebedee, as author of the gospel, are indications from the gospel itself. The author was a Palestinian Jew who was an eyewitness of the events he narrated. He is to be identified with the "beloved disciple," who was closely associated with Peter and who leaned on Jesus' bosom at the Last Supper (13:23). He was present at Jesus' trial (18:15, 16) and at the cross (19:26, 27). The author so frequently refers to Peter, Thomas, and Philip in the third person that none of them could be the author. His brother James was killed early in the history of the church and so is eliminated from consideration. John, the son of Zebedee, is the best remaining candidate.

John's Unique Approach

While it may not necessarily have been John's purpose to supply material left out of other gospels, it certainly was his desire to write a spiritual gospel. In so doing, he stressed the deity of Christ and faith in this divine Person unto salvation. (Various forms of the word *believe* appear about one hundred times in John.) The gospel itself declares: "And many other signs truly did Jesus in the presence of his disciples, which are not written in this book: But these are written, that you might believe that Jesus is the Christ, the Son of God; and that believing you might have life through his name" (John 20:30, 31).

This passage particularly emphasizes the signs or miracles that Christ performed to demonstrate His deity (see 2:23; 5:36; 10:22ff., etc.). But legion are other evidences to the same effect. The author asserts it in the first verses of the book. John the Baptist (1:15–35; 3:25–36), God the Father (5:37–39), and the disciples (6:69) likewise bear witness to His deity. Jesus Himself claimed it (8:46ff., especially v. 58; 9:35ff.; 10:30ff.; 14:6ff. Note also such claims as "I am the vine," and "I am the light of the world.").

Since Christ is presented as deity in this gospel, a number of features that appear in the synoptics are omitted: His birth, genealogy, youth, baptism, temptation, and transfiguration. For deity these have no great significance.

Before outlining the message of John, some comments on the chronology of the book are in order. In the first place, the author narrates events in historical sequence, rather than topically. Second, the book furnishes the basis for a chronology of the life Christ. Taking together the indications of Matthew, Mark, and Luke, we might suppose that the Lord's earthly ministry lasted about one year. In John we learn that its duration was more than three years. We know this in part from the mention of three Passovers (2:12, 13; 6:4; 12:1). Third, John himself does not narrate events occurring on more than twenty days of Christ's ministry. Chapters 13–19, about one-third of the gospel, cover only one day.

Truth Presented in Simplicity

Sublime in its simplicity is the gospel of John. Throughout the twenty-one chapters profound truths are couched in language plain enough for all to understand. Certainly this is a lesson for us as Christian workers. We try to impress our hearers with high sounding phraseology. We develop our ideas in philosophical terms to impress the intellectual. But John the evangelist shuns all that.

Especially impressive is his handling of the preincarnate glory of the Son of God in the first four verses. Note how simply and concisely he introduces Christ's eternality, His fellowship with the Father, His deity, His omnipotence (as evidenced by His creative act), and His exalted position as the source of life.

In the prologue to the gospel (1:1–18), appear statements concerning the preincarnate Son of God, His incarnation, His reception by some and rejection by others, and the announcement of His ministry by John the Baptist. One is tempted to comment at length on this tremendous passage. Every phrase would furnish material for a complete chapter of a book, and then the depths would not be plumbed. It is interesting, however, that verse 14 is all that John has to contribute to the Christmas message, "And the Word was made flesh and dwelt among us."

The Son of God reveals Himself to Israel in the first twelve chapters of the book. In 1:19–4:54, His ministry is launched as John introduces Him, and as He performs His first miracle at Cana, discusses the new birth with Nicodemus, meets the woman at Jacob's well, and heals the nobleman's son. A tremendous amount of ground is covered in this brief section—both geographically and theologically. The disciples were called and water was turned into wine in Galilee; the interview with Nicodemus occurred in Jerusalem at the time of the Passover; the well scene took place in Samaria (forbidden territory for a Jew); and the second miracle was performed in Cana of Galilee, as was the first. Theologically, we observe the first announcement of the passion in 2:19, one of the clearest New Testament expositions of salvation and the results of lack of faith in Christ in chapter 3, contributions to the doctrine of the Holy Spirit in 3:34 and 4:14, 15 (cf. John 7:37–39), a statement concerning the nature of God and true worship in 4:23, 24, and an observation on missions and personal evangelism in 4:35–38.

As this division progresses (chapters 5–12), conflict develops between Jesus and various elements of the Jewish populace. The

struggle begins in chapter 5, when the Jews seek to kill Him for breaking the Sabbath and making Himself equal with God (v. 18), and continues with increasing intensity. The whole process culminates in a
plot of the chief priests and Pharisees to take Him prisoner (11:57).
As a part of this same plot or the development of another, the chief
priests take steps to kill both Christ and Lazarus (12:10, 11).

But by way of contrast, there is also a development of faith in
chapters 5–12. After the feeding of the five thousand, the crowd
apparently made a great show of approval of His ministry (6:15).
Peter confessed Him as the Christ (6:69); the man born blind worshiped him (9:38); many believed in Him at the raising of Lazarus
(11:45); and the crowds hailed Him as "King of Israel" at His entry
into Jerusalem (12:13).

Jesus' Revelation Intensifies

In chapters 13–17, often called the Upper Room Discourse, the
Son of God reveals Himself to His disciples. This He does by showing His true humility in washing their feet, by demonstrating His
omniscience in the prediction of Judas' betrayal and Peter's denial,
and by reminding them of His mission in the reiteration of His
imminent death. He also tells them that He must leave them but
will return again after preparing a place in heaven for them. He
tells them, too, of His essential unity with the Father and that after
His departure, the Holy Spirit will come to comfort and teach
them. Not only does He demonstrate to them His unity with the
Father but also His unity with the believer; the latter He describes
under the figure of the vine and the branches (chapter 15).

In chapter 17, we are permitted a glimpse into the innermost
counsels of trinitarian relationship. Here Christ prays the Father
for our spiritual protection and preservation and progress. This is
indeed the Lord's Prayer. One of the most neglected truths of the
New Testament appears in this discourse of our Lord with His dis-

ciples; it concerns the teaching ministry of the Holy Spirit (14:26; 16:12–15). We tend to depend too heavily on our own intellect, Bible study guides, and the interpretations of Christian leaders for our knowledge of the Word. But the truths of the Bible are available to all—even to those who have rather meager mental ability, and to those who have little opportunity to receive the benefit of Bible study books or the ministry of Christian workers. God Himself will throw light on the sacred page that He has inspired.

Chapters 18 and 19 reveal the passion of the Son of God. Presented here is the culmination of unbelief. Peter denies Him. Jewish leaders condemn Him and demand His death. The crowds cry, "Crucify Him." Roman power accedes to their demands. Jesus appears very much alone at the time of the crucifixion (but see John 19:25–27). This is no doubt due in part to the fact that He was arraigned in Jerusalem, and most of His followers lived in Galilee. Events moved too fast during the latter part of the Passion Week for any of them to have arrived in Jerusalem to support Him.

But chapters 20 and 21 show the culmination of faith in Christ (remember the purpose for which the gospel was written, 20:30, 31) and the final confirmation of the deity of Christ. What greater proof of His deity could be offered than the resurrection? It was this greatest of all miracles, basic to the Christian message, that rekindled the faith of the disciples. He appeared to Mary, to the ten, to the eleven, and to a group of the disciples who had gone fishing on the Sea of Galilee. Fittingly, He drew from Peter a renewed confession of faith.

Since the deity of Christ looms so large in John, a fact that is designed to elicit faith, it may be well to conclude our study with a list of the claims of Christ that appear in the book. Bible teachers commonly mention the seven great *I am*'s Jesus said of Himself: the bread of life (6:35), the light of the world (8:12; 9:5), the door (10:7), the good shepherd (10:11, 14), the resurrection and the life (11:25), the way, the truth, and the life (14:6), and the true vine (15:1). To these may be added His claim to be the Messiah (4:25, 26), to have existed before Abraham (8:58), and to be one with the Father (10:30).

NARRATIVE OF THE LIFE OF CHRIST
AS RECORDED IN THE GOSPELS

As noted above, the gospel of John is especially helpful in constructing a chronology of the life of Christ. An outline of His life on earth follows.

1. The Thirty Years of Preparation: Matthew 1:1–4:11; Mark 1:1–13; Luke 1:1–4:13; John 1:19–2:12
2. Early Judean Ministry (about a year): John 2:13–4:54
3. The Galilean Ministry: Early Period (from imprisonment of John the Baptist to choosing of the twelve, about four months): Matthew 4:12–17; 9:1–17; 12:1–21; Mark 1:14–3:12; Luke 4:14–6:11
4. The Galilean Ministry: Middle Period (from choosing the twelve to withdrawal into northern Galilee; about ten months): Matthew 4:18–8:34; 9:18–11:30; 13:1–15:20; Mark 3:13–7:23; Luke 6:12–9:17; John 6:1–70
5. Galilean Ministry: Later Period (from journey into northern Galilee to departure for Jerusalem; about six months): Matthew 15:21–18:35; Mark 7:24–9:50; Luke 9:18–50; John 7:1–9
6. The Later Judean Ministry (about three months): Matthew 19:1, 2; Luke 9:51–13:21; John 7:10–10:42
7. The Perean Ministry (about three months): Matthew 19:3–20:34; Mark 10:1–52; Luke 13:22–19:28; John 11:1–12:11
8. The Passion Week: Matthew 21:1–27:66; Mark 11:1–15:47; Luke 19:29–23:56; John 12:12–19:42
9. The Resurrection and Post-Resurrection Ministry: Matthew 28:1–20; Mark 16:1–20; Luke 24:1–53; John 20:1–21:25

MIRACLES OF CHRIST

Though the gospels refer to many groups of miracles Jesus performed, they describe thirty-five specific miracles. These are listed below roughly in the order in which they occurred.

1. Turning water into wine: John 2:1–11
2. Healing a nobleman's son at Cana: John 4:46–54
3. Healing a lame man at the pool of Bethesda: John 5:1–9
4. Providing first miraculous catch of fish: Luke 5:1–11
5. Delivering a synagogue demoniac: Mark 1:23–28; Luke 4:31–36
6. Healing Peter's mother-in-law: Matthew 8:14–17; Mark 1:29–31; Luke 4:38, 39
7. Cleansing a leper: Matthew 8:2–4; Mark 1:40–45; Luke 5:12–16
8. Healing a paralytic: Matthew 9:2–8; Mark 2:3–12; Luke 5:18–26
9. Healing a man with a withered hand: Matthew 12:9–14; Mark 3:1–5; Luke 6:6–11
10. Healing a centurion's servant: Matthew 8:5–13; Luke 7:1–10
11. Raising a widow's son: Luke 7:11–17
12. Healing a blind and dumb demoniac: Matthew 12:22; Luke 11:14
13. Stilling a storm: Matthew 8:18, 23–27; Mark 4:35–41; Luke 8:22–25
14. Delivering the Gadarene demoniacs: Matthew 8:28–34; Mark 5:1–20; Luke 8; 26–39
15. Healing a woman with an issue of blood: Matthew 9:20–22; Mark 5:25–34; Luke 8:43–48
16. Raising Jairus' daughter: Matthew 9:18, 19, 23–26; Mark 5:22–24, 35–43; Luke 8:41, 42, 49–56
17. Healing two blind men: Matthew 9:27–31

18. Delivering a dumb demoniac: Matthew 9:32, 33
19. Feeding the five thousand: Matthew 14:14–21; Mark 6:35–44; Luke 9:12–17; John 6:4–13
20. Walking on the water: Matthew 14:24–33; Mark 6:45–52; John 6:16–21
21. Delivering a Syrophoenician's daughter: Matthew 15:21–28; Mark 7:24–30
22. Healing a deaf mute in Decapolis: Mark 7:31–37
23. Feeding the four thousand: Matthew 15:32–39; Mark 8:1–9
24. Healing a blind man at Bethsaida: Mark 8:22–26
25. Delivering a demon-possessed boy: Matthew 17:14–18; Mark 9:14–29; Luke 9:38–43
26. Finding the tribute money: Matthew 17:24–27
27. Healing a man born blind: John 9:1–7
28. Healing a deformed woman on the Sabbath: Luke 13:10–17
29. Healing a man with dropsy: Luke 14:1–6
30. Raising of Lazarus: John 11:17–44
31. Cleansing ten lepers: Luke 17:11–19
32. Healing blind Bartimaeus: Matthew 20:29–34; Mark 10:46–52; Luke 18:35–43
33. Cursing the fig tree: Matthew 21:18, 19; Mark 11:12–14
34. Restoring Malchus' ear: Luke 22:49–51; John 18:10
35. Providing a second miraculous catch of fish: John 21:1–14

PARABLES OF JESUS CHRIST

Scholars vary widely in the number of parables they discover in the gospels. Their lists range from about thirty to eighty, depending on whether they include seeming parables not described by the term "parable" and whether they include shorter parables and parabolic illustrations. A total of fifty-two are noted here. These are arranged in nine categories; in a few cases assignment of a parable to one of these categories is somewhat arbitrary.

    I. The Message of God in the World
        A. Nature of the message
            The patched cloth and the wineskins (Matthew 9:16, 17; Mark 2:21, 22; Luke 5:36–38)
        B. Proclamation of the message
            The sower (Matthew 13:3–9, 18–23; Mark 4:1–9, 13–20; Luke 8:4–15)
        C. Growth of the truth (kingdom) in the world
            1. The seed growing secretly (Mark 4:26–29)
            2. The mustard seed (Matthew 13:31, 32; Mark 4:30–32; Luke 13:18, 19)
            3. The leaven (Matthew 13:33; Luke 13:20, 21)
        D. Corruption of the message and work of God
            The wheat and tares (Matthew 13:24–30, 36–43)
  II. Salvation and Forgiveness of Sin
          1, 2 & 3. The lost sheep, the lost coin, and the prodigal son (Luke 15)
          4. Pharisee and the publican (Luke 18:9–14)
          5. Sons called to work (Matthew 21:28–32)
          6 & 7. The hidden treasure and pearl of great price (Matthew 13:44–46)
          8. The marriage of the king's son (Matthew 22:1–14)
          9. The great supper (Luke 14:16–24)
          10. The barren fig tree (Luke 13:6–9)
          11. The strait gate and shut door (Luke 13:23–30)
          12. The door of the sheep (John 10:1–10)
          13. The good Shepherd (John 10:11–18, 25–30)
          14 & 15. Defilement from without and from within (Matthew 12:43–45; Luke 11:24–26)
          16. Inward light (Matthew 6:22, 23; Luke 11:34–36)

          17. The two roads (Matthew 7:13, 14)

          18. The builders (Matthew 7:24–27; Luke 6:46–49)

III. Treatment of Christ

          1. The wicked husbandmen (Matthew 21:33–41; Mark 12:1–9; Luke 20:9–16)

          2. The rejected stone (Matthew 21:42–46; Mark 12:10, 11; Luke 20:17–19)

IV. Fellowship with God

  A. Prayer

          1. The importunate friend (Luke 11:5–8)

          2. The unjust judge (Luke 18:1–8)

  B. Gratitude

    The two debtors (Luke 7:41–43)

  C. Christ's relationship with His disciples

    The bride and the bridegroom (Mark 2:19, 20; Luke 5:34–35)

  D. Spiritual fellowship and nourishment

    Vine and the branches (John 15:1–11)

  E. Supply of temporal needs

    The rich fool (Luke 12:16–21)

V. Witness or Discipleship

          1. Preparation for building a tower (Luke 14:28–30)

          2. Preparation for war (Luke 14:31, 32)

          3. Salt (Matthew 5:13; Mark 9:50; Luke 14:33–35)

          4. The lighted lamp (Matthew 5:14–16; Mark 4:21; Luke 8:16, 17; 11:33)

          5. Offending members of the body (Matthew 5:29–30; Mark 9:43, 45, 47)

VI. Relations with Others

  A. A forgiving spirit

    The unmerciful servant (Matthew 18:23–35)

  B. Neighborliness

    The good Samaritan (Luke 10:30–37)

VII. Rewards
    1. Laborers in the vineyard (Matthew 20:1–16)
    2. Service (Luke 17:7–10)

VIII. The Return of Christ
    1. Return from the wedding feast (Luke 12:35–38)
    2. Breaking in of a thief (Matthew 24:43, 44; Luke 12:39, 40)
    3. A servant awaiting his master's return (Matthew 24:45–51; Luke 12:42–46)
    4. Householder and the porter (Mark 13:34–37)
    5. The unrighteous steward (Luke 16:1–13)
    6. The sprouting fig tree (Matthew 24:32–35; Mark 13:28–31; Luke 21:29–33)

IX. Judgment
    1. The fish net (Matthew 13:47–50)
    2. The ten pounds (Luke 19:11–27)
    3. The ten talents (Matthew 25:14–30)
    4. The ten virgins (Matthew 25:1–13)
    5. The rich man and Lazarus (Luke 16:19–31)[2]

Notes

1. In our day of emphasis on Christian social action, there is a tendency to assume that in both the Old and New Testaments "the poor" refers always or almost always to the materially poor. As a matter of fact, in a large percentage of cases reference is to spiritually poor.

2. Some prefer to call this a historical incident.

The Growth of the
Young Church

"Power from on High": Acts of the Risen Lord

Acts

WHAT'S IN A NAME?

T HOUGH commonly called the "Acts of the Apostles," this book deals mainly with only two of the apostles: Peter and Paul. Therefore, the name would seem to be inappropriate. Some have dubbed it "The Acts of the Holy Spirit." Certainly the third Person of the Trinity looms large in the book, but we may get a more appropriate title from a study of the first few verses. There we learn that in the gospel of Luke, the author described what Jesus began to do and teach until His ascension. This book intends to continue the account. After the ascension our Lord directed the apostles through the instrumentality of the Holy Spirit. So "The Acts of the Risen, Glorified, and Ascended Lord as Carried Out by the Holy Spirit" might be a more appropriate title, though admittedly too long for common usage.

THE AUTHOR

Unanimously, tradition declares for Luke's authorship. Internal evidence supports this view. Of particular importance in this regard are the so-called "we sections" (16:10–17; 20:5–21:18; 27:1–28:16). The point is that the author was with Paul during the events of these passages. Perhaps, then, we can determine by process of elimination who he was. Several individuals are distinguished from the author in Acts 20:4, 5; so they are automatically eliminated from further consideration. In addition to those mentioned in Acts 20:4. 5, Titus is a possibility. But neither in tradition nor in the book is there any evidence for his authorship. Luke seems to be the only other strong candidate, and we know that he was with Paul in Rome at the time Colossians was written (Colossians 4:14). What is more logical to suspect than that Luke accompanied Paul there on his Roman voyage (note the occurrences of *we* in Acts 27:1–28:16)? The rest of the book is by the same author as the "we" passages, as a careful study of the Greek style will attest.

Since in Colossians 4:14 Luke is distinguished from those "of the circumcision," we must conclude that he was a Gentile—the only author of either the Old or New Testament who was. Probably he was a native of Antioch of Syria, though some argue that he came from Philippi. He accompanied Paul briefly on the second missionary journey but remained at Philippi until Paul returned to Jerusalem at the end of the third missionary journey. From then on he seems to have been with Paul almost constantly to the end of the apostle's life, possibly as a medical adviser, for Luke is known as "the beloved physician."

THE SETTING

Without Acts the rest of the New Testament would be imperfectly understood. In fact, without it we would have no authentic record of apostolic history. Here the unity of the whole Christian movement becomes evident. The narrative involves the entire sweep of events from the ascension of Christ through the experience of Pentecost, the establishment of churches in Palestine and the eastern Mediterranean world, and the imprisonment of Paul at Rome. Paul, Peter, and James are presented and their ministries authenticated. By means of chapters 13–20, we learn how the Pauline epistles fit into the historical framework of the early church. Acts relates the founding of the churches that are addressed in the epistles.

The date of writing is indicated by Acts 28:30. There we have the seeming inference that the book was completed near the end of Paul's two-year Roman imprisonment. Surely Luke would have mentioned Paul's death or release if either had occurred by that time. Well-accepted chronologies of this period in Paul's life vary slightly. Some conclude that the two years in Rome took place 58–60, others 59–61, and still others 60–62. Taking into account all of these, we conclude that the book was probably written in Rome between 60 and 62.

THE MESSAGE

The key verse of Acts is 1:8 (NKJV): "But you shall receive power, when the Holy Spirit has come upon you; and you shall be witnesses to Me in Jerusalem, and in all Judea and Samaria, and to the end of the earth." There the theme is enunciated: the church witnessing. Several questions concerning witnessing are answered.

- Who was to witness? The apostles and other believers.
- How were they to witness? By the Spirit of God coming upon them.
- Of whom were they to witness? The person of Christ.
- Where were they to witness? Jerusalem, Judea, Samaria, and the remotest parts of the earth.

The answer to the last question provides a simple outline of the book:

1. Preparation of the disciples for witnessing, 1:1–2:47
2. Witnessing in Jerusalem, 3:1–7:60
3. Witnessing in Judea and Samaria, 8:1–9:43
4. Witnessing to the remotest parts, 10:1–28:31

During the period of preparation, the disciples, according to the command of the Lord, assembled in Jerusalem for ten days, waiting for the coming of the Holy Spirit. During this time the vacancy in the ranks of the twelve, resulting from the defection of Judas, was filled by the appointment of Matthias. When the day of Pentecost arrived, the Holy Spirit came upon and filled them all, empowering them for ministry. Then Peter was ready to preach his great sermon which, when combined with efforts of the other disciples, was instrumental in leading three thousand souls into the kingdom of God.

Just as great signs and wonders authenticated our Lord's message, so He imparted power to the disciples for the same reason. At the beginning of their ministry in Judea, they healed the lame beggar by the temple. But it must not be supposed that the servant is immune to the reproach of his Lord. Soon the Sadducees and later the Sanhedrin questioned them concerning their teachings and actions. As the opposition increased, the high priest and Sadducees threw several of the apostles in prison. When they escaped by the intervention of the angel of the Lord, the high priest and chief priests took them again and beat them and let them go. Finally, Jewish leaders centered their attack on Stephen, who became the first Christian martyr. Meanwhile, however, persecution had a salutary effect on the believers; several references in this section point up the purity and power of their lives.

In chapters 8 and 9, the witness of the Lord's followers broadens out to include Judea and Samaria. As has often been true in the history of the church since that time, persecution scattered the members of the church abroad so their testimony would be more widespread (8:1). Chapter 8 tells of the remarkably successful ministry of Philip in Samaria and his witness to the Ethiopian eunuch, while chapter 9 describes the efforts of Paul to extend the persecution of the saints to Damascus. But the Lord stopped him and regenerated his heart and life (chapters 22 and 26 also recount his Damascus road experience).

Most of Acts is devoted to the witness "to the remotest parts." Much against his own desires, Peter went to Caesarea, the center of Roman government in Palestine, to lead the Roman centurion Cornelius into a knowledge of the truth. Meanwhile, other believers preached in Phoenicia, Cyprus, and Antioch; and in the latter city the disciples were first called Christians (11:26). Soon persecution arose again, this time at the order of Herod (Herod Agrippa 1, who ruled Palestine A.D. 41–44). He killed James, the brother of John, and threw Peter in prison. But God delivered Peter in answer to prayer and smote Herod with a fatal disease.

The great missionary journeys of Paul begin in chapter 13. On the first journey Barnabas and Paul were traveling companions; their itinerary included Antioch of Syria, Cyprus, Attalia, Perga, Antioch of Pisidia, Iconium, Lystra, Derbe of Asia Minor (modern Turkey) and return by the same route. During this trip Jewish opposition to the gospel constantly manifested itself, and a mob stoned Paul at Lystra and left him for dead. When the missionary party returned to Jerusalem, the question arose as to whether Gentiles must come for salvation by way of the law. That is, must they subscribe to Jewish practices and observe the requirements of the Mosaic Law in addition to placing their faith in Christ? The decision of the council of Jerusalem (chapter 15) was in the negative. It concluded that Gentile believers were only to abstain from eating bloody meats or meats offered to idols and to maintain high moral standards to avoid offense to their Jewish brethren.

The second missionary journey is detailed in 15:36–18:22. This time Paul and Silas traveled together; Barnabas left Paul's company because of a disagreement over John Mark, and he took Mark on

296 THE AMG CONCISE INTRODUCTION TO THE BIBLE

a preaching tour of Cyprus. On the second journey, Paul and Silas revisited churches established on the first journey and then crossed over into Europe, where they founded churches at Philippi (chapter 16) and Thessalonica (chapter 17). Then Paul went on to minister at Athens (chapter 17) and Corinth (chapter 18), where he remained eighteen months.

The third journey is described in 18:22–21:17. Again Paul visited churches established on the first journey. Then he went to Ephesus, where he spent his longest period of ministry (over two years). At Ephesus his great success stirred up the wrath of the silversmiths, who tried to dispose of him. Shortly thereafter Paul made another tour of Macedonia and then returned to Jerusalem.

In all of Paul's ministry he followed a two-pronged strategy. First, he preached to the Jew first. This was natural and logical. He was a Jew and he was concerned for the salvation of his own people. Moreover, Jews were monotheists, had a promise of a new covenant, and a hope of a coming Messiah who would deliver them. In a sense or to a degree they were ready for his message. Furthermore, all the Jewish synagogues had proselytes or "Godfearers," Gentiles who were impressed with Judaism and who, to a greater or lesser degree, had become Jews. Many of these were perhaps as prepared as the Jews for the preaching of the gospel. In the cradle of the synagogue the church was to be born.

Second, Paul's strategy was an urban strategy. He did not just wander from place to place witnessing for Christ. He spent considerable periods of time in large cities where he could reach masses of people who would move out into the surrounding hinterland and beyond. As cases in point, he spent eighteen months in Corinth (Acts 18:11), through which flowed multitudes of people from all over the Mediterranean world; and over two years in Ephesus (Acts 19:8, 10; 20:31), the hub of the whole province of Asia, the wealthiest and most populous province of the Empire.

Urbanization had been a goal of Alexander the Great and his Seleucid and Ptolemaic successors. The Romans had bought the concept and sought to urbanize the entire empire. Thus, an urban center was a place where governmental officials, military forces, economic activity and cultural development could all be concentrated. It could hold down the countryside (or its hinterland) and permeate it with a desired cultural and political program. At the height of Paul's ministry, Rome was well on its way to urbanizing the entire empire. Paul, as a shrewd strategist and a Roman citizen, could be expected to use to the fullest extent this means of evangelizing the empire. From a place like Ephesus, for example, be could reach all sorts of individuals from the province of Asia who would return home to found churches. The fact that he could write an epistle to the church in Colosse, which he probably never visited, is a case in point. Evidently he spent weeks in such centers as Thessalonica or Iconium (see Acts 14:3), preaching with great success.

While in Jerusalem at the end of his third missionary journey, Paul was seized in the temple by Jews because they thought he had taken Trophimus, a Gentile, into the court of the Jews. Roman soldiers rescued him and, upon learning he was a Roman citizen, took especially good care of him. They whisked him away to Caesarea during the night to protect him from a Jewish plot on his life. There Paul appeared before Felix (a procurator, who kept him in prison with the hope of getting a ransom). When Festus, the new procurator, heard his case two years later, he called in King Agrippa (Herod Agrippa II who ruled a territory northeast of the Sea of Galilee) to help decide the case. Agrippa felt Paul should be released, but because Paul appealed to Caesar for justice—the right of a Roman citizen—Palestinian authorities were obliged to send him to Rome. Perhaps Paul took this way of getting to Italy to do evangelistic work. After an arduous journey, which is one of the most dramatic sea voyages on record, he reached Rome, where he spent two years under a kind of house arrest (28:30). Evidently he was kept at the camp of the famous Praetorian Guard on the edge of Rome. It may be supposed that at the end of this time Caesar came to the same conclusion as

Agrippa and released him (for evidence of his release and fourth missionary journey, see discussion under 1 Timothy). After all, the fire of Rome had not yet occurred, and Nero had no pretext on which to execute a Christian.

Without doubt, the historical and geographical detail of Acts has received more careful scrutiny than that of any other New Testament book. The scholar who has done more than any other to verify Luke's accuracy is Sir William M. Ramsay, Scottish archae-ologist, and he started his career as a skeptic. Sir William's many works are nearly all still in print. Especially noteworthy are *The Bearing of Recent Discovery on the Trustworthiness of the New Testament* and *St. Paul the Traveller and Roman Citizen*. But Ramsay only made a beginning. Ever since he laid down his pen in 1939, other scholars have been throwing light on the Lukan nar-rative and confirming its accuracy, and the day of diminishing returns has not yet set in.

"Grace to You and Peace": Paul's Letters to Young Churches

Galatians, 1 & 2 Thessalonians, 1 & 2 Corinthians, Romans, Colossians, Philemon, Ephesians, Philippians, 1 & 2 Timothy, Titus

THE New Testament letters have more than literary interest for the contemporary Christian. They were written under divine inspiration to deal with the everyday problems of ordinary Christians. Therefore they discuss all sorts of issues, such as relations between members of the family, masters and workers, and the state and its subjects. They contain teachings concerning sex, divorce, and ethical lapses of various sorts. They have a lot to say, too, concerning the corporate life of the church: about church government, the officers and their qualifications, the ordinances, and conduct in worship services. But especially they are filled with doctrine, with teachings about the Bible, the Father, the Son, the Holy Spirit, salvation, angels and Satan, humanity, and the future.

Lest we think that these letters were written to another generation very different from our own and therefore are somewhat irrelevant to our times, let us remember these important facts. First, human nature has not basically changed in the last two thousand years; people have much the same drives and concerns and sins as they did in New Testament times. Second, the New Testament was written to a people living under totalitarian government; if principles enunciated in these letters could work for them, they should certainly work for people living in Western democracies or under modern dictatorships. Third, the New Testament was written to people living in a pagan, permissive, sex-oriented society largely governed by situation ethics. Social and religious conditions were far worse than they are today; if Christianity could triumph so gloriously under such conditions, it must be capable of doing the same today. The same Holy Spirit who strengthened first century believers can empower twenty-first century Christians to live victoriously.

WHEN AND WHERE PAUL WROTE HIS LETTERS

The following chart is not offered with any degree of finality. It represents the opinions of a large percentage of New Testament students, who have reached their conclusions on the basis of biblical indications and tradition. Many are the unsolved problems concerning the chronology of Paul's life, however; and new information may in the future alter suggestions made here. Where there is a great deal of uncertainty, a question mark appears after the entry. Arrangement is chronological rather than biblical.

Perhaps the New Testament will make much more sense if we discuss Paul's letters in the order of composition, fitting them into the Pauline narrative.

Book	Place of Composition	Composition Date of
Galatians	Antioch of Syria?	48?
	Macedonia? Achaia?	55? or 56?
1 Thessalonians	Corinth	50 or 51
2 Thessalonians	Corinth	51
1 Corinthians	Ephesus	55
2 Corinthians	Macedonia or Achaia	55 or 56
Romans	Corinth	56
Colossians	Rome	59–61
Philemon	Rome	59–61
Ephesians	Rome	59–61
Philippians	Rome	61
1 Timothy	Macedonia?	62?, 64?, 65?
Titus	Macedonia?	62?, 65?
2 Timothy	Rome	67 or 68

GALATIANS: ATTACK OF A FALSE GOSPEL

Probably in the year A.D. 45 Barnabas and Paul launched the first missionary journey (Acts 13). After preaching through the entire island of Cyprus (Barnabas's home), they attacked the Asia Minor mainland. There they had considerable success evangelizing in the province of Galatia, which occupied a north-south strip of territory in central Asia Minor (modern Turkey). They preached first in Antioch of Pisidia, sweeping many converts into the kingdom of God. When the Jews stirred up trouble for them, they moved on to Lystra where they enjoyed a tumultuous welcome, the populace taking the apostolic pair for Jupiter and Mercury. After making clear that they were not, the apostles again had many converts and again suffered Jewish opposition. This time Paul was stoned and left for dead. However, he recovered, went on to Derbe, and evangelized there. Then Barnabas and Paul returned along the route they had come, organizing the churches they had founded.

Soon after they arrived in Antioch, they became embroiled in a debate over whether or not Gentiles had to keep the Mosaic Law in addition to faith in Christ to attain salvation. Peter and even Barnabas (Galatians 2:11–13) momentarily sided with the Judaizers. Meanwhile word arrived that the same sort of controversy had broken out in Galatia. Fighting to protect the purity of the gospel and his newly founded churches, Paul wrote to the Galatians from Antioch, possibly in A.D. 48. The Pauline position was vindicated at the council of Jerusalem in the following year, when the whole church agreed Gentiles did not need to keep the Law to be saved (Acts 15). Another school of interpretation puts the writing of Galatians after the council of Jerusalem, in 55 or 56.

The occasion for writing this letter appears in 1:6, 7, which may be more fully translated as follows: "I am amazed that you are so readily removing yourselves from him that called you into the grace of Christ unto a gospel of a different sort: Which is not another of the same sort [that we preach]; but there are some that trouble you and would pervert the gospel of Christ."

After Paul's evangelization of the area, a Judaizing element began preaching a gospel of legalism. Their procedure was a logical one. They attacked Paul's work by attacking his right to speak. His reply is logically arranged, too. First, Paul defends his apostleship; second, his message; and third, shows the practical implications of his message. Following this development, the book roughly divides into three sections of two chapters each.

The Defense of Justification by Faith

In defending his apostleship and right to speak, Paul points to his divine call (1:1), the divine source of his message (1:11, 12), the impossibility of getting his message from the other apostles (1:15–17); his independence of the Judean churches (1:18–24); and yet the approval of his message by the other apostles (2:9, 10). In concluding the biographical section of the epistle, Paul introduces the most important fact of Christianity: justification by faith and how it is possessed. Essentially the argument runs like this. The law condemns sinners for their failures. It took Christ to the cross as a representative of lawbreakers. We, by faith, are seen as crucified with Christ and partakers of divine life. If we are crucified with Christ, the law has no more dominion over us, and it cannot any longer condemn. The law cannot exact a penalty twice; Christ has already paid the penalty for which we were liable. This passage must be placed alongside 3:10–16 and Romans 6 for a complete exposition of the doctrine.

As the apostle deals with the theological argument of the epistle, he points out that after all Abraham was justified by faith. The law, which came after the time of Abraham, did not annul this faith arrangement. Actually, it was a temporary arrangement coming between the time of Moses and the death of Christ, its purpose being to prepare the way for Christ. The full implication of 3:24, 25 is not obvious to the twenty-first century reader. The word translated "schoolmaster" is *paidagogos* in Greek. A *paidagogos* was a slave who supervised the child, took him to school in the morning, and left him there. Once he got the boy to school, his job was finished. Likewise, once the law as a *paidagogos* had demonstrated the inability of humanity to meet the righteous standard of God, and once the provision for meeting that standard was made in Christ, there was no further need for the law. Moreover, the point of the next several verses is that now in Christ we have become adult sons. We are no longer like children who need to be led about by a *paidagogos* (the law). In concluding this section, Paul brings to bear a telling argument from the life of Abraham. It runs something like this: "You Judaizers; who claim to be sons of Abraham, remember that Abraham had two sons, Ishmael and Isaac. Ishmael was the son of the bondwoman and was cast out with his mother so he would not have an inheritance with Isaac, son of the free woman. Likewise, you Galatians who put yourselves under the law cannot be heirs or children of the promise, but you will be cast out, as were Hagar and her son."

In the last two chapters, Paul makes the practical application of the doctrine of justification by faith. After a warning lest one's liberty be forfeited in returning to the law system, the apostle further warns against allowing liberty to become license. Then he proceeds to stress the importance of walking by the Spirit. Earlier (3:1–5) he pointed out that believers receive the Spirit as a power for living the Christian life when they put their faith in Christ. Now the individual and social implications of living in the Spirit are presented. For the individual, there will be a manifestation of the fruit of the Spirit. Among the body of believers, there will be a restoration of brothers and sisters who have fallen into sin, a bearing of one another's burdens, and a beneficent life in general. Good works are not the means of salvation, but they certainly will be the product of the life of faith.

Galatians was a favorite book of Martin Luther, and its message of justification by faith became the touchstone of the Reformation.

First Thessalonians: Confusion and Disorderly Living

After the council of Jerusalem, Paul launched his second missionary journey, this time in the company of Silas. Going by land, the pair revisited the churches founded on the first journey. But then they went through a period of uncertainty as to where to go until the vision of the "man of Macedonia" (Acts 16:9, 10) made it clear that God wanted them to preach in Europe. After successfully planting a church in Philippi, Paul and Silas moved on to Thessalonica, the capital and great port of the province of Macedonia. There, too, they had numerous converts. But Jewish opposition was so violent that Paul determined to go first to Berea and then to Athens to wait out the storm. The storm did not abate soon enough for the apostle, however, and he went on to Corinth where he ministered for eighteen months (Acts 18:11).

When Paul departed Berea for Athens, he sent Silas and Timothy (who had joined them at Lystra, Acts 16:1) to assist the newly converted Thessalonian brethren. Later Silas and Timothy joined him at Corinth, and news received of the Thessalonian church occasioned the writing of 1 Thessalonians (1 Thessalonians 3:1–6). Chapters 1–3 tell of Paul's rejoicing over the Thessalonian believers; chapters 4 and 5 provide instructions for them on the subject of the Lord's coming for His saints.

In 1 Thessalonians 1–3 we learn that there was much to commend in the Thessalonian believers. They had readily received the gospel, faithfully served the Lord, and patiently borne the persecution heaped upon them. In fact, so exemplary had been their testimony that it was spoken of throughout Greece.

But, unfortunately, all was not well in Thessalonica. Apparently some had fallen into the moral laxness of their pagan surroundings (4:1–7), and others were guilty of disorderly living (5:14). The issue of the second coming of Christ disturbed many. Seemingly, a few had even quit working because they expected the Lord to return immediately (4:11; cf. 2 Thessalonians 3:10–12). The chief issue, however, centered on the dead in Christ. Some had heavy hearts because their loved ones had passed on and would not be on hand for the rapture of the saints. (The word *rapture* comes from a Latin verb meaning, "to snatch up, sweep up, carry off by force." It is the commonly used term for the event of Christ's coming to gather up His church.) Paul's message to these mourners was that at the Rapture, dead believers actually would precede (*prevent* is the word used in the King James Version) living believers; then living believers would be caught up to join them (4:13–18). The apostle went on to say that since the time of Christ's coming was uncertain, born-again ones as children of light were to abstain from every appearance of evil and to expect His momentary coming. Preparedness for His coming is more than mental awareness; it involves a holiness of life characterized by obedience to the commands detailed at the end of the epistle.

SECOND THESSALONIANS: ISSUES OF THE LAST DAYS

Second Thessalonians continues the general theme of the Lord's return, dealing even more exclusively with it than did 1 Thessalonians. Since in this second epistle Paul reveals a detailed, firsthand knowledge of conditions in Thessalonica, presumably he received the information from Silas and Timothy when they returned to Corinth from delivering the first Thessalonian epistle.

The problems attacked in this epistle differ somewhat from those mentioned in the first epistle. Concern over loved ones who had died before the Rapture seems to be nonexistent. The big question now is whether or not the Thessalonian believers are in the midst of the Tribulation and about to experience the day of the Lord (chapter 2). While there has been definite spiritual growth on the part of the church as a whole, a certain few seem to have become even more shiftless as they anticipated the soon return of Christ. No doubt their attitude was, "If Christ is coming right away, why work?" (3:10–12). The persecution evident in 1 Thessalonians continues to plague the church as this second letter is written.

The outline of 2 Thessalonians follows chapter divisions. In chapter 1, Paul offers thanksgiving and encouragement. There has been marked spiritual growth among the people, for this he is thankful. As they face continued persecution, he reminds them that at the day of the Lord, God will judge those who know Him not.

In chapter 2, the apostle deals with the central problem now before the Thessalonians. Through a forged letter supposedly Pauline, or a teaching falsely attributed to Paul, or a misinterpretation of something the apostle had told them, they have concluded that the rapture had taken place, that they were now in the midst of the tribulation and that the day of the Lord was upon them (2:2). Unfortunately, the *King James Version* conveys an incorrect idea in 2 Thessalonians 2:2, where it speaks of the "day of Christ." *The New American Standard* and the *New International Version* correctly render it "the day of the Lord." The point is this: The day of Christ refers to the rapture of the saints before the Tribulation, while the day of the Lord applies to Christ's coming in judgment at the end of the Tribulation. Scripture presents the Rapture as occurring at any time; no specific event must take place before Christ's return for the saints. Before the day of the Lord, however, a definite order of events will occur, as Paul now proceeds to enumerate: the great apostasy from godliness, the removal of the restrainer, and the revelation of the Antichrist (2:3–12, man of sin). Then at the end of the Tribulation, during which the man of sin will run rampant, Christ will return to judge him and the forces of evil (2:8, 9). Much has been said about the identification of the restrainer. Along with many Bible students of the past and present, the writer believes that he is none other than the Holy Spirit. He lifts His great restraint now operative in the world at the time of the rapture of the church. The pretribulation rapture position does not stand or fall with this identification, however.

While chapter 2 seeks to correct error in doctrine, chapter 3 endeavors to stop error in practice. Paul strongly reproves those who, in the light of the soon return of Christ, have quit work and have become troublemakers to the industrious, even living off the fruits of the labors of the industrious. His dictum: no work, no food. He exhorts the believers to avoid all who walk disorderly, but in so doing to admonish them as brothers and not as enemies of the truth.

FIRST CORINTHIANS: THE GOSPEL IN A PERVERSE GENERATION

After Paul's successful and extended ministry at Corinth on his second missionary journey, he returned to Jerusalem and thence to Antioch of Syria. After a brief stay in the metropolis, he went by land across Asia Minor again, stopping at the churches founded on the first journey. Finally he settled down at Ephesus, remaining over two years. While there he maintained contact with the churches founded in Greece during his second journey. The church at Corinth caused him great heartache because of its instability. Evidently it was especially afflicted with moral laxity and factionalism. In regard to the latter, Apollos had ministered effectively especially among the Jews of Corinth subsequent to Paul's ministry there (Acts 18:27, 28). Apparently Peter had also gone through town and won something of a following. As a result believers had split into factions, some following Paul, others following Apollos, and yet others Peter; while some said they followed Christ.

In addition to the rumors reaching Paul at Ephesus concerning conditions at Corinth, the church there had sent him a gift and had written him a letter of inquiry, sending both in the hands of Stephanas, Fortunatus, and Achaicus (1 Corinthians 16:17). First Corinthians is a response to this letter as well as to matters reported to him orally; he deals in his epistle with much more than the questions raised in their letter.

If the gospel could succeed at Corinth, seemingly it could succeed anywhere. Essential to Corinth's economy was the trade that rolled through her ports. But with this trade came a transient population element that threw moral discretion to the winds. It is bad enough when, in our day, people having some familiarity with Christian principles are torn loose from the inhibitions of community life; but imagine those same people in a society totally unacquainted with Christian morals! During the New Testament period there were at least five temples at Corinth to Aphrodite, goddess of erotic love and goddess of the sea. Though religious prostitution in connection with the worship of Aphrodite apparently was not practiced at Corinth during the New Testament period (as it had in ancient Corinth), her worship did heavily influence the mindset and practices of the region and of the mobile population. Add to this the effects of great material abundance gained under boomtown conditions. "Corinthian morals" became a byword in the

Mediterranean world. The picture of Gentile degradation painted by Paul in Romans 1 may well have been inspired by conditions he witnessed at Corinth. That the Corinthian church was greatly affected by its pagan context is evident from the nature of problems with which Paul dealt in the book.

In general, 1 Corinthians falls into two sections: chapters 1–6, problems reported to Paul orally, perhaps by members of the house of Chloe (1:11; cf. 5:1) and Stephanas, Fortunatus, and Achaicus (16:17); chapters 7–16, problems inquired about by letter. The first part deals with party strife, sexual morality, and litigation before heathen. The second touches on the subjects of marriage, virgins, things sacrificed to idols, public worship, exercise of spiritual gifts, the resurrection of the body, and the collection. Now let us consider each of these divisions in more detail.

Party Factions and Gross Immorality

As the book opens, Paul attacks head on the factious spirit in the Corinthian church. While four parties are named in 1:12, the two most important claim to follow Paul and Apollos. Revealing their Greek outlook, many of these Christians apparently were impressed by the greater eloquence and more philosophic approach of the latter. The apostle points out first the worthlessness of human wisdom in arriving at the truth of God when it is unaided by the Spirit of God. The "natural" or unregenerate person cannot understand spiritual concepts (2:14). Then he shows that neither he nor Apollos is of primary importance in the spiritual ministry; God is the one who brings about spiritual growth. The real answer to factionalism is spiritual maturity. To conclude the matter, he defends his apostolic ministry. In passing, it should be noted that there was no animosity between Paul and Apollos (cf. 1 Corinthians 16:12; Titus 3:13).

Chapters 5 and 6 deal primarily with immorality, with a brief section on litigation. For the former Paul recommends church discipline until the evil is removed and issues a reminder that their bodies are temples of the Holy Spirit (6:19). In connection with the latter, he points out the bad testimony of believers going to law before unbelievers and tells them to settle their differences within their own ranks. The message of 1 Corinthians 6:19, 20 revolutionizes all Christian conduct. Believers have been bought with a price (the blood of Christ) and therefore are not their own. Their bodies, time, talents, and energies all belong to God; and they as good stewards must use all these wisely for the glory of God.

Chapter 7 begins the section devoted to answering the letter from the Corinthian church. Topics are clearly introduced by the phrase "now concerning" or "as touching" (7:1; 7:25; 8:1; 8:4; 12:1; 16:1; 16:12). Chapter 7 contains some passages that are interpreted with great difficulty. Apparently some in Corinth taught that it was wrong to marry. Paul makes it clear that marriage on the one hand is not sinful but on the other is not obligatory. Those who were married to unbelievers should remain with their mates in an effort to win them.

Chapters 8–10 deal with eating meats offered to idols and participation in pagan feasts. Here the apostle points out the privilege of Christian liberty but reminds believers of their responsibility to weaker brothers and sisters. Also, he says the believer has no business participating in pagan feasts along with the Lord's Supper.

Spiritual Gifts

Chapters 12–14 furnish the most extended passage in the New Testament on spiritual gifts. Here it is demonstrated that the Holy Spirit bestows spiritual gifts on individual Christians according to His will, that the same gifts are not given to all but each has a gift and a place to fill in the church, that spiritual gifts are to be exercised in love, and that certain regulations are to control their manifestation. Two observations are in order here. First, the possession of spiritual gifts is not necessarily an evidence of spirituality because the Corinthians are described as carnal believers. Second, if the regulations of chapter 14 were carefully observed today, the excesses of certain groups would disappear immediately. Some who claim to have a corner on spiritual gifts today open their exclusive position to question by violating in their teachings and practice the clear instructions of chapters 12–14.

While this book makes a unique contribution to the subject of spiritual gifts, it also has much to offer concerning the resurrection (chapter 15). As usual, Paul's argument is a logical one. He begins by defending the fact of the resurrection. Then he points to its value as the basis of our faith; a dead Christ would be no Savior. He shows, too, that our resurrection is based on His. Then he goes on to discuss the nature of the resurrection body, the most important factor being its incorruptibility. The chapter ends on a note of triumph and with an exhortation. Being certain of the resurrection, and therefore certain of our faith and our future, we are to be "stedfast, unmoveable, always abounding in the work of the Lord," for we know our labor is not in vain (15:58).

The message of the last chapter is not unrelated to the foregoing theme of the resurrection. "Abounding in the work of the Lord" (15:58) and maintaining the testimony of the church requires financial support for the poor saints at Jerusalem. Instructions are clear as to the time and principle involved in taking the collection, the method of sending it, and its destination.

Now look at the way Paul closed the epistle, "My love be with you all." Though factions among them had bitterly opposed him, he was still able to express his love for them. Such was the magnanimity of the great apostle.

SECOND CORINTHIANS: A PLEA FOR REPENTANCE

Apparently the Corinthians had not been responsive to Paul's first letter nor to the personal efforts of Timothy who delivered it. So, with great heaviness of heart, Paul made a hurried second visit to Corinth to deal with the situation. This is inferred from such references as

2 Corinthians 2:1; 12:14, 21; and 13:1, 2, where he tells of coming to see them a third time. Moreover, it seems he had been poorly received on this second visit (note especially 2:5–8) and shortly thereafter wrote a scorching epistle (now lost to us), for which he was later sorry (2:34, 9; 7:8–12). But it also seems that this epistle was remarkably successful in accomplishing its aim and that there was now a repentant attitude among most of the Corinthian believers. At least so Titus reported as he returned from a mission to Corinth on which Paul had sent him (see 7:6–16). Paul's thanksgiving for this good report, along with a need for dealing with continuing activities of Judaizers at Corinth, led the apostle to write the second canonical epistle to the Corinthian church.

Because Paul's person and apostleship had been so vehemently attacked, he wrote from a more personal standpoint in this epistle than in any other. Here we learn, for instance, of his sufferings (1:4, 5, 8; 4:8ff.; 11:23–33), his weakness of body (10:10), and his unappealing speech (10:10; 11:6). Since matters having to do with doctrine or church order are so largely lacking in the defense of Paul's apostleship and person, one might ask the value of this letter. It lies chiefly in its description of the ministry of the gospel (its motives, problems, sufferings, and future rewards) and in its teaching on giving in chapters 8 and 9.

The unsystematic nature of Paul's treatment makes outlining the book a difficult task. But in general three divisions appear: chapters 1–7, 8–9, and 10–13. The first division describes Paul's concern for the Corinthian church, his difficulties and joys and motives in the ministry, his message, his advice on how to deal with offenders in the church, his appeal for separation from unbelievers and for reconciliation to himself, and his explanation of his change of plans for coming to visit them. The latter, he points out, was not due to fickleness but to spare them his anguish of heart.

Chapters 8 and 9 deal in detail with the collection for the Jerusalem church. Beyond its historical significance, this passage sets forth for us some important principles on giving:

1. Our giving should not lag behind other demonstrations of Christianity, such as faith, knowledge of the truth, and testifying for the Lord (8:7).
2. Giving is a proof of our love and gratitude to Christ (8:8, 9).
3. The manner of giving should be with willingness and cheerfulness (8:12; 9:7).
4. There is a principle of return in giving: reaping according to sowing (9:6).
5. Giving glorifies God (9:13).
6. By means of giving we secure the prayers and love of others (9:14).

While the first nine chapters of the book are conciliatory in tone, the last four are blasting by comparison. This fact has raised questions in the minds of many, with some even suggesting that this section might constitute the "lost" epistle mentioned above. There is not, however, any evidence that this portion was ever detached from the rest of the book. Furthermore, it is quite obvious that Paul is trying to defeat false teachers here; for such he never has any sympathy. While it is readily admitted that one's enemies would not respond to this kind of approach, it must be pointed out that Paul was trying to get at them through the church. Though the strong language is intended as a frontal attack on his opponents, it is also designed as a reminder to the church of its duty toward false teachers. In reading this section, one should note on the one hand Paul's humility when charges are personal, but on the other his passionate defense when the charges involve his office, authority, or message as an apostle.

ROMANS: THE ESSENTIALS OF THE FAITH

Most profound of all the Pauline epistles, Romans was written to instruct a church that the great apostle had not founded and to prepare the way for his coming visit to them (Romans 15:24–32). Presumably Paul wrote Romans near the end of his third missionary journey from Corinth. There is an air of finality about Romans 15:19: he had "fully preached" the gospel from Jerusalem unto Illyricum (modern Yugoslavia), which means he had evangelized in Syria, Cyprus, Asia Minor, and Greece. He had collected an offering for the poor at Jerusalem and was about to sail for Jerusalem to deliver it (Romans 15:25, 26). Now he is thinking about new arenas where he might do battle for the Savior. Rome is very much on his mind as a future locale for service. Apparently he sent this letter to the church there by the hand of Phoebe, the deaconess of Cenchrea (the eastern seaport of Corinth), who was on her way to Rome (Romans 16:1).

How the church there came into existence is a matter of some uncertainty. Roman Jews were present in Jerusalem on the day of Pentecost (Acts 2:10) and they may have returned to the capital to found a church. But perhaps the nucleus of its fellowship consisted of Paul's converts in other spheres of missionary activity, such as Corinth and Ephesus. In this connection, note the fairly large number of individuals he is able to call by name in chapter 16. In the other epistles this would have been a dangerous practice, because omissions could cause hurt feelings. Here it establishes contact with a congregation otherwise unknown to him.

In developing the theme of the righteousness of God, Paul sought to instruct an infant church in the essentials of the faith. No doubt the Holy Spirit had a further aim of instructing seekers after truth and young believers down through the ages. At least Romans proved to be instrumental in leading Martin Luther into a regeneration experience. Through his ministry the floodgates of mercy were opened wide on a Europe that spiritually was drought-stricken.

The History of Sin and Salvation

After a seventeen-verse salutation, the writer launches immediately into the theme of the epistle: salvation by means of divine righteousness. That humanity stands in need of divine righteousness is the burden of the first major section (1:18–3:20). There is seen the unspeakable degradation of the Gentile, the basis on which God judges the peoples of the earth (the Gentile according to the inner law of conscience and the Jew according to the Mosaic Law), and the failure of both Jew and Gentile to live up to the light given them. In short, all are sinners and therefore stand condemned (see 3:23).

However, God does not leave humanity in this dilemma. He provides for us in Jesus Christ a divine righteousness, which becomes ours as we exercise faith in Him. This is the theme of the next major section of the book (3:21–8:39). The section begins by showing that divine righteousness is available by faith and that this offer is open both to Jews and Gentiles. Moreover, justification by faith is not a new idea, because both Abraham (before institution of the Mosaic covenant) and David (who lived under the Mosaic Law) were justified apart from works. The inference is that other Old Testament saints were also. Then Paul shows that there are two great families on earth: Adam's and Christ's. All by physical birth are part of the first and are therefore condemned; by faith in Christ one can become a member of the second and receive justification and life. As the message of the book develops, it soon becomes obvious that justification is not the end of human spiritual strivings. One must arrive at a spiritual maturity wherein daily Christian experience will somewhat approximate newly found standing before God. The apostle beseeches, "Therefore do not let sin reign in your mortal body . . . And do not present your members as instruments of unrighteousness" (6:12, 13, NKJV). Those who seek this life of sanctification, however, can be sure of great inner battles similar to those of the apostle's. Paul groans that the things he wants to do he often is unable to do, and the things he desires to shun he does not have power to avoid. This section closes with a beautiful chapter on the blessings of life in the Spirit; it is the third person of the Trinity who provides the power necessary for victory in the Christian life.

In discussing chapters 3–8, two terms requiring definition have been used: justification and sanctification. The former is the judicial act of God by which He declares or reckons us righteous; this is on the basis of our faith in Christ and of Christ's righteousness being reckoned to our account. The second simply means "set apart" and as used here refers to the fact that the individual is increasingly set apart unto God and from the world by the enabling of the Holy Spirit.

Righteousness for Israel Too

Chapters 9–11 are often considered to be parenthetical, but they actually advance the argument greatly. They concern the relation of Israel to the righteousness of God and the covenant of God. The question arises as to whether concentration on the justification of Gentiles in this age is an indication that God has cast off the Jew. The apostle explains that Israel because of her unbelief is only temporarily set aside in favor of the Gentiles. At the end of the age God will again turn His attention to the salvation of the people of Israel, and great numbers of them will be saved. Meanwhile, however, individual Jews are being converted; God has not completely turned His back on the Jew today.

Practical Righteousness

The last section of the book concerns practical righteousness—the application of the righteousness of God to the daily life of believers. Paul exhorts them first to dedicate themselves unreservedly to God (12:1, 2). Then he presents their duties in the various relationships of life. Especially, they are to exercise their gifts in the church, to avoid taking vengeance on their enemies, to be subject to the state, and to be considerate of their weaker brothers and sisters in regard to doubtful things. In connection with the latter, Paul notes the fact of Christian liberty. But this exercise of liberty is not to be to one's own hurt, to the detriment of another Christian, or to the hindrance of the work of God.

EPHESIANS: FOCUS ON THE BODY OF CHRIST

Paul was to go to Rome all right, but probably not in the way he had originally planned. Upon his return to Jerusalem at the end of his third missionary journey, Jews at the temple sought to kill him, partly for his preaching of the gospel and partly for his supposedly having taken a Gentile into the court of the Jews (Acts 21:27–31). Roman soldiers rescued him, permitted him to make some defense in Jerusalem, and later took him to Caesarea (Roman capital of Palestine) when a plot on his life was uncovered. After hearings in Caesarea during a two-year imprisonment there, Paul appealed to Caesar as the "supreme court" of the Empire. Taken to Rome and shipwrecked on the way, he waited in the capital for two years for his case to be heard (for all this, see Acts 21:32–28:31).

Picture Paul sitting in the Roman prison thinking over his missionary activities in the Eastern Mediterranean world. As he does, a particular burden for the saints of Asia Minor descends upon him. Onesimus, a runaway slave, is with him and must be returned to his master, Philemon. Doctrinal errors face the Colossians. The Ephesian and nearby churches need to be strengthened in the faith. So, under the guidance of the Holy Spirit, the great apostle pens three letters (Ephesians, Colossians, and Philemon) and sends them with Tychicus and Onesimus (Ephesians 6:21, 22; Colossians 4:7–9).

Apparently the Ephesian letter was sent to more churches than the one at Ephesus. Since "in Ephesus" does not occur in the best Greek manuscripts, and since many impersonal elements appear in the letter (though Paul spent about three years in Ephesus, Acts 20:31), it seems best to regard it as a letter to a number of churches of western Asia Minor. Perhaps the apostle had in mind several of the seven churches John mentions in the Revelation.

The central theme of Ephesians is the church, which is defined as the body of Christ (1:22, 23): the universal, indivisible body of believers. The local church, described elsewhere in the New Testament, is not in view here. The development of the book divides into two sections of three chapters each, the first doctrinal and the second practical. Briefly stated, the message of the doctrinal section is that the church is a new thing. In it both Jews and Gentiles are united to form one organism. Entrance into this body is based on the work of Christ and is by means of faith alone. This new body is a mystery in that it was not known in previous ages, and the revelation of this mystery was in a special way committed to Paul. Members of the body of Christ are already positionally seated in the heavenlies, and many other spiritual blessings attend their daily walk.

In the last three chapters of Ephesians, the conduct of the church is in view. Paul exhorts members of the body of Christ to walk worthy of their exalted position (see 4:1, 17; 5:2, 8, 15), and provides instruction to guide them to a more Christlike life (4:17–5:18). As believers are one in Christ, they are to experience a unity of fellowship and spiritual maturity. In order that this unity may be achieved, gifted men (such as pastors, evangelists, and teachers, 4:11–13) are bestowed on the church. Paul sets a pattern for domestic life (5:22–6:4) and labor-management relations (6:5–9) before believers. And he describes the armor available to them in Christian warfare (6:10–18). Clearly this warfare is spiritual and must be fought with spiritual weapons. Throughout the book the apostle emphasizes the work of the Holy Spirit as the necessary enablement for living the Christian life. One is sealed with the Spirit (1:14; 4:30), is to pray in the Spirit (6:18), is not to grieve the Spirit (4:30), is to be strengthened by the Spirit (3:16), and is to be filled with the Spirit (5:18).

The analogy used in 5:18 is extremely important to understanding the concept of filling of the Spirit, so abused in the modern church. It involves control by the Spirit as one may be controlled by wine in the drunken state. One is not an empty receptacle to be filled by the Spirit. The Holy Spirit indwells all when they believe (Romans 8:9; 1 Corinthians 6:19, 20; Galatians 4:6) and have all of the Spirit they will ever receive. The issue in filling is not how much of the Spirit will we get but how much of us will the Spirit get. Will we permit Him to control us?

Ephesians provides an effective antidote to much that is wrong with the church in the twenty-first century. If its admonitions were heeded, strife among the brothers and sisters would cease. We would be one in fellowship even as positionally we are members of one body. Were this realized, the church would be a much more powerful force for evangelism in the world today.

COLOSSIANS: THE HEADSHIP OF CHRIST

Colossians and Ephesians are twin epistles, written at the same time. Both deal with the church, Ephesians emphasizing its nature as the body of Christ, and Colossians stressing its headship in the person of Christ. Both have direct teaching for husbands and wives, parents and children, and servants and masters. In describing similar subjects, much of the phraseology is similar.

In Colossians, Paul comes to grips with three errors that have been disturbing the Colossian church: Greek philosophy, Jewish legalism, and Oriental religious practices. These erroneous teachings centered on the person and work of Christ and actually destroyed the Christian message. To answer them, Paul does not engage in lengthy argument. To the one seeking knowledge by human philosophy, he says that in Christ "are hid all the treasures of wisdom and knowledge" (2:3). To the legalist, he points out that law observances are abolished at the cross (2:14), and the Christian is dead to them (2:20). To the one involved in Eastern religious practices of worshiping angels or spiritual powers, he sets forth the preeminence of Christ (2:19).

In addition to making specific reference to the three errors mentioned, Paul had much to say generally about the preeminence of

Christ. He is the Son of God (1; 3, 13); the image of the invisible
God (1:15); the creator (1:16); the sustainer (1:17); the firstborn
from the dead (1:18); the Savior (1:14, 20, 22; 2:13, 14); the head
of principalities and powers (2:10); the object of the believer's faith
(1:4; 2:5); the repository of the fullness of the Godhead (2:9); and
the agent in the believer's prayer (3:17). Moreover, He is now
seated at the right hand of God the Father (3:1), from where He
shall come again (3:4).

While chapters 1 and 2 are essentially doctrinal, chapters 3
and 4 apply these great doctrinal truths to everyday living. Again
it becomes obvious that our beliefs determine our actions. As
believers we have died and risen with Him (3:1). Our position is
an exalted one, and we need not descend to inferior beliefs and
practices but should rather set our minds on heavenly things (3:2).
We are to avoid the sins of the flesh and to follow holiness, which
includes true Christian relations between husbands and wives, parents and children, and servants and masters. In short, holy living
involves bringing every relationship into harmony with and under
the headship of Christ.

PHILEMON: THE GOSPEL OF RECONCILIATION

Onesimus, a Colossian slave guilty of a crime, ran away from his
master, Philemon, and eventually found his way to Rome. There he
came in contact with Paul and was converted. Therefore, in gratitude, Onesimus waited on Paul; but this situation could not continue. The honest apostle squarely faced his obligation to return the
runaway. No doubt Onesimus desired to return and right the
wrong he had committed. God had forgiven his sin, but restitution
had not been made. Since Roman law offered no protection to wayward slaves, Paul wrote to Philemon in an effort to reconcile master and slave, now brothers in the Lord. That Philemon lived in
Colosse is learned from Colossians 4:9, 17. Probably Apphia was

his wife and Archippus his son (v. 2). At least these sustained close relationship to Philemon.

Evidently Paul wrote this letter from Rome at the same time as he composed Ephesians and Colossians. Tychicus was the "postman" who delivered Colossians (Colossians 4:7) and Ephesians (Ephesians 6:21), and Onesimus (the bearer of this epistle) accompanied him (Colossians 4:9). The date was probably A.D. 60 or 61.

Paul's wisdom and tact are clearly revealed in this brief epistle. Instead of exercising apostolic authority and ordering Philemon to receive Onesimus, he pleads with him as a friend, pointing out that Philemon owes Paul a great deal for leading him to the Lord. Second, the apostle puts this matter in the hands of the church "to the church in your house"). So, if Philemon is indisposed to grant Paul's request, the pressure of the church will compel him to relent. Third, Paul offers to pay for Onesimus' wrongs. Last, Paul anticipates a visit to Colosse; surely Philemon would not dare to face Paul if he refused this request.

This epistle demonstrates also how social problems are treated by the gospel: not by force but by love. The apostle does not defend the institution of slavery; he merely accepts it. He would have accomplished nothing by crusading against it, but in essence he destroys it by putting both Philemon and Onesimus—master and slave—on common ground before the Lord.

The fervor of Christian love in effect melted the chains of slavery and counted master and slave as beloved brothers in the family of God (cf. 1 Corinthians 12:13; Galatians 3:28). Paul neither conceded the rightfulness of the institution of slavery, nor did he campaign to abolish it. Here he tried to nullify its effects; elsewhere he sought to regulate existing relations by pointing out the duties of Christian masters and Christian slaves to each other (Ephesians 6:5, 6, 9; Colossians 3:22–24; 4:1).

The letter to Philemon well illustrates the gospel message. Sin breaks fellowship and is a bondage; a third party (Christ) related in

some way to both the offender and offended steps in to effect a reconciliation. Paul asks that the sin of the offender be reckoned over to
his account (as does Christ), and he places his good name and reputation at the disposal of the offender (note that Christ's righteousness is made available to the sinner). Fellowship is then restored.

PHILIPPIANS: AN APPEAL FOR CHRISTIAN UNITY

Philippians was apparently the last of the prison letters, written
near the end of Paul's two-year incarceration in Rome. Time was
required for the Philippians to hear that Paul was a prisoner in
Rome, for Epaphroditus to come with their gift and for them to
hear of Epaphroditus' illness while in Rome and for his recovery
to take place (Philippians 2:25–28), for the factions to develop to
which Paul referred in Philippians 1:14–18, for Paul's reputation
to spread among the Praetorian Guard (crack troops of the Empire,
1:13), and for the gospel to penetrate Caesar's household (4:22).
Finally, assuming that Paul was released from Roman imprisonment (see discussion under 1 Timothy), he must have written the
letter just before that release because he expected to see the Philippians
"shortly" (Philippians 2:24).

    To many who read this letter "joy" or "rejoicing" seems to be
the central theme (see 1:4, 18, 25, 26; 2:2, 16, 18; 3:1, 3; 4:1, 4, 10).
Others will find the theme to be the gospel (see 1:5 [Greek text],
7, 12, 16, 27; 2:22 [Greek text]; 4:3, 15). Yet others consider Jesus
Christ to be central to the message of the letter. It is the writer's
belief, however, that the message of this book is twofold, to thank
the Philippian believers for their generous gift and to deal with dis-
sension that had arisen among Philippian believers. Apparently
Epaphroditus brought word of this when he presented the gift to
Paul. The apostle does not deal openly with the matter of unity, but
the reader can find allusions to the problem throughout the book.
Several verses include the words "you all" or "all" and indicate

that the apostle wants them to realize that he is speaking to the whole Philippian church and not several factions (1:1, 4, 7, 8, 25; 2:17, 26). Consider also references to his desire for unity, as expressed in the words "one" or "same" (1:27; 2:2; 3:16; 4:2) and his command in 2:14, "Do all things without murmurings and disputings." A passage that, probably more than any other, expresses the thought of the entire letter and therefore serves as the key is 2:1–5. There one finds the basis for unity—blessings of the Christian life; the exhortation to unity—"be of the same mind"; and the means of unity—humility and the consideration of the needs of others.

Paul begins the letter with a salutation "to all the saints in Christ Jesus that are in Philippi." He then continues to emphasize the theme in making prayer for "you all" (1:4); in believing that the Lord would keep "you all" unto the day of Christ (1:6, 7); in declaring his concern for "you all" (1:8); in stating that it is needful for him to abide with "you all" (1:25); in exhorting them to stand fast in *one* spirit, striving for the faith of the gospel (1:27), and to live with singleness of purpose and love and without faction (2:2). His rejoicing is with "you all" (2:17) and Epaphroditus shared Paul's concern for "you all" (2:26). A further emphasis on single-mindedness is found in 3:15, 16; and in 4:2 he exhorts two women who seem to be ringleaders in factional strife to put away their differences.

The greatest passage in the book is 2:1–11. While it centers on the person of Christ, it must be seen here in connection with the truth that all division ceases and harmony is restored when believers have the mind of Christ. This attitude of utter humility (which led Him to divest Himself of the visible glory of heaven and assume humanity) will not permit infringements on the rights of others, and thus full fellowship among the brethren is restored.

Following the theme of unity, main headings of the outline of Philippians are as follows:

1. Introduction, 1:1–11
2. Paul's imprisonment as related to the question of unity, 1:12–30
3. The mind of Christ: the source of all unity, 2:1–30
4. The biographical appeal for unity: answers from Paul's experience to problems causing disunity, 3:1–21
5. Exhortations that will lead to unity, 4:1–9
6. Thanksgiving for their gift: a representation of their unified action, 4:10–20
7. Conclusion, 4:21–23

In conjunction with the general theme of unity, two special problems arise, problems that caused at least a part of the disunity. The first of these relates to Judaism and Judaizers; this is dealt with in 3:1–7. The second problem concerns Christian perfection and is emphasized in several passages. In answer, Paul clearly teaches that perfection in this life is not absolute but progressive. Chapter 3 provides the most extended treatment of the subject (vv. 7–15).

FIRST TIMOTHY: FOR ALL THE YOUNG PREACHERS

The time-honored approach has been that Paul's instructions to young preachers appear in I and 2 Timothy and Titus; for this reason they are called pastoral epistles. One cannot make a dogmatic or unqualified statement about Paul's authorship today, however, because many scholars are convinced that Paul did not write these books. They admit virtually unanimous witness of the church to Pauline authorship from the second century to the nineteenth century but deny it on the basis of internal evidence. Just about the only leader in the early church who rejected Pauline authorship of these three epistles was Marcion, a heretic who excluded them from his canon about A.D. 140. His claim is insignificant, however, because he also rejected Matthew, Mark, John and reworked Luke to fit his purposes; no one rejects those books or their authorship because of Marcion's conclusions.

Internal arguments which rationalists advanced against Pauline authorship in the nineteenth century may be grouped under the headings of historical, linguistic, doctrinal, and ecclesiastical questions.

Historically, the point is made that these books do not fit into the account of Paul's ministry as presented in Acts. The simple answer is that Acts closes with Paul's two-year imprisonment and these epistles fit into a period after that time.

Linguistically, the language of these epistles is presumed to be too different from Paul's other ten epistles to permit his authorship of them. Four forms of answer are possible. First, Paul was physically and mentally old now, if not chronologically old, and presumably also somewhat changed in his thinking. Any writer must be permitted a change of vocabulary and themes late in life. Second, the thesis has been developed that Luke was his amanuensis or scribe when he wrote these books; there are affinities between the Greek of these books and the Gospel of Luke. Third, some argue that during Paul's Roman imprisonment he came under the influence of Latin linguistic patterns and that he deliberately developed his Latin in anticipation of his trip to Spain and points west. There is a claim of similarity between the style in these works and that of Cicero, for example. Fourth, from the argument of historical grammar it can be asserted that the Pastorals are written in first century Greek and therefore do not fit the hypothesis of second century composition.

Doctrinally, there are also evident differences between these three books and the other ten acknowledged epistles of Paul; but he is dealing with more practical matters here, and affinities between these books and the other ten do exist.

Ecclesiastically, there is supposedly a second century stage of church government in these epistles, with talk about bishops and elders and others. But Paul uses the terms "bishop" and "elder" interchangeably in Titus 1:5–7, while they are differentiated in the second century. In Acts 14:23 Paul appointed elders in the churches.

In Philippians 1:1 he addressed bishops and deacons. In the earliest days of the church the apostles established a separate order of leaders, presumably deacons (Acts 6).

In conclusion, all arguments against Pauline authorship of the Pastoral Epistles are answerable, and the traditional view may be accepted with confidence.[1] Following that view, we conclude that apparently the apostle sent out these two young men (Timothy to Ephesus and Titus to Crete) after his release from the Roman imprisonment mentioned in Acts. That Paul was released from prison and that he did have a fourth missionary journey is evident from several factors, four of which follow.

First, Eusebius of Caesarea in his early fourth century history reported that Paul was released from his first Roman imprisonment, after which he resumed his preaching tours. Imprisoned in Rome a second time, he wrote 2 Timothy and was later martyred (*Ecclesiastical History* 2.22).

Second, Philemon 22 and Philippians 1:25, 26; 2:23, 24 evidence a confidence on Paul's part that he would be released from prison, would return to Philippi, and would visit Colosse. If we believe in verbal inspiration, we should probably assume that these were not idle wishes of the author. Moreover, Romans 15:24, 28 describe a prospective trip to Spain, which various early church fathers say he made. In connection with these references we should take into account 2 Timothy 4:7, "I have finished my course." This would imply the fulfillment of Paul's plans and hopes.

Third, in 2 Timothy 4:20 Paul mentions leaving Trophimus at Miletus. If this refers to the book of Acts (20:4; 21:29), it contradicts Acts; there Trophimus was not left behind. The 2 Timothy reference presupposes another voyage.

Fourth, Clement of Rome, about A.D. 95, said that Paul went "to the extremity of the West" (*1 Clement* V). While admittedly he did not specifically mention Spain, it must be implied. Rome, to Romans, was not the extremity of the West, as some claim; it was the center of the empire.

In a brief meeting with the Ephesian elders at Miletus, Paul had warned, "For I know this, that after my departure savage wolves will come in among you, not sparing the flock. Also from among yourselves men will rise up, speaking perverse things, to draw away disciples after themselves" (Acts 20:29, 30). Now, some years later, this prophecy had been fulfilled; and Paul found it necessary to send Timothy to Ephesus to deal with the infiltration of doctrinal error among Ephesian believers. First Timothy 1 clearly indicates the seriousness of the situation. Some had turned from "faith unfeigned"; for these Paul urged practical godliness (1:5, 6). Others were abusing the law; to these Paul pointed out that the law had a lawful use (1:7ff.). Still others had fallen into gross apostasy; apparently Hymenaeus and Alexander led the pack (1:19, 20). To them was administered more stringent discipline. To deal with Ephesian error and to instruct the church in its corporate worship and administration, Paul commissioned Timothy to Ephesus. But in giving instructions concerning official responsibilities, the great apostle felt it necessary to append some personal admonitions. The outline of the book, then, falls into these three divisions:

1. The Ephesian problem, 1:1–17
2. Instructions concerning official responsibilities, 1:18–4:5
3. Admonitions concerning personal behavior, 4:6–6:21

One cannot be sure whether chapters 2 and 3 were written to tackle specific problems at Ephesus; in part they may have been. At least, the instruction they contain was needful for the effective organization of the church there. Paul deals with public prayer, the place of women in the church, the qualifications of bishops (probably synonymous with elders) and deacons. Spiritual requirements for overseeing the flock include being irreproachable in family affairs, personal walk, social relationships, and doctrinal tenets.

That Timothy was relatively young when Paul sent him these instructions is unquestioned (4:12). But if Timothy was about twenty (to pick a figure for the sake of discussion) when he joined Paul, he must have been at least thirty-five when Paul sent him to Ephesus. Perhaps 1 Timothy 4:12 addresses more his inexperience in dealing with leadership functions on his own than actual chronological age. It seems equally certain that he lacked a forcefulness of personality to deal with some issues. Perhaps he was somewhat dismayed by the gigantic task before him. In the last half of the book, Paul seeks to meet these needs in the life of the young minister. In addition, he provides advice on how to treat various kinds of individuals as he carries out his ministerial duties (see chapter 5). Chapters 4–6 provide timeless advice of the most practical nature for the young Christian worker. Among other things, these chapters exhort him to be an example in all his relationships, to be diligent in service, to be judicious in dealing with others, to hold sound doctrine, to be faithful in proclaiming the truth, to flee the temptations of the world, and in general to fight the good fight of faith.

Timothy was apparently born in Lystra of a Greek father and a Jewish mother (Acts 16:1, 3), who brought him up in the Jewish faith, and under whose tutelage he had learned the "sacred writings" from childhood (2 Timothy 3:14, 15). Presumably he was one of Paul's converts on his first trip to Lystra. The young man joined Paul at Lystra on his second missionary journey (Acts 16:1) and remained with him thereafter; already his testimony was outstanding. He shared with Paul the evangelization of Ephesus and so was thoroughly familiar with the situation there. Subsequently he was with Paul in Rome during his first imprisonment in the capital (Colossians 1:1; Philemon 1). As Paul's "true child in the faith" (1 Timothy 1:2), Timothy was then stationed at Ephesus to meet some of the pressing needs of the church (1 Timothy 1:3). After completing his assignment in Ephesus (as spelled out in 1 Timothy), he joined Paul in Rome during his second imprisonment there (2 Timothy 4:11, 21) and was himself imprisoned and later released (Hebrews 13:23).

TITUS: THE IMPORTANCE OF GOOD LEADERSHIP

Apparently while on his fourth missionary journey, Paul left Titus on the island of Crete to organize the church there and to clear up some of the ethical and doctrinal problems that had arisen. That this was no easy assignment is clear from Paul's estimation of the character of the Cretans and the condition that arose because of that character (see 1:9–16). The task was complicated by the fact that the Cretan church had not heretofore received apostolic attention. Perhaps visitors to Jerusalem founded it on the day of Pentecost (Acts 2:11). Titus's job was more difficult than that of Timothy at Ephesus, therefore, because at Ephesus the church had been well organized and grounded in the true doctrine by Paul. But Titus was older and more experienced than Timothy; he had joined Paul early in the apostle's missionary activities (possibly as a Greek convert from Antioch, Galatians 2:1–3), had been sent by Paul to Corinth to quell the turbulent situation there (2 Corinthians 7:6–16; 8:16–24), and had traveled extensively in Macedonia to collect funds that Paul was raising for poor saints in Jerusalem. To be sure, Paul felt a need for counseling Titus, bur he did not evidence the great anxiety for him that he did for Timothy. The instruction in the book of Titus pertains more to the Cretan situation than to Titus' person problems.

The message to Titus is quickly summarized. After the salutation (1:1–4) appears instruction for church officers. Their position of leadership demands a good testimony (in family life, personal temperance, humility, judgment, and spotless character, 1:5–8) and ability to hold fast and defend sound doctrine in the face of doctrinal error and ethical irregularity (1:9–16). Chapter 2 provides instruction for various groups of members in the church: aged men, aged women, young men, young women, and servants. All of these are to live in a way becoming to sound doctrine. Chapter 3 describes the responsibility of Christians as members of society and in relation to heresy. In delivering his instructions, Paul pens two of the great creedal statements of the New Testament (2:11–14; 3:4–7). The latter pertains to salvation by grace and the former to godly living in the light of Christ's appearing.

SECOND TIMOTHY: PAUL'S FAREWELL

Pitiable indeed is the great apostle to the Gentiles as he writes his farewell message. Detained a second time in a Roman prison (perhaps the Mamertine, where political prisoners were kept), he awaits final adjudication and martyrdom (4:6, 7). Alone (except for Luke) he cries for fellowship, "Be diligent to come to me quickly . . . Take Mark, and bring him with you" (4:9, 11). Intellectually starved, he calls for books and parchments (4:13). Dreading the cold winter ahead, he sends for warm clothing (4:13). But Paul is concerned for far more than himself in this epistle. The Ephesian church apparently faces grave dangers, and Timothy needs continued encouragement to deal with problems there.

Paul was probably arrested in Asia and from there brought to Rome. Likely, some of his enemies reported him to the Roman authorities and brought about his detention. Now that Christians were political enemies (after the burning of Rome in A.D. 64), it was possible to dispose of them in this way (Note: Asia has turned against him, Phygellus and Hermogenes particularly opposing him, 1:15. Alexander the coppersmith caused him a great deal of trouble, 4:14).

Throughout this letter there is a weaving together of Paul's reflections on his own life of service and exhortations to Timothy to continue faithful in service for the Lord. For this reason it is somewhat difficult to outline the book. There seem to be three divisions, however: 1:1–18; 2:1–4:5; 4:6–22. Predominant in chapter 1 is the theme of loyalty to the Lord in spite of suffering. Paul avers his own loyalty and encourages Timothy to continue in loyal service. The second section describes the duties of Timothy. Backbreaking is the task which his father in the faith sets before him. Paul's charge includes these exhortations: teach others, be a good soldier of Christ and avoid the snares of this life, hold to true doctrine and the inspired Word in spite of apostasy, mature in spiritual matters, preach the Word, endure afflictions; in short, seek to be a workman approved (2:15). One of the high points of this section is the great text on inspiration of Scripture: 3:16, 17. Every ministerial student and young preacher will do well to consider carefully the admonitions of this section. Here is an inspired pastoral handbook.

Paul makes his farewell in the concluding chapter of the book. This farewell is with no regrets: "I have fought a good fight, I have finished my course, I have kept the faith" (4:7). It is uttered in loneliness and sorrow as he recounts the apostasy of some, but it is also spoken with confidence in the abiding presence and protection of the Lord.

NOTE

1. Extended treatments of this complicated subject (all of which argue for the traditional view) are Donald Guthrie, *New Testament Introduction*, 3rd ed. (Downers Grove, Ill.: InterVarsity, 1970), pp. 584–622; Everett F. Harrison, *Introduction to the New Testament*, rev. ed. (Grand Rapids: Eerdmans, 1971), pp. 351–66; and William Hendriksen, *Exposition of the Pastoral Epistles* (Grand Rapids: Baker Book House, 1957), pp. 4–33.

A Better Way:
The Letter to the Hebrews

Hebrews

WHO, WHEN, WHERE, WHY?

SCHOLARSHIP has virtually given up on the question of who wrote Hebrews. The current attitude is much the same as that of Origen (third century) who said, "Who wrote the epistle God only knows certainly" (quoted in Eusebius, *Ecclesiastical History* 6.25). In addition to Paul, Luke and Barnabas and Apollos are most commonly suggested as authors. But evidence for any of them is inconclusive. Indecision as to authorship does not affect inspiration, however. The message of Hebrews is one of the most elevated in the Bible. As has often been said, here we have the holy of holies of Christian truth.

The dating of Hebrews is closely tied to the question of authorship, but we have a little more definite information in this case. It could not have been written later than the end of the first century because Clement of Rome in his epistle to the Corinthians quotes extensively from Hebrews (Clement wrote about A.D. 95). From such references as 8:4, 13; 10:11; 13:10, 11, it appears that the temple was still standing (it was destroyed in A.D. 70). Though admittedly the writer was more concerned with the ritual of the pre-Solomonic tabernacle than the temple, there is a lack of reference to the destruction of the temple and the cessation of the Old Testament sacrificial system. Moreover, Timothy was still alive and had recently been set free from prison (see 13:23). Possibly this imprisonment resulted from Timothy's journey to Rome in response to Paul's request of 2 Timothy 4:9ff. If so, the epistle probably dates A.D. 65–70. Clearly, Hebrews was not written early in New Testament church development because internal evidence indicates that this is a church of second generation believers.

Likewise, the destination of Hebrews is uncertain. Many have thought it was sent to Jerusalem and Judea to encourage Christians there to hold fast their profession instead of going back to Judaism. Another possibility is Rome. Hebrews 13:24 states "they from Italy greet you?" The writer in this verse may be sending to Roman Christians greetings from some of their friends who are now with the writer, some place outside of Italy. In this connection, Clement of Rome is the first writer to evidence knowledge of the epistle. Moreover, in opposition to a Palestinian destination, some argue that the knowledge the readers had of Jewish ritual appears to have come from the Septuagint version of the Old Testament rather than from firsthand experience of attendance at temple services in Jerusalem. And, according to 2:3, they had neither seen nor heard Jesus during His earthly ministry, as many Palestinian Christians must have done.

MESSAGE: THE SUPERIORITY OF CHRIST

Although the place to which Hebrews was sent is uncertain, the people to whom it was sent is not. They were Christian Jews who had suffered great persecution (see for example, 10:32–39). Having become occupied with their sufferings, they were beginning to wonder whether their Christian profession was worth all it had cost. Furthermore, they no longer had such religious externals as an altar, a priesthood, and sacrifices. For them the danger of apostatizing to Judaism was real. To meet this situation, the writer describes the superiority of Christ and the Christian faith.

He begins by showing the superiority of Christ to the prophets (1:1–3). Note in these verses the finality of the Christian way. Next the writer presents the superiority of Christ to the angels (1:4–2:18). As the argument progresses, tremendous truths concerning the position of Christ and His relation to the Father are introduced. True, Christ became a little lower than the angels at the time of the incarnation, but this was for the purpose of redeeming humanity and was temporary. Now He is crowned with glory and honor once more. The third section of the book sets forth the superiority of Christ to Moses and Joshua (3:1–4:13). While Moses was a servant in the house, Christ is master over the house. While Joshua led Israel into an imperfect rest in the land, Christ leads believers into a perfect spiritual rest.

Next, the superiority of Christ's priestly ministry to the Aaronic priesthood is introduced (4:14–8:5). Christ is sinless; He is a priest after a higher order—that of Melchizedek; and He ever lives to make intercession, while priests of the old order died. The fifth unit of the argument concerns the superiority of the covenant that Christ introduced (8:6–10:39). In the Old Testament, God promised a new covenant; this Christ has now provided. The old covenant demanded a blood sacrifice; the new involves sacrifice, too. Christ Himself has become the supreme sacrifice and as such bore the sins of mankind. While in the old covenant continual sacrifice was necessary, Christ offered one perfect sacrifice, bringing an end to the Old Testament sacrificial system. The Old Testament priesthood and the old covenant with its sacrificial system were merely types that pointed to the new and better way in Christ. They were merely shadows of reality. Now that the veil of the temple is rent (cf. Matthew 27:51; Hebrews 10:20), the way into the holy of holies of fellowship with God is constantly available to the believer priest.

THE SUPERIOR WAY OF FAITH

In the remainder of the book the new and superior way of faith is described. For their encouragement, examples of faith appear in chapter 11, and the outstanding example of the patient endurance of Christ in His sufferings in chapter 12. The book concludes with practical exhortations concerning social and spiritual relations. These include love for other believers, hospitality, the proper use of sex within marriage, avoidance of avarice, acceptance of persecution, obedience to church leaders, and prayer. The superior way of faith involves an impeccable lifestyle.

In describing the superiority of the new and better way in Christ, the author of Hebrews parenthetically issues a number of strong warnings to these Jewish believers who have fallen into a backslidden condition or are tempted to return to Judaism (2:1–4; 3:7–19; 4:11–13; 5:11–6:12; 10:19–31; 12:25–29). Some of these passages present unnecessarily great difficulty for Bible students because they fail to note the purpose for these warnings: deterrents to apostasy and correctives for backsliding.

These warnings are not meant to upset faithful Christians, but to put careless or wavering Christians on their guard lest they turn out not to be Christians at all. Those who have made a degree of Christian profession can, if they are not careful, "neglect" or "ignore" "such great salvation" (Hebrews 2:3), "drift away" (Hebrews 2:1), and ultimately by a willful and final denial fall under irreversible judgment. The point needs to be made, however, that while the warnings of Hebrews decry carelessness, they primarily concern a voluntary apostasy rather than unconscious decline. They involve abandonment of a position of faith, a purposeful rejection of Christ; for such there can be no restoration

(6:6; 10:26). Fickle followers in Jesus' day as now may one day be impressed with His miraculous powers and elevated teachings and on the next chant, "Crucify Him."

The book of Hebrews has much instruction for contemporary believers who may not be faced with the particular problem of a temptation to return to Judaism. It is always difficult for believers to "worship the Father in spirit and truth" (John 4:23). They easily get wound up in externals or aids to worship as these Jewish believers did. This book provides an antidote with its emphasis on the superior way of faith and trust in Christ alone. Moreover, there is a temptation or a tendency for believers not to grow in the faith—to remain spiritual babes. Hebrews, with a series of thirteen exhortations, summons the believer to ever higher stages of spiritual perfection. Though these are especially clearly marked in the Greek text, they are evident in the King James and most of the other versions, each beginning with "let us" (so see 4:1; 4:11; 4:14; 4:16; 6:1; 10:22; 10:23; 10:24; 12:1 (twice); 12:28; 13:13; 13:15). These culminate in 13:13: "Therefore let us go forth to Him, outside the camp, bearing His reproach" (NKJV). This is the ultimate test of devotion to Christ and His Cross.

To All the Churches:
The General Epistles

James, 1 & 2 Peter, 1, 2, 3 John, Jude

THE seven letters discussed in this chapter have been known as catholic or general epistles, at least since the days of Origen of Alexandria early in the third century. The term distinguished them from the Pauline epistles, which were addressed to individual churches or persons. Although 2 and 3 John were not general letters, they became part of this collection because they were so closely associated with 1 John. Unlike the Pauline epistles, the general epistles have a variety of authors, as the following discussion indicates.

JAMES: THE COMPLEMENT TO GRACE

To steer a straight course in a rowboat, one must have two good oars and apply equal strength to each. The oars necessary for steering a straight course in the Christian life are found in Galatians and

James. The former stresses justification by faith and the latter, works as an evidence of faith. These truths are supplementary, not contradictory; and the neglect of either may ground one on the sandbars of spiritual catastrophe. Some have the idea that grace principles permit them to live as they please; James is the antidote to such careless thinking. Certainly grace has its obligations for Christian living. And did not Jesus Himself say, "By their fruits you shall know them" (Matthew 7:20)?

The message and purpose of James have not always been appreciated in the church. An outstanding example of this fact was the opposition of Martin Luther to the book. Obsessed as he was with the message of justification by faith, he reacted forcefully to anything that hinted at righteousness by works. Early in his ministry he called James a "strawy epistle" but later came to understand the corrective James sought to administer and withdrew his objection to it.

The church has traditionally attributed this letter to James, the brother of our Lord. But whether James was the son of Joseph by a previous marriage or the son of Joseph and Mary after the birth of Jesus is open to question. The latter seems more likely. At any rate, James apparently came to believe in Christ near the end of His sojourn on earth. Christ awarded him with a resurrection appearance (1 Corinthians 15:7); he was present with his mother and brothers at the Jerusalem prayer meeting (Acts 1:14); and James rose to an important position among the apostles (Galatians 1:19; 2:9), taking over the leadership of the Jerusalem church after Peter left the city (Acts 12:17ff.), and even presiding over the great council at Jerusalem (Acts 15). That the author could not be James the brother of John is evident from the fact that James met death at the hands of Herod Agrippa I in A.D. 43 or 44 (see Acts 12:2). There is no tradition supporting the idea that James the Less (another of the twelve disciples) wrote the letter.

Since the book pictures Christianity in its earliest stages of development, when it was still tied to the apron strings of Judaism, it is usually dated around 45–49 and would therefore probably be the first New Testament book written. After 49, when the council of Jerusalem met to discuss the whole question of Jewish legal obligations on Christians, the distinction between Judaism and Christianity became more pronounced. As is clear from James 1:1 and the general content, the book is addressed to Christian Jews of the Dispersion. That Jews were widely scattered over the Roman Empire and beyond is underscored in Acts 2:9–11. Some of those Jews who came to Jerusalem for the feast of Pentecost were converted in the tumultuous events recorded in Acts 2 and returned to their homes to preach Christ. The gospel also reached dispersed Jews through the preaching of Christian Jews who were scattered abroad by the persecutions recorded in Acts (cf. Acts 8:4).

The Practical Christian Life

The message of James is practical rather than doctrinal. It provides instructions for meeting the challenges of everyday living. Although the development is not strictly systematic, a certain topical arrangement is clear:

1. The Christian under trial, 1:1–18. Temptation is an opportunity to prove one's faith, and in the midst of it God will give wisdom to know what to do. There is a reward for the overcomer. Temptation to do evil is not of God.
2. The Christian as a doer of the Word and not a mere hearer of it, 1:19–27.
3. The Christian in relation to others, 2:1–13. Avoid partiality; love your neighbor as yourself.
4. The Christians' faith shown by their works, 2:14–26. This is the heart of the epistle. Its message is that one who has experienced the new birth will evidence it by good works. Key to James' argument is verse 14, which Phillips translates, "Now what use is it, my brothers, for a man to say he 'has faith' if his actions do not correspond with it? Could

that sort of faith save anyone's soul?" In other words, a mere *professed faith* accompanied by no evidence that one possesses the faith is useless. James does not contradict Paul's insistence on the necessity of true faith alone in Christ alone as the means or basis of one's salvation.

5. The Christian and the use of the tongue—the deadly danger of untamed speech, 3:1–18.
6. The sinning Christian and victory over his sin, 4:1–5:6. Here the author deals with a number of subjects relating to victorious living. One need not expect answers to prayer when they are offered for the mere purpose of self-advancement. Resist the Devil. Beware of the spirit of envy. Avoid putting confidence in riches and oppression of those less fortunate.
7. The Christian and the return of Christ, 5:7–10.
8. Miscellaneous instructions for the Christian, 5:11–20.

FIRST PETER: COMFORT FOR THE SUFFERING

Peter in his first letter wrote to "the elect who are sojourners of the Dispersion" (1:1; Jews scattered in lands beyond the borders of Palestine). That would seem to designate a Jewish audience, but several references cannot refer to Jews. For example, 2:9, 10 calls the readers a "no people"; Jews were a covenant people. Moreover, Gentile behavior seems clearly in view in the list of Gentile vices in 4:3, 4. Also, "vain way of life" (1:18) and "former lusts in ignorance" (1:14) seem to apply more to a Gentile than a Jewish audience. Probably these congregations were of a mixed character. While a nucleus may have consisted of Jews, there was a significant number of Gentiles among them. Moreover, some of the Jews probably were only loosely attached to Judaism.

The geographical location of these believers was Asia Minor (modern Turkey, 1:1). Where Peter was when he wrote (probably about A.D. 65) is also a matter of some discussion; 5:13 gives Babylon as the location. There was a Babylon in Egypt, the famous

Babylon on the Euphrates, and the name was used figuratively for the city of Rome. Babylon in Egypt was an insignificant place and there is no tradition Peter ever went there. Babylon on the Euphrates was very much in decline in the middle of the first century A.D., and there is no record of a church there at that time or of Peter's having gone there.

Tradition does indicate that Peter died in Rome and Scripture states that John Mark was in Rome during Paul's imprisonment there (Colossians 4:10) and so he could easily have been linked with Peter there (I Peter 5:13). Further, it is argued that the order of the provinces in the address (1:1) indicates that the bearer of the epistle came from the west and thus came to Pontus first. Babylon is used figuratively or symbolically for Rome in Revelation 17, and the early church fathers believed "Babylon" in First Peter referred to Rome.

Peter's authorship of this epistle has already been assumed. The writer describes himself as "Peter, an apostle of Jesus Christ" (1:1) and a "fellow elder and witness of the sufferings of Christ" (5:1). Phrases in 1 Peter are similar to the phraseology of Peter's sermons in Acts. References to Jesus' sayings in the gospels come from incidents in which Peter played a part, and the references to the Shepherd and care of the flock remind us of Jesus' post-resurrection conversation with Peter (John 21:15–18). With all of this internal evidence early church tradition concurs, and there is general agreement today that Peter wrote the first epistle that bears his name. Peter's "stenographer" as he wrote this epistle was Silvanus (5:12), who is sometimes considered responsible for the smoother Greek of this epistle as compared with that of 2 Peter. Silvanus is presumably another form (perhaps Latin) of the name "Silas," probably the Silas who traveled with Paul on his second missionary journey (see 1 Thessalonians 1:1; 2 Thessalonians 1:1; 2 Corinthian 1:19; Acts 15:40–18:5).

The purpose of the book was to comfort Christians who were passing through trials and persecutions (suffering is mentioned seventeen times in the book). Though some think these persecutions originated with the state, the epistle itself seems to indicate that unconverted neighbors of those addressed initiated them. In this regard, note especially chapter 4. For instance, 4:4 states that the neighbors of these believers spoke evil of them for refusing to engage in prevalent social sins. Nowhere in the book is there evidence of imprisonment or martyrdom, which were usually connected with state persecution. The message of 1 Peter may be outlined as follows:

1. Salvation in Christ and the hope of eternal fellowship with Him as an encouragement in the midst of suffering, 1:1–12
2. The imperative of holy living in order that we should suffer innocently; see to it that the trials of life do not result from one's own foolishness, 1:13–3:17
3. The sufferings of Christ and the believer's privilege in partaking of His sufferings, 3:18–4:19
4. The glory to follow sufferings, 5:1–4
5. Suffering common to all believers during earthly sojourn, 5:5–14

As believers face suffering, they are to bear it patiently for Christ's sake, as He suffered for us (2:20–24); to recognize that it has a spiritually maturing effect (5:10); and to view it in the light of the Second Coming (1:7; 4:13).

SECOND PETER: WARNING AGAINST ERROR

Liberal and conservative scholars alike have questioned Peter's authorship of 2 Peter for many reasons. This doubt arises first because of the differences in vocabulary and style between 1 and 2 Peter; the Greek of 2 Peter is not nearly so polished as that of the first epistle. The usual answer to the problem is that Peter used a different amanuensis or stenographer for the second epistle or perhaps wrote it himself. Second, the reference to Paul's epistles in

2 Peter 3:15, 16 does not require a date of composition after the death of Peter and Paul. It could apply only to those epistles of Paul written and circulating at the time; the collection need not have been complete. Third, some argue that a man of Peter's stature would not have borrowed from Jude and someone else must therefore have written the book. But clearly 2 Peter 2 uses the *future* tense in warning about apostasy; Jude describes apostasy *after* it has become a reality. Fourth, some scholars underscore the hesitancy of the early church in accepting Peter's authorship of the book or its canonicity. But the early church did finally accept it as from Peter's pen and the councils of Laodicea (363) and Carthage (397) are important official witnesses to that fact.

The internal evidence for Peter's authorship is strong. His claim to have written the book (1:1) is backed by several marks of genuineness; a forger would not have dared to vary his style so markedly from that of the first epistle as the writer of 2 Peter did. In spite of the differences, there are numerous similarities between 2 Peter and 1 Peter and between the epistles and Peter's speeches in Acts. There is nothing in the epistle that Peter could not have written; conclusive proof of spuriousness is lacking. Its destination, according to 3:1, is the same group of Asia Minor Christians described in 1 Peter 1:1. Peter wrote his second epistle just before he died (2 Peter 1:14), probably in A.D. 66 or 67. Since apparently trustworthy tradition says he and Paul were martyred in Rome at the hands of Nero, we may suggest that the epistle was written there.

The problem of persecution, which the church faced at the time Peter wrote his first letter, no longer posed a serious threat. Trouble now loomed within the ranks of believers in the form of heresy. So Peter sends this letter as an antidote. Second Peter anticipates error (2:1) which Jude, probably written later, views as a present reality. As in Jude, the error here seems to involve a repudiation of Christ as Lord, and moral irregularity (see chapter 2). Many have suggested that Peter and Jude were contending with the philosophy known as Gnosticism. This taught among other things a dualism between matter and spirit, the former evil and the latter good. Since the flesh was considered to be evil, some took the path of asceticism and punished their bodies. Others, such as those addressed in 2 Peter, felt that giving in to the desires of the flesh would not violate the purity of their spirits. This dualism also affected their view of Christ; for them the incarnation was a degrading idea. Moreover, Gnostics claimed a superior knowledge of divine truth, not available to other believers. Peter's approach in this letter is to meet error with truth, to meet false knowledge with true knowledge. The words *know* and *knowledge* appear sixteen times (1:2, 3, 5, 6, 8, 12, 14, 16, 20; 2:9, 20, 21 twice; 3:3, 17, 18).

Along with the problem of heretical teaching and conduct, Peter dealt with the question of the second coming of Christ in chapter 3. Some had apparently grown weary in watching for His coming. Others mocked the very idea that Christ would return. Peter asserts the fact of His coming, which constitutes a purifying hope for present living and an ushering into eternal bliss at His coming. But for the unbeliever it will be a day of judgment.

Briefly the message of the book may be outlined as follows:

1. True knowledge, 2 Peter 1
2. Warning against abandonment of true knowledge, 2 Peter 2
3. The hope in true knowledge, 2 Peter 3.

FIRST JOHN: ASSURANCE OF SALVATION

That John the apostle wrote 1, 2, and 3 John is not a matter of great controversy. External testimony to this effect is fairly strong, especially for the first epistle. The personality of the writer, the language, style, and thought patterns expressed in the epistles are similar to those of the gospel of John. Probably the epistles were written in Ephesus about A.D. 85–90 and were addressed to a church or churches of Asia Minor located near Ephesus.

John gives as his reason for writing the first epistle, "that you may know that you have eternal life" (5:13). This is an advance over the purpose for writing the gospel ("that you might believe that Jesus is the Christ, the Son of God; and that believing you might have life through his name," John 20:31). The gospel provides a historical account of the good news of the coming of Christ and His offer of salvation; the epistle focuses on the realization of salvation in Christian experience. In fulfilling his aim, the apostle gives several tests for determining one's certainty of salvation:

1. Do we keep His commandments (2:3, 5)?
2. Do we practice righteousness (2:29)?
3. Do we love the brethren (3:14, 16, 19)?
4. Do we have the inner testimony of the Spirit that we are saved (3:24; 4:13)?
5. Do we shun a life of sin (5:18)?

Two secondary purposes for writing this letter also appear: to deal with an early form of a philosophical system known as Gnosticism (see comments under 2 Peter) and to correct false views concerning sin. Gnosticism's basic teaching was antipathy between spirit and matter. And, said the Gnostics, "How could a good God, spiritual in nature, have anything to do with a material body?" Obviously, the whole doctrine of salvation, which requires that the Son of God take on human flesh in order to pay the penalty of man's sin, is at stake. John answers this error by declaring the reality of Jesus' humanity (he had heard, seen, and touched Him, 1:1; cf. 1:1–3) and classifying those who denied His humanity as "antichrist" (2:22; 4:2–3) and not of the apostolic circle (2:19).

John also felt called upon to deal with false views of sin. Apparently some were taking advantage of grace teachings and living lawlessly. The apostle made it clear that those who are truly born again do not practice sin or sin lawlessly (I John 3:9, literal translation). The point of 3:1–9 is that those who truly know

God, will have no desire to live in sin. Rather, they will seek to honor their Savior. Moreover, if professing believers demonstrate a great love for the world, they show that the love of the Father is not in them (2:17). However, John does not teach sinless perfection. All do sin occasionally (1:8), but for them the means of forgiveness is available (1:9). Jesus Christ Himself is our advocate with the Father (2:1); He has already made satisfaction (propitiation) for all sins—those of the believer as well as the unregenerate person (2:2).

SECOND JOHN: OF LOVE AND TRUTH

To whom John addressed this epistle is uncertain. Some think he wrote to a Christian lady in whose home a church met and thus translate the address: "to the lady Electa." Others interpret "the elect lady and her children" figuratively to refer to a church and her members. Which of these views, or some other alternative, is correct we cannot say. All the efforts of modern scholarship have thrown no further light on the subject. It seems, however, that the letter is personal correspondence destined for some believer or group of believers living in a town near Ephesus.

Like 1 John, this epistle has much to say about love; verses 4 through 6 encourage the reader to continue in love. But the real purpose of the book seems to be to warn against error and preachers of error. Apparently some itinerant teachers in the area where the readers lived taught a heretical doctrine of the person of Christ, denying His true humanity (v. 7, compare 1 John 4:2). These true believers were not to entertain, for in so doing they would become partakers in the crime of the heretics (vv. 7–11). The warning was as applicable to a well-known woman as to the church at large. The apostle's charge to have nothing to do with these false teachers may seem harsh and ungracious, but it should be remembered that these itinerant preachers were undermining the very foundations of the Christian faith. *Truth* is the keyword of the epistle, appearing five times (vv. 1 twice, 2, 3, 4). The message is that truth must be received, obeyed, and cherished at all costs.

THIRD JOHN: THE IMPORTANCE OF HOSPITALITY

Third John was written to warn against domineering leadership in the church and to underscore the duty of showing hospitality to Christian workers. Historically, the situation was this: many early Christians became itinerant evangelists, receiving their support from hospitable believers in places where they went to minister. In the town to which this letter was addressed, a certain Diotrephes secured sizable control over the church. He greatly opposed these traveling evangelists, even going so far as to excommunicate those who dared to entertain them (v. 10). John had protested against this situation in a previous letter (v. 9), but Diotrephes refused to acknowledge the apostle's authority and even made uncomplimentary comments about the apostle himself ("prating against me with evil words" v. 10, RSV). Now John writes to commend a certain faithful Gaius for receiving these missionary-evangelists in spite of Diotrephes and to threaten drastic treatment of Diotrephes during a future apostolic visit.

Whether the Gaius to whom John addressed this epistle (v. 1) is to be identified with any of the others by the same name referred to in the New Testament (Acts 19:29; 20:4; Romans 16:23) is an open question. Gaius was a common name. Very likely the itinerant workers referred to in this epistle were men whom the apostle John himself had sent out. As they returned and presented their report to John, they spoke highly of the hospitable Gaius and critically of domineering Diotrephes. To receive or reject the emissaries of the apostle was in some sense reception or rejection of the One who had commissioned him.

Reflecting the common authorship of 2 and 3 John, both put much emphasis on truth, both address the issue of hospitality to be shown to Christian workers, in both the writer rejoices over others who walk in the truth, in both the writer states his intention to visit the recipients, and in both he indicates his reluctance to write at length with paper or pen and ink.

JUDE: APOSTASY, LICENSE, AND SPIRITUAL WARFARE

While Jude apparently desired to write about our salvation in Christ, conditions in the church forced him to issue a stem warning against apostasy and an exhortation to contend earnestly for the faith (v. 3). It is interesting that in developing his message, he provides a history of apostasy: the fall of angels, self-righteous Cain, the corrupt Sodomites, rebellious Israel, presumptuous Korah, selfish Balaam, and the apostasy of Jude's day and of the last times. These cases are introduced to illustrate the fate of apostates: severe divine judgment. The way of Cain (Genesis 4) is the way of bloodless sacrifice; the error of Balaam (Numbers 22ff.) is exercising self-will and seeking self-advantage; the rebellion of Korah (Numbers 16) is opposition to divinely appointed leadership in the work of God and seeking fellowship with God on one's own terms.

From the description given in verse 4 ("ungodly men, turning the grace of our God into lasciviousness, and denying the only Lord God, and our Lord Jesus Christ"), it would appear that the particular error which the church faced in Jude's day was turning the grace of God into license for immorality and rejecting the lordship of Christ. This was the opposite of the Galatian heresy (salvation by good works). The church that Jude described was characterized by loose morals (vv. 18–19), corrupt thoughts (vv. 8, 10), opposition to control (vv. 8, 16), boastful language (v. 18), and religious sham (vv. 12, 13, 19).

When contemporary believers grow starry-eyed in their reflections on the New Testament church and express a desire to return to the supposed high level of spiritual maturity achieved then, they need to remember such New Testament books as Galatians with its censure of legalism, Colossians with its exposure of false philosophies, and Jude with its condemnation of a whole catalogue of spiritual waywardness. False teachers (v. 4) had made considerable inroads in the church. S. Maxwell Coder wrote a commentary on this book with the intriguing title *Jude: Acts of the Apostates.*

An important principle for Christian living derives from verse 9. There even the holy archangel Michael recognized that in his own resources he could not tangle with Satan. This enemy of God is so formidable that he can be dealt with only by the power of God. Believers commonly fail to recognize the might of this one who is the god of this world and chief enemy of the God of heaven (2 Corinthians 4:4). In underestimating both his gargantuan stature and his fierce and shrewd and unrelenting attacks (Ephesians 6:16; 1 Peter 5:8) believers tend to rely on carnal or fleshly or natural weapons (2 Corinthians 10:4) rather than supernatural resources (Ephesians 6:10–18). Hence the high casualty rate among the soldiers of God.

Issues of Dating and of the Apocrypha

That the epistle was written by Jude, the brother of James and half brother of Christ, is quite certain. This is the testimony of Scripture. The writer calls himself Jude, "a servant of Jesus Christ, and brother of James" (v. 1). Matthew says that both James and Jude were brothers of our Lord (13:55; cf. Mark 6:3) and Galatians 1:19 asserts that James, the leader of the Jerusalem church, was the brother of Christ. Incidentally, Jude, like the rest of Jesus' brothers, was an unbeliever during His earthly ministry (John 7:5), and his conversion must have followed the resurrection because he was present with Mary and His brothers at the prayer meeting in the upper room (Acts 1:14). Tradition confirms the biblical testimony to Jude's authorship. But when or to whom it was written is an open question. Since verses 17 and 18 appear to quote 2 Peter 3:2–3, we may conclude that Jude was written after A.D. 67 (approximate date of composition of 2 Peter). Some date the book as late as 80. If the letter was written before the fall of Jerusalem (A.D. 70), it may well have been written to Palestinian Jews.

A special problem in the book of Jude is his use of the apocrypha. In verse 14 he quotes from the *Book of Enoch* and in verse 9 refers to a dispute recorded in *The Assumption of Moses*. Jewish writers produced both of these books early in the first century. The question arises as to whether use of apocryphal books gives them canonical authority. Probably the best solution to the problem is that these references should be put on a par with Paul's quotation in his Mars Hill address (Acts 17:28). The writer knew the allusions would carry weight with his audience and would help to illustrate a point for those who had a familiarity with or a high regard for those works. Such use does not necessarily vouch for the inspiration or canonicity of the quoted work as a whole.

PART

VII

The End of
All Things

"A New Heaven and A New Earth": The Revelation of Jesus Christ

Revelation

THE SIGNIFICANCE OF THE BOOK

WITHOUT the book of Revelation, readers of the New Testament would be left hanging or suspended. They would know that Christ had come once and had provided a full salvation for mankind. They would know from isolated passages that He will return some day and that a time of great trouble or tribulation will afflict the earth. But no scheme or pattern of events unfolds to describe how things eventually will end. Moreover, readers would tend to be depressed as they completed the epistles with their prediction of coming apostasy and the spread of evil across the world (e.g., 2 Timothy,

2 Peter, Jude). In human experience, on a day to day basis, evil seems to triumph much of the time, and right is defeated or at least is on the defensive.

Revelation provides an answer for these concerns. It shows how the age will end. In fact, it describes the coming of a new heaven and a new earth and a perfect order. The book predicts the defeat of Satan and his cohorts and the overthrow of the wicked institutions and systems of the world; evil will not always triumph. Christ at His coming in judgment will utterly crush all forms of evil and become King of kings and Lord of lords. Revelation is eminently the book for the end of the age. To a world that has a sense of moving toward destruction with the nuclear threat, air and water pollution, overpopulation and massive starvation, and possible collapse of the international economic system, there is the message that God is in control and will work out His sovereign purposes.

NEGLECT OF THE BOOK

In spite of all that Revelation contributes to the completeness of the New Testament and the understanding of our world and the future, it is perhaps the most neglected book of the New Testament. This neglect is due in large part to its extensive use of symbols, images, and veiled expressions. But there may be a more sinister reason for ignoring Revelation. The two biblical books that describe most fully the activity of Satan and predict his judgment and destruction are Genesis and Revelation, and these are precisely the two books on which enemies of supernatural Christianity have trained their big guns. Liberal scholarship has tried to destroy the historicity of the early chapters of Genesis and even the patriarchal narrative and has riddled a respect for the integrity of the text with its documentary hypothesis. The approach to Revelation seems to be, "The book is so impossible to understand and interpreters agree so little as to its meaning that there is no sense in even bothering to read it."

Focus of the Book

As a matter of fact, the title of the book, "The revelation of Jesus Christ" (1:1), claims that it is an unveiling or a revealing rather than a concealing of truth concerning Jesus Christ. Whether the "of" Jesus Christ is understood to mean that Jesus is the source of the revelation or the object of it, He is central to the book. At the beginning of the book, Christ is the glorified One, Lord of life and death, worthy of all honor and adoration (1:9–20). In chapters 2 and 3 He is walking among the seven churches. In the body of the text He opens the seals and unleashes terrible judgments on the earth. In the latter chapters He descends from heaven as King of kings and Lord of lords to vanquish His enemies. The book ends with Christ enthroned as Alpha and Omega in the new heaven and new earth.

Apostolic Authorship

The author calls himself John (1:1, 4, 9; 22:8) and evidently he was well known to his readers and accepted by them as an authority figure. His acting like a bishop in addressing the churches of Revelation 2, 3 implies apostolic rank. Discovery of a manuscript in the Gnostic library at Chenoboskion in Egypt dating to about A.D. 150 seems to support the view that this John was the apostle. Early church witness to apostolic authorship of the book includes Justin Martyr, Irenaeus, Clement of Alexandria, Origen, Tertullian, and Hippolytus. In fact, belief that this John was the son of Zebedee was unanimous until Dionysius of Alexandria in the third century assigned the book to a John the Presbyter on the basis of some internal considerations and the supposed existence of a second John in Ephesus. John the Presbyter is a very shadowy figure and all reference to him disappeared early in the history of the church.

A careful analysis of the vocabulary and grammar of Revelation and the gospel does show some differences, but it also demonstrates many affinities. The rougher constructions in Revelation could be due to John's own writing without an amanuensis (personal scribe), as he was in exile on the isle of Patmos (Revelation 1:9). He may have had such an amanuensis in composing the gospel and the epistles. The charge that he used bad grammar in the Revelation is not necessarily valid. Some of the suspect constructions have been found in contemporary papyri where they clearly were acceptable in common usage. The grammar of the New Testament should not be judged by the standards of classical Greek. There seems to be no compelling reason for denying that the author of Revelation was John, the son of Zebedee, the great apostle. As to the date of composition, Irenaeus stated it came near the close of the Emperor Domitian's reign, hence about A.D. 96.[2]

PURPOSE AND DESTINATION: THE SEVEN CHURCHES AND THEIR SUFFERING

Revelation is addressed to seven churches of the Roman province of Asia (1:4, 11): Ephesus, Smyrna, Pergamum, Thyatira, Sardis, Philadelphia, and Laodicea. The book may well be described as a circular letter. Why John singled out these churches when the gospel had certainly reached other places in Asia demands some comment. They were located on the great circular road that bound together the chief centers of the province. Ephesus was the most prominent. The order in which they are mentioned corresponds to the route a messenger would take in delivering the book. Probably, also, these were the churches John had especially under his care as he ministered at his headquarters in Ephesus. Though the writer has in mind primarily the needs of these churches, he foresaw distribution of the book to a much wider Christian public.

The writer's purpose is first of all to deal with internal conditions in the seven churches. He warns against or condemns spiritual deterioration, immoral environments, false teaching, and the effects of material prosperity. But he also has much to commend, and he ends each message with a promise. Second, he seeks to fortify the churches, to console them, and to encourage endurance in the face of increasing persecution. The time was the reign of the Emperor Domitian (A.D. 81–96) who demanded worship of himself as "Lord and God." John had been exiled for reasons we do not know and styled himself as their "companion in tribulation" (1:9). Smyrna was "about to suffer" and to "have tribulation ten days" (2:10). Antipas had suffered martyrdom for his faith at Pergamum (2:13). Thyatira was warned of "great tribulation" (2:22). Philadelphia was to be exempted from "the hour of trial" (3:10). Encouragement of believers comes in the form of a panorama of the end times which involves judgments to fall on Satan and all the forces of evil and the ultimate triumph of Christ and the Christian church. The book is a beacon light of hope for those passing through or about to pass through severe trial and is an encouragement to all believers down through subsequent centuries who may be called on to suffer for the Master's sake.

THE VARYING INTERPRETATIONS OF REVELATION

Four methods of interpreting Revelation are common in the church today.

1. The *Preterist* school holds that the conflicts described in the book raged between the early church and the Roman Empire and that its predictions were fulfilled during the first Christian centuries. Therefore we need look for no further fulfillment of the prophecy. Though this approach has appeal in its relevance for the early church, it suffers embarrassment from the fact that many of the predictions were not fulfilled in that epoch. The Roman Empire did not fall, Jesus did not return quickly, and there was no world tyrant for Him to destroy. On this view, not only did the book turn out to be mistaken, but also there is no provision for elements of predictive prophecy. The majority of liberal scholars have

followed this interpretation. They see in the book an expression of the writer's indignation as he spoke of future judgment on pagan persecutors of Christians, and they infer his use of pagan mythology.

2. The *Idealist* school views the book as portraying in a general way the age-long struggle between the forces of good and evil—between ideals—and the eventual triumph of Christianity. It strips the Revelation of all predictive value and dissociates it from historic events in the past or future. The book then has value only as a promise of ultimate victory for the cause of righteousness.

3. The *Historicist* view holds that Revelation symbolically outlines the history of the church from Pentecost to the return of Christ and the final judgment. Thus some teach that the breaking of the seals pictures the destruction of the Roman Empire, the locusts from the bottomless pit portray the hordes of Muslims conquering the Near East and the Mediterranean world, the beast represents the Papacy, etc. Many of the Reformers and a majority of the older commentaries held this view. These interpreters tend to be postmillennialists (believing that Christ would return after a golden age or millennium brought on by the preaching of the gospel) or amillennialists (denying a literal millennium on earth). The historicist position has against it the fact that its adherents have about as many interpretations as there are commentators. Its utter subjectivity raises the suspicion that there is no real validity to the approach at all. Moreover, it is doubtful that God would so specifically portray a history of the world which had little bearing on the consummation of things.

4. The *Futurist* view holds that the bulk of Revelation deals with a Great Tribulation, followed by the return of Christ, the millennial kingdom, the judgment of the wicked dead, and the institution of the eternal state. The book is interpreted as

literally as possible. Some futurists believe that the seven churches of Asia in chapters 2 and 3 represent eras of church history and to this extent are historicists. Others think that the first three chapters concern the era in which the book was written.

This writer holds that the events prophesied in Revelation 4–22 are yet future. While it is true that symbolic language appears in these chapters, the events described are of a magnitude far beyond anything the world has yet known. Therefore, it seems best to refer them to the great tribulation period at the end of the age. Perhaps it should be pointed out that the last three chapters of Revelation are relatively free from the symbolism employed in the rest of the book. Chapter 20 tells of the millennial age, the battle of Gog and Magog after that period, and the great white throne judgment. Chapters 21 and 22 describe the destruction of the old heaven and old earth and the appearance of the new heavens and the new earth. Before this sequence of events, the second coming of Christ and vengeance on His enemies is described in chapter 19 (see vv. 11, 12ff.). Preceding the second coming is the Great Tribulation. This order of events tallies well with that of Matthew 24 and 25 (where the Tribulation is followed by the Second Coming, a judgment of the nations, and the kingdom age) and 2 Thessalonians 2 (where the Tribulation is followed by a return of Christ and judgment of the atheistic world ruler of the tribulation period).

Message of Revelation: Things Shortly to Come to Pass

As noted above, the book of Revelation clearly states that it is a revelation of Jesus Christ concerning "things which must shortly come to pass" (1:1). One way of outlining the book is to focus on the four times the writer speaks of being "in the spirit" as introducing main divisions of his work (1:10; 4:2; 17:1–3; 21:9, 10).

Following that approach, there is a prologue (1:1–8), four main divisions (1:9–3:22; 4:1–16:21; 17:1–21:8; 21:9–22:5) and an epilogue (22:6–21).

Though every phrase in the prologue invites comment, two observations are especially cogent. First, "things which must shortly take place" (1:1, NKJV) does not mean what the English appears to say. "Shortly" (soon) translates a Greek word that indicates the suddenness of the action, whenever it takes place, not necessarily the immediacy of it. It did not teach the early church that all that follows was due to happen right away. Second, there is a blessing for those who read and respond to the message of the book (1:3). This is not a book merely to satisfy the curiosity of its readers concerning the future but it is a practical lesson to encourage those who suffer for the faith and to warn those who oppose it.

The First Vision: The Omnipotent Christ

In the first vision (1:9–3:22), John is on the isle of Patmos and catches a view of Christ among the seven churches. He is the truly awesome One, who so totally overwhelmed the writer with the glory of His person that he fell down as one dead (1:17). A glimpse of the infinitely glorious One will always have the same effect (cf. Paul in Acts 9:4 and Isaiah in Isaiah 6). The descriptives of Christ come from Daniel and Ezekiel and provide an overwhelming impression of omnipotence. He speaks with a thunderous voice of authority (v. 15), sovereignly holds in his right hand the messengers of the seven churches (v. 20), and acts as all-powerful judge as symbolized by eyes like a flame of fire, bronze-like feet stamping out judgment, and a sharp double-edged sword proceeding from his mouth with a cutting action of condemnation. His face shining with the brilliance of the sun speaks of the glory of His deity.

Chapters 2 and 3 contain messages for seven churches of Asia (the Roman province of Asia). Each begins with a reference to the exalted Christ who addresses the church, proceeds with commendation (except for Laodicea and Sardis), continues with details about the condition of the church leading to a rebuke and warning (except for Philadelphia and Smyrna), and concludes with a promise to believers who overcome. The messages to these local assemblies provide instruction for other first century churches and for all other churches down through history. Some believe that the churches represent stages or eras in church history, from the apostolic church (Ephesus) to the contemporary church reduced to a lukewarm condition by affluence and apostasy (Laodicea).

The Second Vision: Of the Great Tribulation

In the second vision (4:1–16:21) John is caught up to heaven, where he beholds the throne of God, the symbol of government and power, and a host of heavenly creatures; worshiping Him. In His right hand God holds a book (whether a scroll or codex is not clear) with seven seals on it. A minor emergency occurs when no one appears able to open the seals. But the slain Lamb of God, the Redeemer, the ever-living One, steps forward to loose them. When He does so, He pours out on the earth three series of seven plagues each, described as seals (6:1–8:5), trumpets (8:6–11:19), and bowls (12:1–16:21). While it is natural to treat these as sequential, some consider them to be consecutive. With these plagues, the Great Tribulation begins.

The Seven Seals

The first four seals form a group, the so-called four horsemen of the Apocalypse (6:1–8). The white horse probably represents the world ruler or antichrist, who dominates the tribulation period; the red horse, warfare; the black horse, famine; the pale (green) horse, death. Seal five (6:9–11) involves the persecution and martyrdom of saints, possibly as scapegoats for the trouble caused by the four horsemen. Seal six (6:12–17) visits God's wrath on the earth in the form of seismic and celestial disturbances (cf. Matthew 24:29, 30; Mark 13:24–26; Luke 21:25–27). Seal seven (8:1, 2) involves a silence in heaven as preparation for sounding of the seven trumpets and thunder, lightning, and earthquakes on earth as symbolic precursors of judgments about to fall on earth. Between seals six and seven occurs a parenthetical statement about the sealing of the 144,000 (7:1–17), Israelites from every tribe of Israel, that will be protected in the tribulation about to occur.

The Seven Trumpets

The trumpet judgments are far more severe than the seals. With the first trumpet (8:7), hail and fire or lightning descend on earth, consuming a third of the flora. At the blowing of the second trumpet (8:8, 9) a burning mountain or erupting volcano falls into the sea, turning it to blood and destroying a third of the sea creatures and the ships plying its waters. At the sound of the third trumpet (8:10, 11) a blazing star or meteorite descends on the fresh water supply of earth, poisoning a third of it and causing widespread loss of life. With the fourth trumpet (8:12, 13), celestial disturbances result in eclipses that diminish the light of heavenly bodies by one-third (cf. Amos 8:9). The blowing of the fifth trumpet (9:1–12) brings the opening of the bottomless pit by a star (probably Satan) that has fallen from heaven to earth. The released demons as locusts with tails like scorpions torment human beings five months so that they seek death to escape but are not permitted to die. The sixth trumpet (9:13–21) introduces a specific geographical region, the course of the Euphrates River, where four demonic horsemen lead an army that slaughters one-third of mankind. So confirmed will humanity be in all their evil that their trials will not move them to repentance (9:20, 21). The final trumpet (11:15–19) involves the turning of the kingdoms of this world into the kingdom of Christ. Between the sixth and seventh trumpets the writer interjects a parenthetical section

(10:1–11:14), the first part of which is designed to prepare for the final outpouring of God's judgements, and the latter part to record the ministry of two unidentified witnesses later in the tribulation.

Key Apocalyptic Actors

Before the seven bowl judgments John introduces several important personages. In chapter 12 a woman (apparently representing Israel) gives birth to a child (Jesus). A dragon (representing Satan) with his hosts seeks to destroy the child, who is caught up into heaven (the Ascension). Then the woman enjoys protection from satanic persecution for 1260 days in the wilderness during the latter part of the Tribulation (probably a reference to the protection of the 144,000). In chapter 13 two beasts appear. The first presumably, is the political head of the revived Roman Empire and the second (false prophet) is the religious head or antichrist. There is a brief description of their rule. Later, in 19:20, both are thrown into the lake of fire.

The Seven Bowls

The seven bowl judgments (15:1–16:21) represent plagues that probably come in rapid succession near the end of the Tribulation:

1. Malignant sores on worshipers of the beast
2. Turning of the sea to blood and death of marine life
3. Turning of rivers and springs to blood
4. Scorching heat of the sun
5. Darkness and pain on the throne of the beast and his kingdom
6. Drying up of the Euphrates and preparation for Armageddon
7. Earthquake, thunder, lightning, and hail, bringing the downfall of heathen powers.

THE THIRD VISION: CHRIST TRIUMPHANT

In vision three (17:1–21:8) John is caught away into the wilderness to observe Christ in conquest. Chapters 17 and 18 celebrate the destruction of Babylon, which presumably is symbolic of Rome. Hence destruction of the revived Roman Empire is in view. Chapter 17 announces judgment on the Mother of Harlots, the pseudospiritual force or the official religion of the state. Even though this religious system had supported the political arm, God put it into the mind of the political forces to destroy the apostate religious system (17:17). Then chapter 18 focuses on the destruction of commercial and political Babylon-Rome.

The stage is now set for the return of Christ with power and judgment to accomplish what has just been envisioned. Portrayal of Christ in all His majesty and power defies description, but three details deserve special mention. First, His clothing has been dipped in blood, symbolizing His redemptive work. Second, His name is called the "Word of God," the eternal One who created the heavens and earth and who became incarnate to solve the sin problem of humanity (John 1:1–14). Third, He has the title "King of kings and Lord of lords," symbolizing His ultimate supremacy and victory over all His foes. In the war (not "battle") of Armageddon, on the great plain of northern Israel, He will devastate the forces drawn up against Him and will cast the beast and false prophet into the lake of fire (19:20) and bind Satan in the bottomless pit for the duration of the Millennium (20:2). At this point there is a resurrection of the righteous dead, who will reign with Christ for the thousand years of the Millennium. Righteous living persons (as "sheep" or "brethren") will continue on into the Millennium, as passages such as Matthew 25:31–46 demonstrate.

Millennium, of course, means "a thousand years" and the passage, taken literally, teaches that Christ will reign for a thousand years. Many argue that one should not be so literal in interpreting a book full of symbols; they point out that this is the only place in the Bible that mentions a Millennium. But the Old Testament again and again predicts a glorious age of peace when the Messiah will reign in righteousness; Isaiah especially alludes to such a time (e.g., Isaiah 9:6, 7; 11; 30:15–33; 35). Moreover, as noted, Matthew 25 mentions a kingdom on earth to follow a second coming. If one concedes that a thousand years might be symbolic of a very long time, the force of the prediction of a kingdom on earth when Messiah reigns is not blunted.

Not everyone born during the Millennium will voluntarily bow the knee to Christ. The number will increase sufficiently that by the end of the period, when Satan is loosed, he will be able to put together a massive host that as Gog and Magog will do battle with the saints. God will devour this army and cast Satan into the lake of fire, where the beast and false prophet already lie (20:10). Following this final triumph occurs the Great White Throne judgment of the wicked dead and the dissolution of the present heavens and earth and the creation of the new heavens and earth.

THE FOURTH VISION: A CITY ILLUMINATED BY THE GLORY OF GOD

In the fourth vision (21:9–22:5) John is caught up into a high mountain where he has a chance to see the city of God and the Lamb as central to it. Here Christ is revealed in the eternal state. The New Jerusalem comes down "out of heaven" and so is not identical with it. It is a holy city because everyone in it is holy. Its beauty defies description. The nearest that human language can come is to compare the composition of its wall to jasper, the gates to pearl, and the city itself to gold. The city will be brilliantly illuminated by the glory of God, with no need of the light of sun or moon. In the eternal state believers will serve God (22:3), will see His face (v. 4) and will reign with Him forever (v. 5).

The epilogue (22:6–21) closes the book with a command to keep the words of the prophecy of this book (to heed its ethical implications, v. 7), an invitation to eternal life (v. 17), a curse on anyone who tampers with the text or message (vv. 18, 19), and a promise of and prayer for Jesus' return.

Jesus' promise to "come quickly" (vv. 12, 20) does not mean that Jesus will come soon but suddenly—events will occur so fast that they will take many by surprise.

Admittedly, the interpretation of Revelation is fraught with problems. But one fact is clear—one which is of great import to us in this day of international distress. God is still in sovereign control over the world, and some day Christ will return, will judge the forces of evil, and will initiate His rule as beneficent despot.

Moreover, though in past centuries the book may have seemed fanciful or impossible, technological advances in weaponry, communications, and thought control now make possible or even feasible the massive destruction, one world government, or even ersatz religion that the book predicts. The book of Revelation is relevant to the contemporary man or woman on the street.

Notes

1. Everett F. Harrison, *Introduction to the New Testament,* rev. ed. (Grand Rapids: Eerdmans, 1971), p. 467.

2. Irenaeus, *Against Heresies*, V.xxx.iii.

FOR FURTHER NEW TESTAMENT STUDY

ONE could go on almost indefinitely listing books on the New Testament. It would seem, however, that a list in a book of this sort should be brief and that it should consist of publications that are in print or at least readily accessible, fairly recent and non-technical, and theologically conservative. It should also include materials on Bible study methods.

Four books will prove to be especially helpful in providing background information on such matters as authorship, occasion for writing, date, and place of composition: Henry C. Thiessen's *Introduction to the New Testament* (Grand Rapids: Eerdmans, 1943); Everett F. Harrison's *Introduction to the New Testament* (Grand Rapids; Eerdmans, 1964); Donald Guthrie's *New Testament Introduction*, 3rd ed. (Downers Grove, Ill.: InterVarsity, 1970); and D.A. Carson, Douglas J. Moo, and Leon Morris' *An Introduction to the New Testament* (Grand Rapids: Zondervan, 1992).

Among the finest full-length New Testament surveys are Merrill C. Tenney's *New Testament Survey*, 2nd ed. (Grand Rapids: Eerdmans, 1961); *The New Testament Speaks* by Glenn Barker, William Lane, and J. Ramsey Michaels (New York: Harper, 1969); Robert H. Gundry's *A Survey of the New Testament* (Grand Rapids: Zondervan, 1970); and *New Testament Survey* by Robert G. Gromacki (Grand Rapids: Baker Book House, 1974). A wonderful mine of information on the gospels is W. Graham Scroggie's *Guide to the Gospels* (London: Pickering and Inglis, 1948).

Two of the newer works on the life of Christ are Everett F. Harrison's *A Short Life of Christ* (Grand Rapids: Eerdmans, 1968) and Howard F. Vos' *An Introduction to the Life of Christ*, rev. ed. (Nashville: Thomas Nelson, 1994).

Three of the best one-volume Bible commentaries are the *New Bible Commentary* edited by D. Guthrie and others, rev. ed. (Grand Rapids: Eerdmans, 1970); *The Bible Knowledge Commentary*, New Testament Edition, edited by John F. Walvoord and Roy B.

Zuck (Wheaton, Ill.: Victor Books, 1983); and the *Wycliffe Bible Commentary* edited by Everett F. Harrison and Charles F. Pfeiffer (Chicago: Moody Press, 1962).

A biographical work of some interest is Joan Comay's and Ronald Brownrigg's *Who's Who in the New Testament* (London: Weidenfeld and Nicolson, 1971 with reissue in 1993).

Several publishers are producing inexpensive paperbound commentaries on individual books of the Bible. Of course Bible students should learn to study the Bible for themselves and not depend exclusively on commentaries produced by others. Materials of help in this regard are *Effective Bible Study* by Howard F. Vos (Grand Rapids: Zondervan, 1956); *Independent Bible Study* by Irving Jensen (Chicago: Moody Press, 1963); Bible Self-Study Guides begun by Grace Saxe and revised and continued by Irving Jensen (Chicago: Moody Press); and the *Teach Yourself the Bible* series by Keith L. Brooks and others, rev. ed. (Chicago: Moody Press, 1991). Both the Saxe-Jensen's and Brooks's series are paperbound and consist of separate titles on individual books of the New Testament.

A Simple Technique for Learning Old Testament History

I HAVE COME upon a simple way to help my students learn Old Testament history—to find their way through the Old Testament. First, I ask them to learn the names of the first sixteen books in order. Then I proceed to ask questions about the names of the books (something like that which follows). In order to avoid the tiresome repetition of the words—*question* and *answer*—the questions are merely stated here and the anticipated answer appears in italics.

What is the first book? *Genesis.* What does the word Genesis mean? *Beginnings.* Beginnings of what? *Heaven, earth, and humankind.* What major individuals appear on the scene? *Abraham, Isaac, Jacob (the patriarchs).*

What is the next book? *Exodus.* What does the term Exodus mean? *To go out.* To go out from where? *Egypt.* How did they get into Egypt? *They left Canaan because of a famine.* When they left

Egypt, where did they go? *They went into the wilderness.* What was the outstanding event in the wilderness? *They went to Mt. Sinai and received the Law.*

What is the third book? *Leviticus.* What were Levites? *Priests.* What did the priests do? *Made sacrifices and led the people in worship.* Where? *In the Tabernacle.* According to what? *The Law.* So now we have the priesthood, the tabernacle, and the Law—the basic institutions of Israel.

What is the next book? *Numbers.* Where were they then? *Still in the wilderness, where a census was taken.*

What is the next book? *Deuteronomy.* And this word means what? *The second Law.* Where were they at that time? *Still in the wilderness.*

What is the next book? *Joshua.* What sort of activity did Josuha engage in? *Conquest.* Conquest of what? *Canaan.*

What is the next book? *Judges.* What did the judges do? *Judged or ruled the people.* Who was the last of the judges? *Samuel.* When Samuel passed off the scene, how did he arrange for his successor? *Appointed a king.*

What is the next book? *Ruth.* When did the story take place? *In the days of the Judges (see Ruth 1:1).* What is the special significance about the story of Ruth? *It gives the ancestry of David, the great king of Israel. He was an ancestor of Jesus Christ.*

What is the next book? *1 Kings.* Who was the first king? *Saul.* Who was the second king? *David.* Who was the third king? *Solomon.* After 1 Kings, what is the next book? *2 Kings.* What is 2 Kings about? *Kings, lots of kings.* So after King Solomon what happened? *The one kingdom split into two kingdoms: Israel (the northern kingdom) and Judah (the southern kingdom).* Prophets were active during those days. What did they warn about? *Idolatry.*

What are the next books? *1 & 2 Chronicles.* What are they about? *A repetition of much of what appears in 1 & 2 Kings.* According to Kings and Chronicles, what happened to Israel and Judah? *They went into captivity.* Where did Israel go into captivity? *Assyria.* Where did Judah go into captivity? *Babylonia.* Then did God simply wash His hands of the Hebrews? *No, He promised a return to the land.*

What is the next book? *Ezra.* What is that book about? *The return to the land from Babylonia.* What did they do after returning? *They rebuilt the temple.* What is the next book? *Nehemiah.* What is that book about? *Rebuilding the walls of Jerusalem.*

So now the Hebrews are back in the land and their temple and the capital city of Jerusalem are rebuilt. Along the way prophets ministered and their books appear in the latter part of the Old Testament. The last writing prophet was Malachi, about 435 B.C. And Malachi is the last book of the Old Testament.

About the Author

HOWARD F. VOS is Professor Emeritus of History and Archaeology at The King's College, New York City. He holds the Th.D. from Dallas Theological Seminary and the Ph.D. from Northwestern University and has authored 25 books. Dr. Vos and his wife make their home in Philadelphia, Pennsylvania.